TONY HADLEY

TONY HILLERY
A LONG
STORY
SHORT

TO CUT
A LONG
STORY
SHORT

Pan Books

First published 2004 by Sidgwick & Jackson

This edition published 2005 by Pan Books
an imprint of Pan Macmillan Ltd
Pan Macmillan, 20 New Wharf Road, London N1 9RR
Basingstoke and Oxford
Associated companies throughout the world
www.panmacmillan.com

ISBN 0 330 42741 5

9 8 7 6 5 4 3 2 1

A CIP catalogue record for this book is available from
the British Library.

Typeset by SetSystems Ltd, Saffron Walden, Essex
Printed and bound in Great Britain by
Mackays of Chatham plc, Chatham, Kent

To my dad,

PATRICK WILLIAM HADLEY

Picture Acknowledgements

While every effort has been made to trace the copyright holders of illustrations featured in this book, the publishers will be glad to make proper acknowledgements in future editions in the event that any regrettable omissions have occurred at the time of going to press.

Parade promotional flyer © Eric Watson

Sun newspaper cutting © News International

Photograph of Tony Hadley, Gary Kemp and Martin Kemp on *The Tube* appears courtesy of Granada Media Group Ltd

Hadley, Norman, Keeble photograph © Rod Shone

Photograph of military trip to Falklands appears courtesy of Matt Glover

Reborn in the USA photographs appear courtesy of Granada Media Group Ltd © Granada Media Group Ltd

Page 16 of plate section © Rod Shone

This book would not have been possible without the patience, countless hours of interviews, and writing skills of Maria Malone.

John Keeble, my friend for many years, also helped unlock all kinds of memories (mostly good) in recent months.

Very special thanks go to both of them.

I could thank God, the world and the universe, but somehow I don't think that's really me, so I'm going to keep the acknowledgements for this book as short as possible (no offence to anyone).

To my family, friends and acquaintances, I thank you for your love, support and understanding. I'm a fairly easy-going bloke, but I do know that I can be (and have been) incredibly frustrating over the years. Your patience has been duly noted.

This is a work of non-fiction. All the characters are real. Any resemblance to people living or dead is intentional.

Foreword

It might have been said a million times before but, from the moment we're born, life is one long series of events, whether they be painful, joyful, exhilarating or just plain dull. And, yes, I believe you can have a dull event. I should know; I've been to enough of them.

You try to do the best you can, and most people try desperately to be happy throughout their lives, balancing that happiness against hurting those people closest to them, and some even not too close.

As I began work on this book about my life so far, someone asked me, 'Do you have any regrets?'

I replied, 'No, none at all. I just wish I hadn't made so many mistakes.'

I suppose that's the way it is for all of us.

Introduction

The mail clattered through the letterbox, mostly hand-written envelopes, a few late Christmas cards. The last delivery for a few days. Everything was about to close down for the holiday. One envelope caught my eye. It had the hallmarks of an official document. I turned it over, curious. There was nothing on the back to give away the sender. I put the cards to one side and tore it open.

It was a writ, a threat of legal action, the latest development in a battle raging over Spandau Ballet. Almost three years after a court case over publishing royalties, things were worse than ever. The cost of court action already ran into hundreds of thousands of pounds. I had hoped that was the end of it, but apparently not.

It was Christmas Eve, 2001.

I'd like to be able to say that, in the light of what had been going on since the original hearing, I wasn't surprised, that such things were not unusual, but I can't. I *was* surprised. The writ struck me as a sign that things had sunk to new depths.

At the heart of the fall-out has been a row with Gary Kemp over publishing royalties, something that had affected every other member of Spandau Ballet. There was more than money at stake, there was a principle. It struck me as fundamentally wrong that royalties once paid to us had stopped and I was prepared to fight it – whatever the outcome. My old band mates, John Keeble and Steve Norman, felt the same. Together, we had faced Gary Kemp in the High Court – and lost. Afterwards, as far as we were concerned, it was over. We had done what we believed was right. End of story. All that remained was to pay back what we owed in costs.

The postscript was that we formed a band, calling ourselves Hadley, Norman and Keeble, with the sole aim of raising the money to clear the court debt. We billed ourselves ex-Spandau Ballet. That was clear enough, we thought. Not everyone agreed. Gary Kemp and his brother Martin took issue. We had no right, allegedly, to let the people who came to see us know that our roots lay in Spandau Ballet. It struck me as absurd, ludicrous. At the same time, we also knew it was deadly serious.

The writ further tainted my memories of Spandau Ballet, the band that for so long meant so much to me – to all of us. For more than ten years, the five of us had been a gang, mates that grew up together. Now, all that had fractured, once and for all.

There was no going back.

Chapter One

My roots are in Islington, North London. I grew up in Percy Circus, a quiet circle of imposing terraced houses that faced onto a small, tree-lined park enclosed by railings. The properties in my street were typical for that part of London – Victorian structures with long sash windows and heavy front doors. When I was small, all the streets looked drab, everything painted a practical, uniform brown.

We lived in rented rooms on the top floors of one of the houses. The Kidbys – a couple and their two sons – had the ground floor and basement. On the first floor, the rooms belonged to Mrs Hornsby, who lived alone. Everyone lived more or less on top of each other. At times there was friction, the kind of rows that flare up between people living too close to each other. There wasn't a great deal of privacy. To get to our rooms we had to pass everyone else's. If the couple downstairs fell out, we knew about it. Voices carried up and down the stairs.

We were the only ones in the house with a bathroom, thanks to my dad. He built a partition in the kitchen and plumbed in a bath. It was the height of luxury. If you didn't have a bathroom – and few of our neighbours did – you used the facilities at the local public swimming baths.

I was born on 2 June 1960 at the Royal Free Maternity Hospital on Liverpool Road. My mum, Josephine Rose, and my dad, Pat, had been married five years by then. I was two when my sister, Lee, was born. I don't remember anything about that. My brother, Steve, came along when I was five. The first time I saw him was in hospital. He was just a few hours old, lying in a cot with a see-through side, wrapped in a blanket; a tiny bundle with a face poking out. My new baby brother. He was just one of the newborn babies, all lined up in a row of identical cots. I thought you just went in and picked the one you liked. At five years old, I had no idea where babies really came from.

For the next few years, I shared a room with my brother and sister. It was the same for all of my friends. Space was tight. I was ten when my dad put up a dividing wall, at which point Lee got her own room. I don't remember having any serious fights with my brother and sister when we were growing up.

Forty years ago, Islington was not the fashionable area it is now. It was mainly rented properties, families making ends meet, getting by on relatively little. There was a real sense of community though, and a pride in the neighbourhood. You'd see people out, washing windows, scrubbing their front doorsteps, keeping the place clean and tidy. Everyone knew everyone else. They looked out for each other.

Although we weren't wealthy, I don't ever remember feeling hard up. My dad, an electrical engineer at the *Daily Mail*, was doing pretty well. There wasn't money to burn, but we were comfortable. The difference between then and now was that we lived within our means. We didn't have credit cards or an overdraft. I don't think my parents even had a bank account at that stage. My dad brought his wages home in a brown envelope at the end of the week and my mum got her housekeeping money, which had to last until the next pay day. I don't doubt there were times when it was a struggle and money was tight, but my parents managed. If there were difficulties, they kept them from us. All I remember is being happy and secure.

I came from a lovely home; we had stylish furniture, a television. All three kids had smart clothes. In the bedroom I shared with Steve, my dad had built a cupboard, which was crammed with toys. We were never spoiled, but life was good. There were things we didn't have, like a washing machine, but no one else had one either. Every week, my mum would load the laundry into a pram and wheel it down to the Merlin Street washing baths. All the women did the same. While they did the weekly wash, they caught up on each other's news. There were few secrets in our neighbourhood, as I discovered when I was growing up. If I got into a scrape, the chances were my mum would find out sooner rather than later.

I was never cheeky to my parents, never answered back, although occasionally I overstepped the mark without even knowing. My mum remembers taking me into the cake shop one day to choose something as a treat. The shop was full of people who knew us. I frowned at the rows of sticky buns and fresh cream cakes. 'I'll have that fucking one,' I said. All the chatter in the shop stopped. Everyone in the queue craned to get a better look. My mum went pale. She said, 'What did you say?'

I pointed at a vanilla slice, thick layers of fresh cream sandwiched between flaky pastry, topped with pale lemon icing. 'That fucking one. Please.'

My mum blinked. The woman behind the counter slipped the cake into a bag with a wry smile and handed it over. No one said a word.

Outside, my mum gently explained that some words – *swear* words – aren't nice. She didn't know where I'd learned to talk like that, but she didn't want to hear it again. I nodded. I was only five and I didn't know what I was saying. All I was bothered about was getting stuck into my cream cake.

Sunday was always a family day. After breakfast, we'd walk from Percy Circus down Farringdon Road, to visit my mum's family. Her father, Bill Tee, grew up in Clerkenwell Dwellings, a block of flats built at the end of the nineteenth century. My great-grandparents, and some of my aunts, still lived there. A flight of worn stone steps led to my great-grandparents' front door. My aunts, Nelly, Maggie and Mary, lived in the flat opposite.

Once a week, we got together, all in our Sunday best. My parents always looked a million dollars, my dad in tailored flannel trousers and a jacket, my mum in a dress. She carried a smart handbag, with a metal clasp that fastened with a click, and matched her shoes. My outfit was invariably a pressed shirt, shorts with a knife-edge crease, long socks and shoes that had been polished until they shone.

I knew my great-grandfather as Pop. He occupied a brown leather chair by the fire, a tin of tobacco within easy reach on one side, a roll-up machine on the other. I don't remember seeing him anywhere other than in that chair. Pop never said much, but he fascinated me because he had a wooden leg. I would get him to roll up his trouser leg so I could play with it. It kept me amused for hours, levering his leg up so it stuck out at an angle, pressing the button that released the mechanism. Up and down, up and down. Every now and then, I'd glance up at him for signs he was getting fed up, but he never seemed to mind. He just chuckled at me and left me to it. I can't have been more than about five years old. Lee was just a toddler and Steve was a baby.

Some Sundays we went to visit my dad's mum, little Nanny Hadley. My grandad on that side had died before I was born. My nan had a flat on the top floor of a high-rise block, next to the Arsenal ground at Highbury. You could see a corner of the pitch, a tiny bit of the Clock End, from her balcony. With my dad coming from Highbury and my mum from Clerkenwell, there was never any doubt that I'd be an Arsenal fan. There was no other team. These days I play for the celebrity eleven side whenever I can.

Little nan was tiny, less than five feet tall. She loved jellied eels. We'd always take her some. They turned my stomach. Even now, I can't touch them; the sight of aspic makes me ill.

I had knock knees when I was little. For months, at bedtime, my mum strapped padded splints to my legs, to straighten them while I slept. They were heavy and uncomfortable; I hated them. Once they were on, I could barely walk, but they did the trick. By the time I started at Clerkenwell Parochial Primary School, I no longer needed the nightly splints.

I loved primary school. Mine ran on traditional High Church of England principles. We were taught by a mixture of nuns and lay people. Religious Education and daily prayers, led by Sister Constance and Sister Edna, were part of the fabric of the school. For the first couple of years I joined in, then it started to bother me. I wasn't sure who we were meant to be praying to. The idea of God was all a bit vague. One day, I refused to pray.

Around me, all my classmates had their eyes shut and their

hands joined in prayer. There was a lengthy silence. I glanced at Sister Constance. She nodded at me. 'Put your hands together.' I shook my head. 'No, Sister.'

I was sent straight to Mr Hamilton, the headmaster, a big man in tweeds and Oxford bags held up with braces. He wanted to know what I was playing at. It was simple: I had started to question God and religion. The more I thought about it, the less sense it made. I was the kind of child who wanted answers to my questions. When it came to religion, no one seemed to have any, as far as I could tell. You had to take an awful lot on trust. At home, we were not a deeply religious family. At school, the whole subject of God left me confused. I tried to explain this to my headmaster. 'I'm sorry, but I can't see God. I can't touch him; I can't feel him. Unless someone proves to me that God exists, I don't see the point in praying.'

He sat forward in his chair. He straightened the knot in his tie and frowned at me across the desk. No doubt, he was wondering what to make of me, trying to work out if I was being truthful or just plain cheeky. I waited for a telling-off, but none came. The school decided to make light of my crisis of faith. They hoped that, left to my own devices, I might conform of my own accord. I never did.

Although I wouldn't say prayers, I was happy to sing hymns. Our singing teacher, Mr Sheffield, stood in front of the class, conducting us, mouthing the words, in an exaggerated manner. We stood in a row copying him.

The words of the hymns, written in big letters on huge sheets, were hauled up in front of us, one at a time. We must have been a decent enough choir because we sang on a regular basis in three of the neighbouring churches – St James's, Our Most Holy Redeemer and St Mark's, the church I was married in.

I never looked for trouble, but somehow it seemed to find me. From an early age, I hated the idea of bullying. If I saw someone being picked on, I'd step in, sometimes with disastrous results. Half the time, the bullies I took on were a lot bigger than I was.

At primary school there was a lad who was the same age as me, but built like a bloke. He always picked on kids that were smaller than him, which wasn't difficult since he was twice the size of the rest of us. I hated it. Our fights followed a familiar pattern. He would pick on some kid, and I'd wade in to stop him. That was the idea, anyway.

I'd say, 'Right, you've got a fight after school.' I was always squaring up to him, a skinny kid with a death wish. He beat me every time. I never worked out that it would have made sense to keep out of his way. That sums me up, even now. If I get knocked down, my instinct is to get straight back up and go back for more.

It's not always a good thing, but that's the way I am.

One day, round the back of the school, he was doing his usual demolition job on me, jabbing away at my face. *Thump, thump, thump.* I was little more than a human punch bag. I'd had enough, but I wasn't about to say so. Tears ran down my cheeks. Maureen Henry, a neighbour from Percy Circus, spotted us and, thankfully, stopped it. She was one of my mum's best friends and went straight round to tell her what was going on. Maureen was always tipping my mum off if she spotted me misbehaving. I'd get home and be pulled to one side. 'A little birdie came to my window and told me . . .' was my mum's classic way of letting me know I was in trouble. My parents weren't too thrilled to hear I'd been fighting. They went round to see his folks and, between them, sorted things out. He stopped tearing me apart, which was a relief, and, eventually, we became friends.

I was constantly falling out with another of the lads in my class, Clive Scorgie. We had run-ins over all kinds of stupid stuff. One day he accused me of putting a hole in his jumper (I hadn't). After school, we did our best to knock lumps out of each other. We were always at it. The final straw came when we started a scrap outside the front of the school over something petty. I can't even remember what it was. We didn't really need a reason; by then, we just didn't like each other. Anyway, there we were flailing about, when I grabbed him and swung him off his feet. Clive Scorgie was no muscleman. He smashed his head on the pavement. There was blood everywhere. It caused absolute ructions. Both sets of parents came to the school. By now, the teachers were sick of the pair of us. The solution seemed to be to separate us. They decided I was the brighter of the two and moved me up a year into Mr Hyams' class.

Suddenly, I had a new, older set of mates. I fell in with Gregory O'Shea, Kevin Thompson, Johnny Harris, John Devitt. I fell for girls like Maxine White, Pamela Grubb and Karen Blackshaw. I was besotted with Karen Blackshaw, a slim, pretty girl with long, dark hair cut in a bob. She was gorgeous. I went on my first school journey to Norfolk with my new classmates and spent most of the time dawdling along country lanes at the back of the group gazing at Karen Blackshaw. I was an old romantic, even at nine years old. For a while, I forgot about fighting, but I still got into trouble.

One afternoon, a supply teacher came in to cover for Mr Hyams. It didn't take long to work out that discipline wasn't her strong point. We decided to push our luck. I spoke up. 'Miss, is it all right to go out to play if you've finished your work?' She looked unsure. I said, 'Only Mr Hyams always lets us.'

It was a barefaced lie, but she fell for it. Off I went to play with Johnny Harris and John Devitt. While we were gone, Mr Hyams came back. By the time we sauntered back in, he was furious. He sent us to the Head.

Mr Hamilton wasn't nearly as understanding as he'd been the first time I went to see him. The three of us stood in front of his desk. We had no excuse. As far as he was concerned, we were in serious trouble. There was only one thing for it. He would cane us. It was the first time anyone had been caned for years. I was nine; the others were a year older. He sent us out to wait in the corridor. One at a time, he called us in for six of the best on the arse. It hurt like hell. We were all trying to be brave but tears streamed down our faces. It was the worst punishment I'd ever experienced. The most I got at home was the odd verbal slap. When Mr Hyams saw the state of us, he was shocked. I think he'd expected a telling-off, not a thrashing. It wasn't as if we'd set fire to the supply teacher; all we'd done was pull a fast one. Still, we didn't complain, and I didn't go crying to my mum and dad. I don't think I'd have got much sympathy. Deep down, I thought it served me right, although, when I think back, it was pretty medieval.

I grew up in the age of *Thunderbirds* and *Flash Gordon*. Space held a huge fascination. No one knew what was out there and, as a kid, I was happy for my imagination to run riot. I knew the stories of H.G. Wells and John Wyndham and believed in aliens and Triffids. It didn't seem all that far-fetched. The Sixties was the era of the space race. Anything was possible.

On 20 July 1969, *Apollo 11* landed on the moon. At home, we drew the curtains to shut out the daylight and tuned into grainy pictures of the moon landing on our black-and-white TV set. It was unbelievable. A slice of science fiction, only real. These were pictures from *space*, beamed back from nearly

250,000 miles away. For a nine-year-old, it was beyond belief. I watched with my mum and dad, and Lee and Steve. No one knew what would happen when the lunar module landed. I was on the edge of my seat. I suspect the team at NASA was too. We were all venturing into the unknown. Maybe the surface of the moon wasn't solid. I half expected the spacecraft to sink, swallowed up in some kind of evil, bubbling quicksand (too much *Flash Gordon*, probably). Thirty-five years ago, technology was primitive. The entire mission felt touch and go. The whole time Neil Armstrong and Buzz Aldrin were on the moon, my heart was in my mouth. I couldn't help wondering about the third astronaut, the *Apollo* Commander, Michael Collins, left behind in the spaceship, one eye on the rear-view mirror, engine ticking over, ready for lift-off. Fancy going all that way and not getting out. He must have been pretty pissed off.

Even when they returned to Earth, it was all anyone was talking about. They were back, but were they safe? When I found out that the astronauts were going into quarantine, I dreamed up all kinds of deadly space diseases. Maybe a killer spore, capable of wiping out mankind, had come back with them. *Revenge of the Spore!* You have to remember I was only nine.

The furthest I went at that point was on school journeys, usually to Norfolk. I never minded being away from home, although I remember some of my classmates crying themselves to sleep at night.

By the time I was ten, my old class had caught up with me. I had buried my differences – whatever they were – with Clive Scorgie. It was our final year at primary school and we went off on our last trip to the Fens.

By the end of the week, I was dangerously ill.

On our last night, instead of going to bed, I sneaked into

the girls' dormitory. Suddenly, someone hissed a warning; Mr Hyams was on his way. I ran back into the boys' dorm and dived into my bunk, banging my right knee on the bedpost. Pain shot through my body. I rolled about in agony. By the morning, I could barely stand. As soon as I put any weight on my knee, I doubled up in pain. I hobbled about as best I could. Not surprisingly, Mr Hyams wasn't about to waste his sympathy on me. He knew what I'd been up to the night before and had no reason to suspect there was anything more than a nasty bruise to worry about.

That day, we packed up and went home. By the time the coach pulled up outside the school, I was in a bad way. I couldn't walk. My dad met me and carried me home on his shoulders. My parents were so concerned they took me straight to the casualty department at the Royal Free Hospital, which was on Gray's Inn Road in those days. The doctor said my knee had taken an awkward knock. There was severe bruising. I was sent home to rest. In the early hours of the morning I woke up screaming. At ten years old, it was the worst pain I had ever experienced.

We didn't have a car, so my dad carried me to the hospital. I screamed the place down. The doctor did blood tests straight away. He knew there was something seriously wrong. As a precaution, he started pumping me full of antibiotics.

His swift action probably saved my life.

It turned out I had a condition called osteomyelitis. Bacteria had made a home in the marrow of my right knee and had been multiplying, probably for months, forming a large colony, without my knowing. The bump had disturbed the bacteria and sent it flooding into my bloodstream. By the time I was admitted to hospital, septicaemia had set in. Left untreated, I would have suffered heart failure. It was caught just in time. In theatre, the infected tissue was removed from the marrow surrounding my knee. I didn't know it, but my parents were frantic with worry. Although doctors had stabilized the condition, they warned them I still might lose my knee joint. For a while it was touch and go. I had no idea how serious things were; my parents kept that to themselves. There's still a chance the condition may flare up again although, so far, I've been fine. In fact, my left knee gives me more trouble. Years of playing football and running have worn away the cartilage.

Whenever I hear Mungo Jerry's 'In The Summertime', it reminds me of the two months I spent in hospital in 1970 (and the nurse I fell in love with). Once I started feeling better, I had the time of my life. Being a patient was never a hardship. There were other kids to get to know and, every day, I had visitors. My mum spent hours with me. My Aunt Sylvie got into the habit of bringing in crusty buttered rolls and bananas, which was a real treat. I loved it. I kept up with my schoolwork as best I could. I was on the ward so long I got to know all the nurses. They spoiled me rotten. If I couldn't sleep, they would sit with me and play Frustration late into the night. For the first two weeks, I was bed-ridden, then I was up and about on crutches, racing up and down the ward.

When I was finally discharged, I got around on walking sticks. It was six weeks before I was able to walk unaided. On my first night at home, I remember my dad coming in from work, hurrying up the stairs. I was waiting for him in the living room, leaning on my walking stick, grinning.

He said, 'Come on, boy, let's see you walk then.'

I took a few unsteady steps towards him.

Tears ran down his face. That's one of the few times I ever saw my dad cry.

Chapter Two

My dad was a big, powerful man, not in the least bit slushy. A lot of the time, he kept his feelings bottled up. His view of life was simple and traditional: he was the provider, out to do the best he could for his family. He was incredibly conscientious and, I suspect, pushed himself too hard at times. The work ethic never let up. I don't ever remember him taking a day off, however sick he was. At home, he was strict with us, but incredibly kind and generous too. I inherited my dark hair and brown-green eyes from him – as well as a good deal of my outlook on life. He was the best dad I could have had. I thought the world of him.

I suppose it must have been a struggle for my parents, bringing up three young children, but we weren't aware of it. If times were hard, they were expert at keeping it from us. What sticks in my mind more than anything are the good times: the holidays and unexpected treats.

For years, we had a black-and-white television. One day my parents ushered the three of us into the living room. My dad beamed with pleasure. He nodded round the room. 'Do you notice anything different?' We all looked round. It looked much the same. I frowned in concentration. No new furniture, as far as I could see. I shook my head. My dad said, 'Come on, kids, *look.*'

Eventually, I stared at the TV set. There was something

different about it. 'Is it a new black-and-white TV?' My dad nodded. 'Go on, turn it on then.' We stood in a line waiting for the set to warm up while my mum and dad exchanged looks. A picture started to form on the screen. A *colour* picture. Our jaws dropped open. We had a *colour* TV. We jumped around the room in excitement.

My favourite shows at the time were *The High Chaparral* and *The Man from U.N.C.L.E.*, although I rarely got to see them since all the best programmes started just as it was my bedtime. I would try to stay up, sometimes managing to catch the first few minutes, but that was about it. My dad would clap his hands, which meant time for bed. There was no arguing.

Not long after the colour TV arrived, I came home one day to find a bike parked up in the passage. It was beautiful. A twenty-four-inch frame painted blue, and brand new, as far as I could tell. I had no idea whose it was. One of the Kidby boys, maybe. I went upstairs. My parents had some good news. The bike belonged to my cousin, Robert, who'd outgrown it and passed it on to me. I couldn't believe it. It wasn't even my birthday. It was the best present I had ever had. I kept that bike so clean; I was forever polishing it.

I had a happy childhood. No, it was more than happy; it was idyllic. I had a lot of freedom when I was growing up. I was always out, playing football, messing around with my friends. In the school holidays, we'd meet up after breakfast and stay out all day. I was born fifteen years after the Second World War ended, but the devastation left by air raids over London was still in evidence as I was growing up. Just down the road from Percy Circus – now the site of the Royal Scot Hotel – the area had been flattened. We roamed the bombsites, breaking into old buildings, lighting fires and setting up camps. Looking back, the places were deathtraps. We'd clamber about on floor joists held together by a few splintered bits of wood, and race up and down staircases that shifted under our weight. Now and then, an older gang would turn up and you'd have to get on your toes and run for it. One day we broke into an old chemical factory, only to find security guards patrolling with dogs. A snarling Alsatian chased us back over the fence.

We were always up to something, the more reckless, the better. We took our lives in our hands, speeding down Great Percy Street in home-made go-karts knocked together from old pallets and wheels we picked up in the yard of Macready's, an engineering company at the back of Bevin Court flats. We 'steered' with a bit of string. Those things didn't half move. How none of us was ever badly hurt, I'll never know.

Most of the time, I managed to keep out of trouble although, occasionally, things got out of hand. One summer, I was playing with my mates at Hackney Marshes. The grass was several feet high and bone dry. For some reason, we had an absolute fascination with fire. We were always setting things alight. This particular day, we turned some old brooms into flaming torches and started swinging them round our heads. Sparks flew and the grass caught fire. We dropped the brooms and watched in horror as the flames spread. There was a factory nearby and, a few yards away, a mound of coal. We had visions of the whole lot going up. All we could think to do was to pee on it. We stood there, eight of us in a circle, making a feeble attempt to douse the flames. Smoke belched into our faces. The heat was unbearable. In the end we ran and watched from a distance as fire engines arrived and tackled the blaze.

A lot of the time, we did stupid things. We went through a phase of emptying the gunpowder from fireworks to make our own explosives. It was asking for trouble. We loved playing with bangers and rockets and never took any notice of the instructions about lighting them and standing well back. We ran round the streets throwing them at each other. One of the craziest things we did was to set fire to rockets and hang onto them as the fuse burned its way to the gunpowder. It was an endurance test to see who dared keep hold the longest. I burned my hand badly playing that mad game.

I spent a lot of time with my best mate, Roy Harold. When his family got a flat on the new Pakenham Estate, off Essex Road, in Islington, I was devastated. I thought I wouldn't see him any more but, of course, I did. The first time I visited his new home, my eyes practically fell out of my head. It was a brand-new flat with a proper bathroom and a beautiful kitchen. I had never seen anything like it.

My grandparents, Bill and Rose Tee, were also on the move. Their house on Green Terrace, in Clerkenwell, was due for demolition to make way for a new school. They got a flat on the twenty-first floor of Michael Cliffe House, a brand-new block, just off Rosebery Avenue. We couldn't get over the fabulous entrance hall and their spacious rooms with views across London. Just a couple of years later, though, the whole block had been vandalized. The entrance was shabby and the stairwells stank of piss. They ended up moving out.

My parents were thrilled when I passed the eleven-plus and won a place at Dame Alice Owens Grammar School. They weren't so happy when, a couple of years later, I was almost expelled.

Dame Alice Owens was a traditional school with a strict uniform code. On my first day I turned up in a blazer, slightly too big, with the school crest on the breast pocket, a white shirt, black tie with a red stripe, and my first pair of long trousers.

Everything felt new and strange, especially the trousers. When I left primary school I was still running round in shorts. I didn't see why I needed proper trousers for grammar school. My mum talked me out of wearing shorts on my first day. I'm glad she did. I would probably never have lived it down.

In the beginning, I loved my new school. It felt like I was stepping into a different world. There was a school song. The teachers wore gowns. Latin was compulsory. The whole place was steeped in tradition. At the end of term we lined up to collect 'beer' money, a practice begun by the school's founders, the Worshipful Company of Brewers. It was also a tradition to spend the money on a couple of pints in the pub round the corner. On the last day of term, the place heaved with under-age drinkers, school ties stuffed into blazer pockets, as if that was going to fool anyone.

I liked the ethos of the school, with its emphasis on individuality, equality and independence. We were encouraged to believe in our own potential. There was an interesting mix of pupils, council-estate boys rubbing shoulders with the well-to-do. It didn't matter where you came from; we were all there on merit.

I was starting to get into music around the time I started grammar school. I bought my first single, 'Double Barrel' by Dave and Ansil Collins, in 1971. My parents gave me a tape recorder with a microphone, and I started experimenting with it. I was into Iggy Pop, Lou Reed and Roxy Music. I loved bands like the Clash, Generation X and the Buzzcocks. A family friend who had a record shop gave me a David Bowie album. As far as I was concerned, Bowie had it all: a unique voice, an original sound and an image kids everywhere wanted to copy. I started recording myself singing along to his songs. His was the only poster I stuck on my bedroom wall.

Later, I got into Elton John and Queen. I thought Freddie Mercury's voice was amazing, and I loved the arrangements of the Queen songs. The first time I heard the instrumental version of 'Seven Seas Of Rhye' I was knocked out. I wasn't just into pop music though. Even as a kid I was a fan of 'crooners' like Frank Sinatra, Tony Bennett and Jack Jones.

At school, I got a part in the choir of *Joseph and the Amazing Technicolor Dreamcoat*. I started to enjoy singing. The school did a production of *The Boyfriend* and I went along to the auditions. I wanted to try for a part but, in the end, I lost my nerve.

For the first two years at Dame Alice Owens, I thrived. My favourite subjects were biology and history. I sailed through my exams with marks that put me in the top five in my year. I wanted to study medicine. During my stay in hospital I'd become fascinated with the idea of being a surgeon.

It was in the third year that everything started to change.

My grades slipped, and I got involved in a stunt that almost got me expelled.

I started to hate school, and I stopped working. I was being bullied, something tons of kids go through, although in my case the bully was a teacher.

My new maths teacher, Mr Copping, made my life a misery, although I still don't know why. He picked on me at every opportunity. At thirteen, I was already almost six feet tall and towering over my classmates, which is probably what caught his eye. At the time, though, I thought there had to be a more sinister reason for him hating me. My self-confidence took a nosedive. I couldn't believe a teacher could be so vindictive.

I dreaded his lessons. He would haul me out in front of the class and throw questions at me I couldn't answer. I would stand there, wishing the ground would open up and swallow me, while everyone laughed. The more I squirmed, the more he seemed to enjoy it. He was meant to be teaching us, but half the time he was pulling me apart. It was horrible. I grew to hate him, with his nicotine-stained teeth, and his shiny demob suits that stank of stale pipe smoke. He wrote me off as a halfwit. Thicko Hadley, he called me. The label stuck. Once he'd had his fun, he would send me back to my seat to jeers of 'wanker' from the rest of the class. Mates like Freddie Capon, Mark Corker, Gary Ashmore and Noah Tucker stuck by me, but I still had a miserable time.

I would sit at my desk smarting, feeling helpless. I had no idea how to deal with him, or the taunts that had started following me round the school. I could no longer be bothered to make an effort with my schoolwork. There seemed no point.

One day, in class, I turned round and blacked Billy Perrin's eye for calling me 'thicko'. I was sent out, which suited me. From then on, I became disruptive in every lesson. It worked. Time and again, I was excluded. I used to go down to the basement and have a cup of tea and a biscuit with Mrs Williams, the caretaker's wife. She was kind, even though she must have suspected I was a bit of a troublemaker. I never told her what was really going on.

Things came to a head one day in the middle of a French lesson. I enjoyed French, and I liked the teacher, Mr Clarke, but my stomach churned when he called me out to jot something on the board. The last thing I wanted was to face the class. As I got out of my seat, the jeering started. A couple of people whispered 'wanker' under their breath. Everyone laughed. Mr Clarke, oblivious to what had been going on, handed me a piece of chalk. I froze. Under normal circumstances, I wasn't bad at French, but my confidence was in shreds. I couldn't think straight. In front of everyone, I broke down and ran out of the classroom.

I went to the basement, but I didn't look for Mrs Williams. I didn't want her to see me in that state. I stayed down there on my own for ages. Once I'd pulled myself together, I went and hung round in the cloakroom. Eventually, Mr Clarke found me. He wanted to know what was going on. I told him I was having problems in another class, and that the name-calling had got out of hand. He was a decent bloke and he did his best to sort things out. For a few weeks, it died down. Then it started again.

I realized nothing was going to change. I could either put up with it or do something. I decided from then on I would take on anyone who called me names, and I did. I was always fighting. I got into all kinds of trouble and I earned a dreadful reputation. One day I picked up a chair and belted someone with it. I didn't care. I was horrible.

I just didn't fit in. It's only now that I've discovered how many performers go through a rough time at school. Perhaps something inside sets you apart, I don't know. Ask any singer, and they'll say the same. I didn't choose to be the odd one out, but that's how it was. Maybe the teacher who picked on me thought he saw an arrogance that wasn't there. Until he came along, I was hard working, a high-flyer. In the space of a few months, all that changed. Still, I'm thankful to him now. He just made me even more determined to succeed.

I toughened up and vowed not to let anyone push me around. I developed a thick skin and an I'll-show-you attitude. I stuck two fingers up to anyone in authority who gave me a hard time. I promised myself that the people who'd written me off would one day see I'd made something of my life, in spite of them.

By then, any ideas I had about doing well academically were rapidly going out of the window. Forget medicine. I had decided I was going to sing instead. I had been away to a holiday camp in Devon with my parents and, for the first time, had sung on my own in public. There was no backing, so I sang a cappella. I was so nervous I almost didn't go through with it, but forced myself onto the stage and launched into a version of the Beatles' song 'Lady Madonna'. Halfway through, I forgot the words. There was an awkward silence. I stared out at the audience. Four hundred people stared back. I cursed myself, apologized, and, as calmly as I could, left the stage. To my amazement, everyone applauded. Some of the younger kids wanted my autograph. A couple of people encouraged me, told me I had a decent voice. It gave my confidence a boost. Best of all, I ended up with the girl I'd had my eye on all week – Beverley from Camberley. As we sat on the beach that evening, watching the sun go down, she asked what I was going to do with my life. I said, 'I'm going to be a famous singer.' She looked at me and said, 'I just know you will.'

The next week, still at the camp, I bumped into someone who played the guitar. All he could manage was a few basic chords, but I asked if he would accompany me. I got up and sang the Joe Cocker version of 'A Little Help From My Friends'. I was so terrified I'd forget the words I wrote them out in big, bold letters, and propped them on a music stand at the side of the stage. Even now, I still struggle with lyrics; in the past I've jotted them on my hand before going on stage. At thirteen, and on the verge of my second solo performance, I was racked with nerves. Although I felt awful, once I got up there, the churned-up feeling in my stomach disappeared. I discovered I loved singing. I thought, in time, I'd get over my nerves, but I never have. I still have to force myself to take deep breaths before each performance.

That night at the holiday camp was a turning point. I got through the song without fluffing the words, which gave me the confidence to start entering competitions. To my amazement, I started winning. From then on, every time I went on holiday with the family I won us another break at a camp somewhere else, which kept everyone happy.

At school things continued to go from bad to worse. I was on my way back from the science block after a biology lesson one day with my mate Freddie Capon when the giant fire hose reels fixed to the wall caught my eye. I said, 'Freddie – I'll take you on,' nodding at the reels.

He stopped in his tracks. Freddie was always game for a laugh. He said, 'You what? Come on then.'

We dropped our books, grabbed a hose each, ran to opposite ends of the corridor, and turned them on. Jets of water shot into the air. We soaked the place. Water poured down the walls and swamped the corridor. We were caught red-handed, by now dripping wet, and hauled in front of Mr Jones, the head-master. He was livid. He wanted to expel us. I dread to think how much damage we had caused. It probably ran into thousands of pounds. The water had seeped through to the dining room below, where the wallpaper was starting to peel off. It was an almighty mess. The only thing that saved me was that it was the first time I'd been up in front of the Head. My parents were angry and upset. They had been so proud of me for getting into the school, and I had almost thrown it all away with a single act of madness.

At home, I was also getting into the odd scrape. One day I went off to the flats at the Barbican with my mate David Harris. We took an airgun up on to one of the balconies and started taking potshots at the fishpond below. What we didn't know was that a guy in one of the flats below was also firing at the same target, with a high-powered air rifle. As pellets ricocheted off the side of the pond, one of the neighbours called the police. Two patrol cars pulled up. We were hauled off the balcony, shoved into the back of a squad car, and taken to the station. The guy from the flats was also taken in. We got a right telling-off and a caution. I begged the police officer not to tell my parents. I was more scared about what they'd say than anything. Predictably, they were furious. I was thirteen and I had a police caution. I wasn't allowed out for a week and had my pocket money stopped. That sort of punishment was dished out at home a fair bit.

Most of the time I managed to keep out of trouble, although there were plenty of gangs roaming about and all kinds of rackets on the go. A few of the lads got into serious trouble and ended up in Borstal. I remember a gang smashing open parking meters with a hammer and nicking the contents. They went away for six months for that. One of my mates did a stint in Borstal and came out with some awful tales.

I was never part of the gang culture, but it was all around. Sometimes, trouble found you, whether you were looking for it or not. One day I was messing about with a mate at Bevin Court flats. We weren't doing any harm but the caretaker, an old boy called Fred, took exception. The next thing they were squaring up to each other, swinging punches. I tried to get between them but, before I could, my mate had smacked Fred. He went down like a sack of spuds. We ran off, terrified. Later we heard Fred was in hospital with a broken leg, and within a few hours we were in the local nick at King's Cross, making statements. The police were satisfied it was an accident, but that wasn't the end of it. Some of the local gangs were out to get us. A lad called Micky, a couple of years older than us, and with a reputation for being able to handle himself, wanted a word as well.

Things kicked off a few nights later at St Peter and St Paul's social club. I was with Peter Kresowaty, one of my mates from Percy Circus, and I could tell things were about to turn ugly. I can smell trouble a mile off. There was a gang of lads eyeing us up.

'Let's just go,' I said.

Peter wanted to stay. 'It's fine, I know these lads,' he said.

He wandered over and had a few words. I watched from a distance. It was obvious that while Peter was being friendly they were taking the piss. I didn't like the look of it.

He came back over. 'They're all right,' he said.

I still wasn't happy. 'Peter, I really think we should go. Just trust me.'

By the time we left, there was a gang of ten lads trailing us. Every now and then, someone would shout, 'Arsehole.' Then, a few paces on, I felt a boot up the arse. We walked on. Boot. Another kick up the backside. I looked at Peter. I said, 'Look, this is not going to go away. The next time he kicks me, I'm going to hit him – then run as fast as you can.'

Boot. I wheeled round, smacked the guy, and we took off. They chased us through the streets. When we got to Margery Street flats we fled up the stairs and lost them. Everything went quiet. We cut along a balcony and headed down a different staircase. At the bottom, we walked into Micky, who poked a screwdriver against my throat. It wasn't my night.

He was in a rage over Fred. I spent ages apologizing, insisting it had been an accident. The whole time, he pressed the screwdriver into my neck. We weren't getting anywhere. I decided to give him a shove and make a run for it. Over my shoulder, I saw he now had Peter pinned to the wall. I went back. It took about an hour to persuade him to let him go.

I never wanted to be part of that local gang culture. When things started getting serious, I ducked out. Talk of pinching cars and going on nicking sprees up the West End didn't interest me. Some of my mates went off the rails and started sniffing glue. One fell to his death from the top of Michael Cliffe flats. It was terrible, absolutely devastating. A few years later, another lad from the neighbourhood died the same way. Like me, he had also been trying to make it in a band. Meanwhile, I cut my ties and looked for something else to do. I got myself a part-time job on the maintenance team at the Royal Scot Hotel, just down the road from Percy Circus. I'm not entirely sure how I was taken on to do maintenance work. I didn't know the first thing about it. To this day, I'm not very good at DIY. It didn't matter, though, because I never had to do much more than clean the air filters in the bedrooms. It wasn't especially difficult or hazardous work, although occasionally I'd let myself into a room with the passkey at an awkward moment. I walked in on a few half-dressed guests. Once a woman opened the door to me naked. She wanted more than the air filter serviced. I didn't hang around. At fifteen, I was way too innocent for that.

I had some good times at the hotel though. The kitchen staff looked after me. They knew that if they had any problems, they just had to call me – not that I'd have been a lot of use, I suspect. In return, I got to choose my meals from the guest menu. Everyone else got standard staff meals, which were awful.

Every week I went skating at Streatham or Queensway ice rinks. It was great, and a good way to meet girls. I got quite good at skating. I'd weave around, showing off for the girls.

There was a steward to keep an eye on things, make sure there was no speed skating, which wasn't allowed during normal sessions. He was constantly blowing his whistle, sending people to the 'sin bin' for bad behaviour. I spent a fair bit of time in there.

I couldn't afford my own skates, but I found a pair of boots in a junk shop on Upper Street, in Islington. I bought a pair of blades separately and ended up with a good pair of figure skates for hardly any money. That's how we did things. No one had much spare cash, so we'd find a way round it. I knew people who put bikes together like that. They'd start with a frame, pick up a tyre from here, a set of brakes from somewhere else. There was no shame in having something second hand.

At school, by the time I was in the fourth form I had a terrible reputation. At that point, we had started mixing with the girls' school. Of course, they'd heard all kinds of stories about me getting into trouble. It took me ages to persuade them I wasn't as bad as they imagined.

Sometimes it was hard to stay out of trouble. Fights were often as much about saving face as anything. I never enjoyed fighting, but I learned from experience that sometimes it was the only way. Often I was up against someone bigger and stronger – and I did take some beatings – but that's just the way it was. Where I came from, you stood up for yourself, or risked having some vicious sod walk all over you. I never backed down when it came to bullies, whether or not the odds were stacked against me. I'd take my chance.

In my neighbourhood, fighting was part of the culture. It might sound brutal, but you couldn't always sort things out by talking them over.

Despite that, it was a good place to grow up. The bullies were in a minority. Mostly, people were decent.

One day, Steve, my brother, came home in tears. He was about ten years old. One of the older lads from the area had given him a hiding. My hackles went up. I said, 'Right, let's go and sort this out.' He sounded doubtful. 'He's a big lad.' 'How big?' I said, as I laced up my Doc Martens. Steve shrugged. 'Big.' Suddenly, I wasn't sure I wanted to play the hero, but I couldn't back out. All the kids were waiting for Steve to come back with his brother and sort out the bully. When we got there, a crowd had gathered. I said, 'Which one is it?' Steve craned his neck. He pointed. 'The one in the middle.' I looked. My opponent was a big, solid lump. I felt my stomach tighten. What I really wanted to do was turn round and go home. I said, 'Right, come on.' I sounded a lot braver than I felt. I walked up to the lad. 'Have you got a problem with my brother?' He said, 'He thinks he's a flash git.' I said, 'Well, I'm a flash git as well.' Introductions over, I beat the living daylights out of him.

I never minded sticking up for Steve, but at times he asked for trouble. He could be such a pain in the arse. The last thing I wanted was my little brother hanging round, winding up my mates. He was good at that, but he pushed his luck a bit too far the day he picked on Andy Dunn. Andy was one of those cool characters who always looked immaculate. He had all the latest gear, and bowled around like he owned the place. We called him The Bowler. My brother started having a dig at him one day.

Steve said, 'You think you're really hard.'

Andy shrugged. 'I can handle myself. Nothing bothers me.'

Steve said, 'Nothing bothers you?'

Andy shook his head. 'It takes a lot for me to lose my temper.'

I was starting to wonder where this was leading. Without warning, Steve swung a punch and smacked him in the face. 'Lost your temper now, have you?'

Andy stared at him, too stunned to say anything. It was one of the funniest things I'd ever seen. I cracked up. Another mate, Roddy Forbes, was on the floor, crying with laughter. Steve – who wasn't daft – took off. Andy went mental. 'I'll fucking kill him!' He chased after Steve. I thought, Shit, he *will* kill him. I ran after the pair of them. Luckily (for Steve), Andy didn't catch up with him. It took me ages to smooth things over.

These days, Steve and I are good mates. In fact, he's one of the best blokes you could ever wish to meet. We've worked together on numerous occasions. I love my brother to bits.

I remember Steve having a few run-ins with a lad over the road. It was just two kids falling out, but it got completely out of hand, with his dad having a go at my dad. There were some nasty rows. My dad didn't want to make a scene, but our neighbour wouldn't let it drop. The whole thing was stupid. It ended up with him putting the word out that he was going to sort my dad out once and for all. My grandad, Bill Tee, who thought the world of my dad, got to hear about it. Things came to a head in the street one day. Our neighbour appeared with a mate, the pair of them tooled up with chains. They meant business. It was like something out of a gangster film. My dad knew how to take care of himself, but he was outnumbered; he wouldn't have stood much of a chance.

Suddenly, a van pulled up and a load of blokes spilled out. It was my grandad arriving with the cavalry. He got hold of our neighbour and had a quiet word. The basic message was to stay well away. He did. A few months later, he moved out of the area.

Now and then I'd find myself a bit too close to the gangs for comfort and it frightened the living daylights out of me. There was always a sense that things could kick off. You just needed to be in the wrong place at the wrong time and you'd be in the thick of it. When I was sixteen I saw a guy stabbed just a few feet in front of me.

A couple of friends, Celia and Becky Cole, had thrown a party. Amazingly, their folks had agreed to go out and to leave them to it. The Cole family was a bit out of the ordinary. Barry, the father, was a poet. His daughters were progressive. On the night of the party, it was more or less open house. Inevitably, a few of the local faces showed.

I was in the hallway when things turned nasty. Someone pulled a knife and suddenly there was blood everywhere. It all happened so fast, I barely saw it. Everyone was screaming and scrambling out of the way as glasses and bottles went over. I grabbed a couple of girls and shoved them in the front room. In the hall, there was a complete scrum. Then the trouble was over as fast as it started. The place emptied. All the trouble-makers legged it. There was no sign of the guy who'd been stabbed. We looked round. The place was a tip. There was blood all over the wall. Glass had been trampled into the floor. The Coles were the only people I knew with hessian flooring instead of carpets. It was trendy, but a bugger when it came to broken glass. The splinters had got right into the fibres.

It took us until 5 a.m. to clean things up.

Looking back, I went off the rails a bit around this time.

I was making no effort at school, always misbehaving. On

my way to see my best mate, Pete Hillier, in High Barnet one day, I decided to skip the train fare. When I got off, there were a couple of inspectors checking tickets. I had a story ready about the ticket office being closed when I'd got on a couple of stops back. It didn't sound all that convincing, even to me. I was taken to one side. They wanted my name, address and telephone number. I made something up, thinking that would be the end of it. The next minute, they were calling the number I'd given them. I swallowed. Shit. Maybe no one would answer. No such luck. Predictably, the person on the other end had no idea what they were talking about. I shrugged. I said, 'I'm sorry, I'm just a bit scared.' They tried again. Name, address and telephone number. I was confident they wouldn't check a second time, but they did. Before they finished dialling the number, I owned up. A few days later, I got a summons to appear before the Transport Police at King's Cross. My dad came with me. He said, 'What were you thinking, giving an inspector a false name and number?'

I said, 'I thought I was being clever.'

My dad said, 'Twice? You silly sod.'

I was let off with a caution.

Chapter Three

By the time it came to sitting my mock O levels I was making almost no effort at school. I sat my English exam without doing a stroke. I knew nothing, but I still managed to answer every question. I remember our teacher, Mr Sparrow, walking round the class handing back the marked papers. He saved mine until last. He was utterly perplexed. Finally, he said, 'Hadley, this is brilliant. It would have got you an A-plus . . .' he paused, '*if* the book you refer to in here actually existed.' He tapped my paper. 'It's utter fabrication. What on earth were you playing at?'

Since I hadn't read any of the set books, I had relied on my imagination. My entire exam paper was a work of fiction. I said, 'Sorry, sir, I didn't have time to revise.'

Fortunately, he saw the funny side, although he did point out it wouldn't get me a GCE pass when the time came.

The fact was, I couldn't be bothered to study. At the end of the fifth form I managed four O levels. I decided to stay on and do A levels, but my heart really wasn't in it.

Meanwhile, the school was on the move. Under a plan to redevelop the original site, the building was earmarked for demolition. My year was the last intake in London. From then on, the number of pupils steadily shrank.

A new school went up miles away, in suburban Potter's Bar in Hertfordshire. Princess Anne opened it, commenting on what an improvement it was on the Islington site. Actually, I preferred Islington. The new school was in the middle of nowhere. It was a train journey away and the nearest pub was a hike. By the time we switched sites, the first four years were already established at Potter's Bar. Suddenly, the sixth form arrived, loud, loutish London riff-raff disturbing the peace and quiet. At least, that's probably what it looked like. We were a nice bunch, really. The fourth-form girls certainly thought so. The fourth-form boys weren't so sure.

One positive effect of the move was that it threw together the lower- and upper-sixth years. Since we all felt a bit like outsiders in a strange, unfamiliar place, we tended to stick together. There was more mixing between the two years than was usual, which was instrumental in bringing together the various elements that eventually became Spandau Ballet.

One lunchtime I was messing around on the drums in the music room when Steve Norman came in with Gary Kemp, Michael Ellison and John Keeble. John kicked me off the drum kit straight away. That was his territory. There were a couple of girls with them. I knew Steve. He was in my class, a funny, likeable lad. Gary was in my year, although I didn't know him well. John was in the year above. So was Michael Ellison. I don't think he was particularly friendly with anyone, but his brother had a PA, which was useful.

I watched them start playing, Gary and Steve on guitar, Michael Ellison on bass, and John on drums. After a few seconds, I gave up any ideas I might have had about being a drummer. John was good. They all were. The only thing that let them down was that the girls couldn't sing.

A couple of days later, during break, Steve Norman said they were thinking about forming a band, but they needed a singer. I was in there like a shot. 'I can sing.' I'm not sure he believed me, but he told me to come along to the music room the next day. I sang 'Oh Carol', and I was in. We called ourselves the Roots.

John and I hated each other in the beginning. I thought he was a moody git, he thought I was a stroppy so-and-so. He had his reasons. He knew my reputation for getting into scrapes. He had seen me in the fourth form gatecrashing the Cloisters – a common room reserved for the upper school – to the annoyance of the sixth form.

On one occasion I was in there when my mate, Ian Fordham, balanced a bucket of water above the door. We thought this was hilarious – until the door opened and a teacher walked in. Of all the members of staff, this teacher was possibly the least likely to see the funny side of a daft practical joke. He was also one of the teachers no one dared cross. The bucket tipped over, narrowly missing him. No one laughed. He lined us up and poked the cane in our faces, demanding to know who was responsible. Ian burst into tears, which gave the game away. He was pulled aside and thrashed.

My earliest memory of hanging around the Cloisters was as a first year. It was a no-go area for the younger lads and I thought I was being cool, nipping up there at lunchtime to see Charlie MacNair, who was in John's year. I was a bit lippy, and I sensed I was pushing my luck spending time there. One lunchtime a big, scary sixth-former rounded on me. He'd had enough. He said, 'Right, Hadley, two choices – you can either fight me or go through the tunnel of love. That's the only way you're getting out of here.'

I didn't stand a chance against him, so I chose the tunnel

of love, not that I had a clue what it was. I watched while the entire upper school formed an arch, which I had to walk through. They kicked and punched me all the way. By the time I came out the other end, I was in tears.

Eventually I got the message and kept away from the Cloisters. None of this had endeared me to John, though.

In the music room at Potter's Bar, we started putting together a set, mostly Sixties' hits, such as 'Young Girl', 'All Day And All Of The Night', 'We Gotta Get Out Of This Place', 'I Wanna Be Your Man'. We played everything at about 100 mph.

In December 1976 we set up our kit on a makeshift stage in the corner of the school dining room and played our first gig for the fourth-form girls' disco. We got a strange thrill from seeing our gear on a stage for the first time. John Keeble had actually carried his drum kit in on the train, bit by bit. It dominated the stage, sparkling red and gold under the disco lights. As usual, I felt sick with nerves before we went on. This was our first public outing and we all wanted it to be great. We went on stage to loud cheers from the fourth-form girls, and my nerves did a disappearing act. Although we were only on for about twenty minutes, our short, sharp set went down well. Suddenly we felt like a proper band. We were just starting out, but we sensed we had the makings of a strong unit. The school booked us to play again, this time for the first- and second-year disco. Everything seemed to be happening fast.

With a couple of gigs under our belts, we were ready to spread our wings. Before Christmas, we had our first public gig, in the function room at the Queen's Head in Turnpike Lane, a big old boozer with sticky carpets, stained velvet seats, and bored-looking drinkers propping up the bar.

It was here that the cracks began to show. Michael Ellison

– nicknamed Deafie, because he was hard of hearing (so cruel) – never really fitted in. He was in the band because he could play bass. And because of his brother's PA system. He also had a guitar – a Les Paul copy – he was willing to loan us, which came in handy. And he'd managed to get us the gig at the Queen's Head. The night we played there his dad helped with the gear. I don't think he was impressed. I remember him having a go at Gary, who was struggling to tune his guitar. We couldn't afford tuners in those days. They ended up shouting at each other. We didn't even manage to complete our set. The DJ pulled the plug because we were too loud. In the confusion, the Les Paul copy got knocked over and broken. It wasn't going well.

Still, Michael Ellison came up trumps in the New Year. He knew Tom Robinson and managed to get us a gig supporting the Tom Robinson Band at the George Robey in North London. It wasn't the most exciting gig. Support bands don't command a great deal of attention, but we got through the set without incident, which was an achievement, and celebrated with a couple of pints. The main thing was we'd proved we could handle a gig. We felt like we were on our way. A week later, we supported them again at the Golden Lion in Fulham, when the high point of the evening was sighting Led Zeppelin's Robert Plant and John Bonham in the audience. The low point was having the plug pulled on the set (again) for being too loud. Tom, generously, offered us the tube fare home. I think we told him where to get off.

By this time a clear split had developed in the band, with Michael Ellison on one side, and the rest of us on the other. We had nothing in common. He didn't even drink, which was a major worry. In his favour, he had set up a few gigs, but it wasn't enough, so we asked him to leave. Or maybe he decided to go. I'm not sure which, but it was a relief to everyone – including him, I suspect – once we parted company.

The next time we played, it was as a foursome with Steve on bass. We changed our name to the Cut, did a couple of gigs at the Pinder of Wakefield in King's Cross, and found a new bass player, Richie Miller. Richie was in my year at Dame Alice Owens. He was a gifted player and a lovely bloke. To mark the new line-up, we decided on a new name, the Makers. Steve went back to playing guitar.

At that stage, Steve Norman and Gary Kemp were busy writing songs. I was happy to leave them to it. I was the singer, and I wanted to concentrate on that. I think John Keeble felt the same about playing drums.

We had no master plan. Like so many bands starting out, we were finding our feet, learning as we went along. We were naïve and inexperienced but we shared the same dream. We loved playing and performing. Perhaps we were rough around the edges, but we had energy and we improved with every gig. We wore drainpipe cords, hand-painted geometric T-shirts and Chelsea boots, and played four-to-the-floor power pop – an energetic mix of covers and original tracks. Our early set was influenced by bands like the Kinks and the Rolling Stones. One reviewer compared our material to songs on the Beatles' album, *Rubber Soul*. We thought we were the business.

It was the late Seventies and the punk movement was starting to move aside for the next wave of bands coming through. Soon to emerge were the likes of Midge Ure with Ultravox, Steve Strange and Visage, Boy George and Culture Club – and us. We all wanted success and we were prepared to work at it.

I was seventeen and supposed to be studying for History, English and British Constitution A levels, but I wasn't doing any work. One day, I set off for school with Pete Hillier and ended up in the pub instead. We had got to know each other in the fifth year and become best mates. We complemented each other – Pete's very logical, I'm a bit of a dreamer – but we had one important thing in common: we were sick of sitting in classrooms.

For two weeks, I went out every morning to go to school. I never made it. I was like one of those executives who gets the sack but can't bear to own up, so goes out 'to work' every day, then sits on a park bench until it's time to go home. Except I wasn't spending the day on a park bench; I was going for a few pints with Pete instead. Eventually, a letter arrived at home from the school. That was the first my parents knew about my lengthy absence. They were not happy. They thought I was throwing away a great opportunity to get some qualifications. I didn't want qualifications, though. I wanted to be a singer. I decided to leave school.

When I dropped out of my A-level course it was a major let-down for my parents. A few years earlier, I'd been talking about wanting to study medicine. They had always hoped I would make the most of my education. To see me throwing it all away struck them as an incredible waste. My mum is an intelligent woman and I don't doubt she would have gone to university had things been different. She wanted me to have the opportunities that weren't there for her. But I had no interest. I was going to be a singer. Mum and Dad probably wondered what had got into me and where, if anywhere, it would all lead. They'd seen me walking off with prizes for singing at holiday camp talent nights, so they knew I could do it, but there was no tradition of singing in the family. The closest we came was getting round the piano at family parties. Under the circumstances, they were remarkably tolerant.

Having dropped out of school, I needed a job. I went to the Churchill Rooms in Mayfair to see if they'd take me on as a singer, but I was too young. Both my dad and my grandad, Bill Tee, had spent years in the print industry. My grandad pulled a few strings, and got me a job with IPC magazines, working in the warehouse.

I made the tea and packed boxes. I earned £23 a week.

At that time the print industry was a strange, murky world filled with the kind of people it was best to keep on the right side of. There were plenty of decent blokes, but some were hard as nails. More often than not, there was an undercurrent of something not quite legal going on. One of the guys in the warehouse was accused of conspiring to rob a string of jewellers. It was heavy stuff. We'd have regular visits from the Van Man, who'd arrive selling cut-price electrical goods of unspecified origin. It all took a bit of getting used to.

I was the new boy, the posh grammar school kid. For a while, I was the butt of everyone's jokes. One day, I was bundled onto the packing shelf, my trousers yanked down, and paste slapped on my bollocks. There was nothing about that in my terms and conditions. It was their way of making me feel welcome, I suppose.

I clashed with the SOGAT union rep, John Davison, early on. He was a big pal of my grandad, but he and I just didn't get along. It was a hard, blokey culture and he loved to make me squirm. From day one, I was in trouble. I turned up late, disappeared to the offices upstairs to chat up the girls, idled away my time in the pub. I was never where I was meant to be.

One day I was having lunch in the canteen with a girl who worked on one of the IPC magazines. A guy came over and asked if either of us had done any modelling. I was a bit wary, but he turned out to be from *My Guy*, a teen magazine. He wanted us to be the couple in one of their photo love stories. It seemed harmless enough. I didn't realize how popular those things were until, shortly afterwards, I went on holiday with the family. All these young girls recognized me from *My Guy* and wanted an autograph. It was great. The rest of the band was less pleased. Soppy photo love stories weren't quite the image they were after. I took a bit of stick for that. I took even more when, a couple of years later, the national press raked it up again. It went against the grain of our new, pretentious image as Spandau Ballet. Still, it could have been worse. Around the same time as *My Guy* went on sale, my mum tried to persuade me to get involved with a new TV game show. One of her friends was a producer and was looking for families. There were some good prizes on offer, and a chance to win thousands of pounds in cash. My grandad was up for it and my mum was keen. The show was *Family Fortunes*. I thought it over and decided if that came out a few years down the line when we had made it the band would never forgive me. I turned it down. *Uh-urr.*

I was always close to my nan, Rose Tee. She was an amazing woman. The two of us could talk about anything. After I'd dropped out of school and landed a job in the IPC warehouse I went to see her. She made us tea and asked what I planned to do with my life. Did I really see my future in the print trade? When I told her I wanted to be a singer, she didn't seem too surprised. She said, 'Do you think you've got a chance?' I told her how hard we were working to get the band off the ground. I thought we had every chance. I said, 'Nan, I think we can do it.'

Once she knew I was serious she was right behind me. She said, 'If that's what makes you happy and you think you can make a career out of it, then you have my blessing.'

Her only concern was what she'd heard about drugs in the music industry. By then, I'd smoked a bit of pot, but hadn't gone near anything else. I'm quite an addictive, excessive person. My nan knew that if I dabbled with drugs I'd end up in trouble. She made me promise never to go near them. I never have.

When I was seventeen she went into hospital for an operation. I never found out what was wrong. According to my mum, it was 'women's trouble'. I got the impression she wanted me to mind my own business, so I did. No one seemed too worried. I never suspected for a moment there was anything seriously wrong. She seemed to get better and went on holiday with my grandad. I remember going with my mum and dad to meet them at Waterloo Station when they came back. They were in such good spirits. We all went back home with them to Yardley Street, and sat drinking tea. My nan always used sterilized milk. None of us liked it, but we never said anything. My grandparents looked so well. They were full of tales of their holiday. We all sat there, laughing as they told one story after another.

Three weeks later, my nan was back in hospital.

I went in to see her almost every day. Some days she was cheerful. We'd chat, and she'd assure me she was on the mend. Not that I even knew what was wrong with her. Other days she didn't seem to know who I was. She was completely out of it. I later discovered she was on morphine to keep the pain at bay. I tried talking to my mum, but she wouldn't tell me what was going on. Thinking about it now, she was probably too upset.

One day, I went to the hospital determined to get some answers. I looked in on my nan, and found her in a deep sleep. The morphine was doing its work. I went looking for the ward sister. In a private room, I waited for news of my nan's condition. I now know that when hospital staff show you to a private room it's a sure sign of bad news; at that stage, I hadn't a clue. I was not prepared for what I was about to find out. I said, 'I need to know what's wrong with my nan. Sometimes she doesn't even know I'm here. Is she going to be all right?'

The ward sister looked at me. She said, 'Hasn't anyone spoken to you?'

I shook my head. 'No one will tell me anything.'

She said, 'I'm sorry, but your nan's got terminal cancer. She's not going to live.'

Her words floored me. It was the last thing I had expected to hear. She must have registered the shock on my face. I was distraught. I walked out of there and, for the next few hours, wandered the streets, sobbing.

Two weeks later, my nan died.

That was the first time I had lost someone close to me. I felt my outlook on life change at that point. Until then, I'd never even thought about death, about losing the people I loved. My nan hadn't seemed old enough to die. She was sixty-seven and, just a few weeks earlier, she was full of life. There were fifty years between us, but no generation gap. If I had a question, the chances were she would come up with an answer that made sense. I had taken it for granted she would be around for a while longer. I wanted her to see what I did with my life, and it saddened me to think she wouldn't. It put an awful lot of things into perspective.

A week later, my mate Bobby Watts was due to marry Lynn Farrell. Bobby was eighteen and I'd given him a hard time about being too young to tie the knot. I'd gone out with Lynn briefly when Dame Alice Owens moved up to Potter's Bar, but it didn't work out. I was just too clumsy. Captain Chaos. Every time I went round to see her, I'd knock a cup over, or leave muddy footprints all over her mum's carpet, and she'd end up in tears. It was all too stressful.

A big gang of us went out on Bobby's stag night. I remember my mum didn't want me to go. She thought it was too soon after losing my nan. That didn't make sense to me. From what I could see, my nan had packed as much into her life as she could. I knew she'd have wanted me to get on with mine. I went out that night and proposed a toast to her. Round the table, twenty-five of my mates got to their feet and raised their glasses. We all got roaring drunk. In the early hours, we took Bobby home to Russell Square, left him outside, barely able to stand, and rang the bell. His parents, not best pleased at being woken up, came down to find Bobby tied to the gate naked, and his mates running away across the square.

As for my parents, by 1978 I'm sure they were tearing their hair out. I was out all hours, wearing T-shirts I'd designed myself with skin-tight fluorescent trousers (usually green), and looking less and less conventional. One night, getting ready for an Iggy Pop concert, I'd been in the bathroom for ages, experimenting with a sachet of hair dye. By the time I'd finished, my hair was standing on end in lurid red spikes. I was pleased with it. I was pretty sure my parents wouldn't be.

When I tried to sneak out without them seeing me, they knew something was up. My mum caught a glimpse of shocking red as I scurried past the kitchen, and burst into tears. I kept going but my dad came after me. He shouted down the stairs, 'What are you doing? Come back here.' He was furious. I did go back – but not until after the concert.

My mum told me recently that for two years she was worried sick. As far as she was concerned, I showed all the signs of turning into some kind of delinquent. I was staying out late, drinking, seeing girls. My parents never knew when I would be home. I wasn't getting into trouble, but they didn't know that. I was just finding my feet and I was doing it in an era when it was easy to shock people just by wearing make-up and weird clothes. If you looked strange, people did a double take, which was the whole idea. No one would give you a second glance now. I'm not sure it's possible to shock any more. We've seen it all. But then the sight of me in my green punk trousers and make-up was mortifying.

I think it was worse for my dad. Working in the print industry was a tough environment and his job meant handling heavy machinery, mixing with hard individuals. Here was the son he hoped would go to university dyeing his hair.

In the early days of the band, I remember meeting my grandad at Waterloo Station. We were off to join my parents and my brother and sister at a holiday camp on the south coast. I was just going for a couple of days. My grandad always took a great pride in his appearance. That day, I turned up in a pair of Arab-style trousers, all baggy round the bum and gathered at the ankles – shit stoppers, my grandad called them – and ballet shoes. I was wearing an embroidered shirt with a little mandarin collar. My hair flopped over my eyes. My grandad was apoplectic. He couldn't believe his eyes. 'What the bloody hell do you look like? Look at the state of you. If you think I'm getting on that train with you, you've got another thing coming.' He ranted on and on.

When he got on the train, he wouldn't sit with me. We were in separate carriages all the way.

I didn't set out to embarrass him, but the whole point was to dress for effect. The fact it sent him into orbit was exactly what I wanted. When he went off the deep end, I knew I'd got my outfit exactly right.

Chapter Four

I love driving, but I've never had much luck with cars. The day I passed my test I almost rear-ended someone in my dad's Vauxhall Victor on Upper Street in Islington. I managed an emergency stop just in time. A few months later, in my dad's car again (this time his 'new' second-hand Hillman Hunter) I pulled out at a junction and *smack* – someone ran into the side. We both jumped out. I blamed the other driver; he blamed me. Looking back, it was probably my fault. I hadn't looked properly. I dreaded going home and telling my dad I'd smashed up his car, his pride and joy. He was so upset when he saw the side all dented, but it could have been a lot worse. When it was in for repairs, the garage discovered the floor was rotten. It was a write-off. I remember saying, 'See, Dad, I've done you a favour – the floor could have dropped out while the family was in it.'

He wasn't very happy, but he couldn't argue.

My first car was a pale blue Vauxhall Viva, with a red stripe running through the middle. It looked like an Embassy packet on wheels, but it came in handy for getting gigs. Effectively, John Keeble and I managed the band in the beginning. We knew the gigs wouldn't come to us so we went looking for them. It wasn't a job anyone else wanted to take on. Three nights a week we trailed round pubs trying to get bookings. It was a slog. We went to some awful places, and dealt with some rough people. We got gigs by lying that the band was better known than it was, and promising to pack the place out. Then we crossed our fingers. We were learning as we went along, and it was a steep old learning curve.

We weren't choosy. We played some real dives. Sometimes we came away with a few quid, sometimes we settled for a couple of pints. Occasionally, we got nothing. In amongst the shit holes, we landed some good gigs. My grandad knew the owner of the Roxy in Covent Garden and managed to get us a gig there. The Roxy was a basement venue with standing room for around 300 people. It was a dark, cramped, sweaty club but it represented a breakthrough for us in terms of credibility. The Sex Pistols and Siouxsie and the Banshees had played there. We were still in our power-pop phase at this point, performing our own songs, most of them written by Gary, and a few by Steve. Our style was high-energy, thrashing, catchy pop.

It wasn't long before we became familiar faces on the circuit and started attracting some attention. One night, waiting to get into the Nashville to see Midge Ure's band, the Rich Kids, I heard someone say, 'There's Tony Hadley.' I thought, Fucking hell, we're on our way.

Our first review appeared in *New Musical Express* in December 1977, after a gig in King's Cross. It made us think we were on the right lines with our brand of four-to-the-floor pop. 'The Makers are a new band. A kick in the groin band. A needle in the arm band. An everything you've always wanted but never thought you'd hear band.'

It was all looking good. Around us, other bands, like Secret Affair, a five-piece mod-revival band, were landing deals. I thought that Ian Page, their lead singer, was incredibly cool. They went on to have a hit with 'Time For Action', which became something of a youth anthem in 1979. It felt like everyone else was being signed. Bill Hurley, a mate of mine from IPC, had given up his job to concentrate on music full-time. He was in a band called the Inmates. One day my mum came home from her weekly trip to the washing baths. She had been chatting to Bill's mum. The Inmates had landed a record deal. I was pleased for them but hoped we wouldn't be too far behind.

We carried on playing, appearing on bills with bands like Johnny Curious and the Strangers, and Gene October's Chelsea. Gene tried to poach John Keeble. It must have been tempting for him as Chelsea had a record deal, but in the end, out of loyalty, he decided to stick with the Makers. Like the rest of us, John believed we would make it. It was all about timing, although there were moments of sheer frustration along the way. In early '78 we headlined at Middlesex Polytechnic. Even the support act, the Monos, had been signed. It was starting to depress us.

There had been hints of a publishing deal with EMI and, as far as I was concerned, that was as good as a record deal. I didn't know the difference. In the end, it didn't happen. I was so disappointed, I sat on the end of my bed sobbing. My dad found me, smoking and crying. All he worried about was that there was no guarantee we would ever make it. He didn't want to see the bottom fall out of my world every time something went wrong. Plenty of bands came and went. Meanwhile, all he could do was advise me to keep my feet firmly on the ground. For the next few months, we continued to play gigs in venues like the Rock Garden and the Hope and Anchor.

In 1978, we booked our first recording session in a BBC studio in Langham House – now a hotel – in the West End. The atmosphere and technical paraphernalia felt peculiar. For the first time, we performed wearing headphones – cans. Once we got used to the strangeness of being in a studio, we settled down and recorded thirteen tracks, all power pop, built around a powerful drum and bass line. They were raw, and it was weird hearing takes played back, but we were happy. The recording captured the energy of the band. More than twenty years on, it still sounds pretty good.

By then, Steve Dagger was on the scene, hanging out with us and coming to the gigs. He had also been a pupil at Dame Alice Owens, a couple of years above us, and became friendly with the band through Gary. I wasn't sure of the connection but, according to John Keeble, they met when Steve helped roadie a gig for the Same Band – the band Gary played in before we all got together. John's usually pretty good on details, but I wouldn't like to swear to that one. In all the time I knew Steve Dagger it was pretty obvious he had no idea what a road crew did. Still, he was good company and he thought the Makers had something. I'm not sure exactly when he eased into the role of manager; it was all pretty informal then.

Steve thought we should drop Richie Miller as the bass player and replace him with Gary's younger brother, Martin, who had also started hanging around with us. It was an idea that came out of nowhere. Richie was a mate and he played well. Why drop him? Dagger argued that Martin looked the part. Maybe we weren't landing the record deal we wanted because we had the wrong image. Having Martin in the line-up might make all the difference.

I'm not even sure Martin could play bass at that stage. He was playing guitar in a punk band called the Defects. We mulled over what Dagger had said about image. It goes without saying that Richie wasn't part of these discussions. We wanted success, but we had reservations about dumping our bass player. It felt wrong, although we could see that Martin would fit into the line-up. He was seventeen and a good-looking lad, with striking blue eyes. It was probably less of a dilemma for Gary. He made no secret of the fact he wanted his brother in the band.

Steve Dagger was a clever guy and persuasive. I trusted his judgement. He was older and wiser. We went along with him and decided that Richie would be dropped. He played his last gig with us at the Hope and Anchor in May '78. It earned a good review too in *Sounds*. 'They size up as a currently very typical pop/rock band laced with statutory energy and with beautifully cut hair.'

Of course Richie didn't know that was his last gig and no one wanted to tell him. We didn't have the guts. It was all pretty underhand, and I'm sorry for the way it was handled. We set up a band meeting at a pub in Islington, which we had no intention of attending. When Richie arrived, Steve Dagger was waiting for him. While Dagger told him he was no longer required, the rest of us sat hunched over our pints somewhere else, feeling guilty. It was appalling. I still feel ashamed about that whole episode.

Being realistic, things did work out with the new line-up. Maybe we'd never have become Spandau Ballet otherwise. With Martin in the band, we ditched the Makers and started calling ourselves the Gentry.

It was while I was working at IPC that I fell in love for the first time.

One day, at the start of my shift, I was on the loading bay when I caught sight of a beautiful girl walking past the warehouse. Tall, with short, dark hair. Fine, chiselled features. I dropped what I was doing and ran after her. My supervisor,

Joe Kent, yelled at me, 'Where do you think you're going? Come back.' I spun round – 'Joe, I'll be back in a second.' The girl vanished through the door that led to the offices upstairs. I chased after her, and caught up just before she got to her office. I blundered in. 'Hi, you don't know me, but I work in the warehouse. I'd really like to take you out.'

She stared at me as if I was mad. She said, 'Are you serious? It's eight thirty a.m.'

I said, 'I'm *really* serious.'

She said, 'I'm sorry, I've got a boyfriend.'

I said, 'Get rid of him.' I was a cheeky sod.

For the next couple of weeks, I delivered magazines to her office, perched on her desk, and pestered her for a date. She wasn't interested. She kept reminding me she already had a boyfriend. I wasn't about to take no for an answer. I told her to ditch him and go out with me instead. I can be incredibly persistent. Eventually, she admitted she had finished with the boyfriend. I was over the moon. That was how I started seeing Alison Montgomery.

I was eighteen. Ali was twenty-three. For nine months, we were inseparable. I was mad about her. I'd always had this romantic notion of waiting until the right girl came along to lose my virginity. Ali was that girl. She came from a different, well-to-do world. Her father was a diplomat. We had nothing in common, but we fell in love although, at times, our differences surfaced. I remember she didn't want to take me to a party because she didn't think I'd fit in. Of course, that made me want to go all the more. It turned out to be a boring affair, with lots of serious people locked in dull conversation in the kitchen. One or two spoke to me. 'And what do you do?' 'Oh, I pack boxes in a warehouse.' They tended to drift away after that.

Out of boredom, I decided to make my own entertainment.

I rounded up a few people and we ended up outside, lying on the pavement, looking at the stars. It was a lovely clear night. I was in my element. When Ali found me, she was not amused. She accused me of disrupting the party and threw a drink over me.

I didn't like to say, but I thought that was far more disruptive than my stargazing.

While I was seeing Ali, I was always coming in late. My parents worried themselves sick. If I wasn't home when I said I'd be my mum couldn't sleep. She tossed and turned, afraid there'd been an accident. I wasn't very good at ringing to say I'd be late. Sometimes, I'd come in at 3 a.m. to find my mum sitting at the top of the stairs in tears, convinced something terrible had happened to me. My dad went mad. When I think about it now, I feel really awful about putting them through all that. I just never realized how late it was. Anyone who knows me won't be surprised to hear that my time-keeping has never been good.

A couple of years earlier, my parents had gone out for the evening. I was left in charge, baby-sitting. They were due back around 12.30 a.m. I put Steve to bed, then waited with my sister, Lee, for them to come home. It got to 1 a.m. and there was no sign of them. We sat at the top of the stairs waiting, checking the time every few minutes. At 2 a.m. they still weren't back. I was frantic by then. At 2.15 a.m., the front door opened. We shot down the stairs. There were my mum and dad, all smiles, after a good night out. I couldn't believe my eyes. I said, 'Where the hell have you *been*? You said you'd be home *hours* ago!'

They looked at me in amazement. I never spoke to them like that. Then they started laughing. My dad could hardly contain himself. He said, 'Now you know what it's like.'

It's true, I did, and I still managed to drive them up the wall with worry.

At that stage, we were playing whatever gigs we could as the Gentry – a more soulful version of the Makers – although we didn't seem to be making much progress. It was all very frustrating. One night we played the Red Cow in Hammersmith. On the way home afterwards, Ali started pulling the band apart. I didn't want to know. She had a few choice words about Steve Dagger. Still, I thought she was out of order. By the time we pulled up outside her place in Putney, I'd had enough. We had a huge row. It felt as if Ali was testing my loyalty, and the band was winning.

Not long after, we broke up.

We still thought we were on the brink of making it as the Gentry. In early 1979 we were booked to play a Saturday night in Basildon. We'd done a gig there a few weeks earlier, which went down well, but second time round, it had disaster written all over it. My car was out of action. My dad's car was not available. That just left John Keeble's van. There was no way we would get all the gear into that. Our only option was to make two trips. We loaded up, did one run to Basildon, then came back for the rest.

The best was still to come. At the end of the night, Steve Dagger broke the news that we were not being paid. The bloke running the place had some feeble excuse about there not being as many people in that night as he'd hoped. He was a lot bigger than Dagger, who didn't feel like arguing. We loaded up John's van. Thankfully, some mates had turned up to see us, which meant we were able to get back to London in one go, all of us swearing that we would never play that venue again, however bad things got. We never did.

We were all wondering what we needed to do to get the breakthrough we needed. The Gentry didn't seem to be setting the world alight. We reached the point where we had just three dates left in the diary. In May '79, we played the Rock Garden, the Hope and Anchor and the Marquee, all sweaty, packed, standing-room-only venues. Then we started to think about what to do next.

Somewhere along the way, I had left the warehouse at IPC in a hurry after a fall-out with John Davison. If I had stuck around, things would have got ugly. I had visions of broken bones (mine, not his). It was time to find another job, fast. By then, I knew most of the people working in the offices upstairs. I went up one day and cast around for work. One of the guys bailed me out on the spot. I became a sales executive on *Electronics Weekly* and *Electrical Review*.

I also became deputy father of the chapel for the print union, NATSOPA – at nineteen, one of the youngest union officials at that level in the country. I loved the meetings, getting round the table with other officials, negotiating with management. Most of the union reps were a lot older, and a lot more left wing. Among my union colleagues was John Davison, who represented SOGAT. Having been glad to see the back of me in the warehouse, I don't suppose he was thrilled at having to deal with me at union meetings. It didn't bother me. One of the directors at IPC expressed concern at my union dealings. I didn't see the work in political terms. I was never a militant. It was more to do with principles, making sure people were treated with respect. I enjoyed taking things on; if I saw an injustice, I'd tackle it. To the irritation of the other reps, I wasn't always conventional. I walked through my own picket line one day, because I disagreed with the strike.

I was doing all right financially, though. My union work meant business lunches here and there. I could pick up sixty or seventy pounds for a single Saturday-night shift at one of the Sunday papers. Some weeks, I was coming out with more than a hundred pounds, which was serious money for a nineteen-year-old in 1979. I still have my union card.

I was living in two utterly different worlds. By day, a sales executive and union rep, neatly turned out in the kind of uniform every office worker wore. By night, one of the so-called bright young things, a singer in a band I reckoned was going places. I wore frilly shirts and trousers tucked into knee-length, fur-trimmed boots.

I wasn't the only one. The New Romantics were coming.

Chapter Five

By 1979, a small, sweaty club called the Blitz in Great Queen Street, Covent Garden, had become the hub for London's bright young things. By day, the Blitz was a wine bar, a haunt for business people. I used to go there with some of the guys from IPC for expense-account lunches now and then. The waitresses always looked after me. On Tuesday nights, it opened its doors to a different, more exotic crowd.

The Blitz was the brainchild of Steve Strange, who ran the best clubs in London. Steve was heavily into the music scene. He'd worked with the punk band Generation X, and later formed Visage with another Blitz regular, Rusty Egan. They went on to have a hit with 'Fade to Grey' in 1980. Steve set the tone with his own unique style of dress, glamour make-up and a hairstyle that defied gravity. He became an icon in his own right. Steve manned the door. If you didn't look the part, you didn't get in. Gary, Martin, Steve, John and I were all regulars. It was rumoured that Steve Strange turned away Mick Jagger at the door one night. I never found out if that was true, but it wouldn't have surprised me. As word spread, the Blitz became the coolest club in London. It was just a couple of hundred people getting together, but it felt like the centre of the universe.

I loved the atmosphere of the place. It was like stepping into a different world, a world which encouraged oddity. There was an element of fancy dress, with girls in bouffant frocks and too much make-up, a look that later became known as New Romantic. Most of the guys wore make-up too. It was all very theatrical, a bit like a costume drama with different periods thrown together. You could easily feel underdressed at the Blitz, even in your most outrageous gear.

A bar ran the length of the room. At the far end was a dance floor. Upstairs, too many people squeezed into the VIP area. Each week it was the same crowd, drinking and dancing to an eclectic soundtrack that veered from Kraftwerk to Roxy Music and the B-52s. The mix was the work of Rusty Egan, then drummer with the Rich Kids, whose lead singer Midge Ure – also a Blitz regular – went on to form Ultravox. Designers like Melissa Caplan, Simon Withers and Stephen Linnard were regulars, as were Boy George and Marilyn.

We all got to know each other.

A myth grew up around the place that it was a hotbed of intellectuals. The idea that everyone was discussing Nietzsche and Jean-Paul Sartre was laughable. The Blitz was more about dressing up, drinking Schlitz beer, taking speed and meeting girls, than anything else.

In that kind of atmosphere it was hard to stand out from the crowd, but one night a girl walked in who caught my eye straight away. She was tall and slim, striking, with curly strawberry-blonde hair. Fresh-faced. I shot over to speak to her. She had a strange name I couldn't quite get to grips with. Léonie. I spent hours talking to her, trying hard to impress her. I think she had her doubts, initially. I was dressed as an Edwardian gent, complete with coat. It was far too hot for a coat but I wouldn't take it off in case it spoiled the look. She later told me she thought I was a bit odd. Eventually, I took a chance and kissed her. It wasn't exactly a polite peck on the cheek – more of a lunge. Without warning, I pounced, pinning her to the fruit machine. She seemed a bit taken aback, but by the end of the night I had her number.

I can remember calling her, and struggling with the French pronunciation of her name. It took a while to get the hang of it: Lay-own-ee. It turned out she was living in Clapham, South London, which threw me. I'm not very good south of the river. I can just about find my way to Elephant and Castle. Beyond that, I'm lost. I arranged to take her to a funfair for our first date and roped in my mate, Nicky Sibley, to make sure I actually got to Clapham. Léonie had her sister, Gail, in tow.

As first dates go, it was a success. Nicky and I made it to her flat without getting lost and, when she answered the door, she looked amazing. I think she was relieved to see I'd ditched the Edwardian gear. It turned out to be a fantastic day. I was so proud this gorgeous girl was with me and I was out to impress. I managed to win a goldfish on the shooting range, and dragged her on just about every ride, the scarier the better. She went along with it, although I later found out she's not really one for scary rides. (Then again, a couple of years later, she did agree to marry me, which probably qualifies as the scariest ride of all.) By the end of the day, we'd made plans to meet again.

In some respects, we made an unlikely couple. I was nineteen; she was twenty-three. I was working class; she was posh. I was in an unsigned band; she had a well-paid job at the BBC. Our backgrounds were chalk and cheese. Léonie had lived in Singapore and Canada, and been to boarding school, but our differences didn't seem important. There was no awkwardness between us. Before long, I was smitten. We started spending as much time together as we could.

There was still no sign of a record deal. It was frustrating and depressing. All around us, other bands were being signed. We didn't want to spend the rest of our lives playing the Hope and Anchor, but there was little to suggest a breakthrough. We suspected we needed to reinvent ourselves. By now, we had decided to drop the Gentry. I'm not sure where the name came from in the first place, since we all seemed to hate it. We agreed we didn't want to keep playing the same venues any more as we weren't getting anywhere. We took ourselves off the gig circuit and, for several months, rehearsed in private, working on new material. Most weekends, we got together and worked on songs at a rehearsal studio in Holloway. We were regulars, as were Iron Maiden and another band soon to change their name too – from the North London Invaders to Madness.

At that point, we weren't sure what to call ourselves. For a while, we were a band with no name. But though we weren't doing as well as we hoped, no one wanted to give up. There was a good spirit about the band, an optimism. We were a tight unit, held together by a desire to succeed and a belief that one day we would. We were all excited about the music, which now bore the hallmarks of what would later become Spandau Ballet. It was pop with a solid bass line, a dance rhythm, and distinctive vocals. Our set included 'To Cut A Long Story Short' with its repetitive synthesizer line. We spent hours playing, improving the songs. We all wanted the same thing, to make the songs as good as they could be. Everyone pretty much mucked in on all levels. If we needed guitar strings or a pair of drumsticks, we chipped in. I didn't think it would ever be any different and that was our strength. There was a strong sense of loyalty. We counted on each other, sensing that any breakthrough would depend on the five of us. We needed each other.

At this point, no one wanted to go back to playing pubs and clubs, on the off chance one of the music papers might give us a good review. We had tried all that. We needed to find a different way. By then, we were all part of the Blitz scene. Similar clubs were springing up around London and elsewhere in the country. Those people were our audience. It made sense to gauge their reaction to the new set.

We decided to go out on a limb and arranged a gig at the rehearsal studio we had spent our time in over the past few months. One Saturday morning in November 1979, before an invited audience of around thirty people, mainly mates from the Blitz, in a studio at Halligan's, on Holloway Road, we played our set. I still don't think we were calling ourselves New Romantics at this point. Although we knew the audience – who looked like they'd been up clubbing all night – we didn't expect an easy ride. The set went down well, but you have to remember we were playing to people who prided themselves on being cool. While they were appreciative, they didn't exactly jump up and down.

Afterwards, in the pub next door, we discussed our next move. At that stage, we still didn't have a name for the band. Robert Elms, the journalist, suggested Spandau Ballet. He had seen it scrawled on the wall of a toilet in Berlin, and thought it had a ring to it. Everyone liked it. It was different. It felt right. There and then, we buried the Gentry for good and became Spandau Ballet. Span-dow Bah-lay. It was a while before we got the pronunciation of the new name right.

From then on, we played a different circuit, concentrating on the clubs in town. In December '79 we played the Blitz.

By now the music press were fed up with us. They accused us of being elitist. I suspect what they really hated was that we were making a name for ourselves without their help. They felt left out. It was the same for the record companies. If they wanted to see us, they had to tune in to what was happening on the club scene. Even if they heard about a gig, there was no guarantee they'd get in. Most of the clubs operated a strict – and peculiar – dress code.

The night we played the Blitz, Chris Blackwell of Island Records was in the audience. Afterwards, he came to meet us; he liked us very much. He was interested in signing us to Island. We all thought we had made it. In the New Year, everyone gave up their jobs. Everyone, except me. Gary, Martin and Steve were in the print trade. John Keeble was working as a bank clerk. My dad persuaded me not to resign. He was cautious. I'm not sure he thought being in a band constituted a proper job. Despite the interest from Island, he still wasn't convinced that the dream of being a pop star would become a reality. He wanted me to keep working until we had something solid; a signed record deal. It made sense, although we all believed that was about to happen.

Before we went to Island – to sign, so we believed – we met with Brian Carr, our legal advisor. Carr, recommended by Chris Blackwell, briefed us over lunch in a Chinese restaurant in Hammersmith. At that stage, we didn't know the terms of the Island offer, and we didn't care. There was an excitement round the table. We had spent the past three years slogging for this, served our time playing shitty pubs all over London, gone through four name changes. Now, at last, we were about to get our reward.

We would have signed anything.

Brian Carr told us that if at any stage during the meeting he said, 'Gentlemen, I think we should leave,' we were to do just that, without argument. It was a precaution in case anything went wrong. Not that it would. We were confident. A couple of hours later, midway through the meeting with Island, before anyone had a chance to sign anything, Brian Carr got to his feet. 'Gentlemen . . .' We all stared at him. No. He couldn't be leaving. He picked up his belongings. He was. We trudged behind him in utter disbelief. This was not what we had expected. It turned out Island was offering a standard contract. Brian Carr believed we could do much better. Our dreams were in pieces. We were devastated. The five of us, plus Dagger, went back to Gary and Martin's house, where there was an almighty row. Everyone was screaming. Dagger bore the brunt. John Keeble was furious. He had given up a well-paid job in a bank, believing a deal was imminent. Dagger stood his ground. If Brian Carr thought the Island offer wasn't up to scratch, that was good enough for him. I sided with Dagger. He was our manager. We had to trust him. If Island wanted us, someone else would. We had to believe that the next time a record company approached us, it would be on the right terms.

Léonie and I were seeing as much of each other as we could. In the early days of the band, I had a lot of free time. Whenever I got a chance, I would call in at the BBC to see her, dressed in my New Romantic gear. I looked a sight. At the time, I had a favourite pair of boots decorated with chains. Léonie's boss, Bobby Jay, said he always knew when I'd turned up because he could hear me clanking my way along the corridor.

While I was hanging around, waiting for Léonie, I'd bump into some of the Radio 1 DJs. I got to know Simon Bates, Dave Lee Travis, Steve Wright and Peter Powell. Peter was always a big champion of the band. Before Spandau landed a deal, he played our demos and gave us a lot of encouragement. The two of us became friendly.

Léonie was doing well at the BBC. She landed a job on-screen, as the scorer on the quiz, *My Music*, with Frank Muir and Dennis Norden. I was so proud of her.

There was only one sticky moment when we came close to calling things off. Although I thought the world of her, I still wanted to spend time with my mates. At twenty years old, I hadn't quite got the hang of making arrangements with my girlfriend, and sticking to them. Sometimes, instead of seeing Léonie I'd end up joining the lads for a session instead. Not surprisingly, it got on her nerves. In the end, I overstepped the mark once too often.

One of my mates called to see if I fancied a few pints. I did, but I had a date with Léonie. I called her. 'Listen, love, I know I'm meant to see you tonight, but do you mind if I go for a drink with the lads?'

It was the final straw. She said, 'Do what you want. But if you're seeing them, you don't see me.' The line went dead. I stared at the receiver in disbelief. She had never hung up on me before.

I went back into the front room. Everyone else was watching *Top Of The Pops*. My mum took one look at my face and said, 'Is everything all right?' I nodded but, inside, I was in a terrible state. My stomach churning, I forced myself to sit there until the end of the programme. As the credits rolled, I got up. 'I just have to pop out,' I said, and headed off to see Léonie. I was furious with her for hanging up on me. 'Don't ever put the phone down on me again,' I said. She was just as angry. 'If you keep blowing me out for your mates, what do you expect?'

It dawned on me that she wasn't about to put up with being messed around. She had too much self-respect. Léonie had no problem with me seeing my mates, but a date was a date. It was that simple. If I kept letting her down, it would be over between us. I was in danger of losing her, and the thought made me feel sick. It was the last thing I wanted. She meant too much to me. I was in love with her. I couldn't imagine life without her.

I decided to get my act together.

The band had been booked to play a two-week residency at a club in St-Tropez. The timing could not have been better. In London, there was increasing interest in us from various record companies. Since the deal with Island had fallen through, however, there were no firm offers on the table.

We all told ourselves it was only a matter of time.

Meanwhile, we were growing impatient. We had seen so many of our contemporaries, bands like Pleaser, getting deals while we remained unsigned. Pleaser were a bit like a Beatles pastiche band, in terms of their style and sound. We felt our drum and bass sound set us apart, as well as our vocals. I don't suppose everyone liked my voice but most people seemed to agree it sounded different to any of the other singers around at the time. At that point, getting a deal was the be all and end all. It seemed that way, anyhow. Privately, I had moments when I wondered if it was ever going to happen. Three years had gone by since I'd cried my eyes out over the collapse of the EMI publishing deal and it was months since we had walked away from Chris Blackwell and Island Records.

Still, the profile of the band was good. People were talking about us. Although we had played relatively few gigs in our new guise as Spandau Ballet, our reputation had spread beyond the club scene. In the spring of 1980 we had played the Scala Cinema in the West End. The venue, better known for obscure art-house films than pop bands, suited us down to the ground. It was about as unconventional as we were. There was no support band, just some cult film with sub-titles. Instead of the Scala's usual crowd of earnest film buffs, were people from the Blitz. In their midst, doing their best to blend in, but not quite managing it, were those record company executives who'd managed to get hold of tickets.

The venue worked to our advantage. As we played, blurry images flickered on a screen behind us. Shafts of white light threw the band into sharp relief.

The whole thing was done on the cheap, but the effect was striking.

It gave the record companies something to think about. I'm not sure they knew what to make of us. We had an unusual look, and we could play, but we stuck two fingers up to the music industry. Under normal circumstances, bands chased record companies, not the other way round. It must have driven them mad. That was the idea, of course. We wanted a deal, but we wanted the right deal. The only way to get it was by holding out. The record companies were beginning to get the message. I suspect they hated us for it, arrogant little shits that we were. Actually, the reason we dug our heels in was only partly to do with arrogance; it was more about doing things on our own terms. Record company executives swam in shark-infested waters. If they expected us to get in with them, we wanted lifeguards standing by. We preferred to deal with people we knew we could trust, in other words, each other. When it came to outsiders, executives in suits, we were wary.

By the time we played the Scala, there were record companies ready to sign us. We weren't ready to sign, though. Steve Dagger and Brian Carr continued to play it cool, waiting for the balance of power to shift even more in our favour.

A few weeks later, it did.

We returned to play the Scala in May 1980, this time, with

a television crew from a show called *Twentieth Century Box* in tow. The series, produced by Janet Street Porter for London Weekend Television, deemed us worthy of a show all to ourselves. For an unsigned band, it was manna from heaven, although there was the odd hitch during filming. A power failure halfway through the set knocked out the PA system and plunged the place into darkness. It could have been much worse. It turned out that a single 13-amp plug was carrying the load of our equipment, the PA and the lights. I'm surprised we didn't burn the place down.

The resulting documentary, shot in black and white, condensed a day in the life of Spandau Ballet into a slick thirty minutes. It was scheduled for transmission a few weeks later.

We began to plan our trip to the South of France.

It was a huge adventure for all of us. Other than the odd school trip or package holiday, no one had spent much time abroad. We were hardly seasoned travellers, any of us, but we were unfazed at the thought of driving hundreds of miles to the French Riviera. A few months before, I had gone to Luxembourg with John Keeble. We had delivered a van-load of tiles for his dad, Stan, who was off work recovering from a hernia operation. That trip had taught us all we needed to know about driving on the right-hand side of the road. We were practically old hands.

Only John and Steve Dagger were old enough to hire a van. They went up to Tottenham Hale and picked up a ten-seater Toyota. Dagger had only just passed his test. He climbed into the driver's seat. John got in beside him. Dagger stared at the instrument panel. He peered at the gear stick, which was on the steering column. He frowned. Anyone would have thought he was attempting to pilot the *Starship Enterprise*, rather than drive a van. John waited for him to start the engine. Nothing happened. Dagger turned to face him. There was a look of utter incomprehension on his face. John said, 'Shall I drive?' They swapped places. That was the only time John ever saw our manager behind the wheel of a vehicle. Any thoughts of a three-way split on the drive to St-Tropez went out the window there and then. John and I did it between us.

As we loaded the van, we began to have doubts about whether it was big enough. We took out a row of seats, and began to shoehorn everything in. A roof rack was looking like a good bet. It would have been a squeeze with just the band and Dagger, but we'd invited a few more people along. From the Blitz crowd was Bob Elms, the journalist, photographer Graham Smith, and Simon Withers, who, for the next couple of weeks, would be our lighting director. Some mates from Islington – Paul Devaney, Ricky Stanborough and Lee Cleary – came too. Neil Matthews, another mate from school and the Blitz, came along on his motorbike.

The van was groaning under the weight of the luggage, equipment, lights and bodies. The roof rack added several more feet to the height of the vehicle. Everyone else was in by the time it pulled up outside my place. There was only one place for my case to go. We heaved it up onto the roof and secured it as best we could. The luggage formed a small, unsteady tower. It didn't look safe. I had visions of looking in the rear-view mirror on the way down the motorway, in time to see our clothes disappearing under the wheels of the vehicles following us. The one consolation was that there was so much gear in the van I couldn't actually see out of the rear-view mirror.

Inside, it was a jumble of bodies. Not everyone had a seat. A couple of people were roughing it on top of the amps. The sliding door at the back of the van was completely hidden. For the duration of the trip – about twenty-four hours on the road – it stayed shut. Anyone in the back wanting to get in or out had to squeeze through the window. The van was an absolute death trap. We didn't care. We were off to St-Tropez.

I took the wheel for a couple of hours, then swapped with John. We kept going like that all the way. Every time we pulled in at a service station, we checked the roof rack. For all it looked like it would topple off, it stayed put. On the final leg of the trip, at the end of the autoroute, I was behind the wheel. John had retreated into the back with a bottle of wine. There was a steep camber on the road and it crossed my mind that, above me, the roof rack was probably leaning dangerously to one side. Suddenly, there was a loud bang and the van slewed. The rear tyre on my side had blown. The van slid away from under me. I hung onto the wheel. We lurched across the carriageway, then swung back again. My hands gripped the wheel, which spun through my fingers. The van listed to one side. I thought, We've had it. In the back, everyone was quiet. Our speed began to drop. I touched the brake. Gradually, we came to a stop. I was shaking. We all got out. The back tyre was shredded on the rim. We found the spare, but no jack. We were stuffed.

We stood at the side of the road flagging down passing cars. No one stopped. We must have looked a sight. A rag-bag of blokes in funny clothes, with a van listing to one side. Eventually, a lorry pulled up. In bad, broken French, we asked for help. The driver was English. He promised to stop at the next service station and get someone to come out. We thought, That's the last we'll see of him, but he was as good as his word. While we were still wondering what to do next, a breakdown truck pulled in beside us. The van was so heavy we couldn't jack it up. Everything had to come out. We piled our belongings on the side of the road, changed the tyre and loaded up again. A couple of miles further on, the road narrowed as it took us high into the hills. We looked at each other. All that separated us from a sheer drop was a narrow strip of earth. I gripped the steering wheel and gave thanks.

I wasn't the only one thinking we were lucky to be alive.

The Papagayo Club was one of the smart clubs on the marina. It still is. Out front, there were so many yachts moored, it was difficult to see the sea beyond the rows of gleaming hulls. The place reeked of money. We thought we'd arrived. Inside, the club looked ordinary. A small stage at one end. A dance floor. Flock wallpaper and heavy velvet drapes. Dust in the air. As with most clubs, it needed people to bring it to life. The deal was we would play two sets a night, which posed an immediate problem. We only had enough material for one. We decided to play the same set twice, in a different order. Which is what we did, night after night, for two weeks. No one noticed.

We had been promised an apartment next to the club for the duration of our stay. Since St-Tropez was the playground of millionaires, and we'd landed a gig in an exclusive club, we anticipated something special. What we got was a couple of rooms with mattresses on the floor. As soon as we started to unpack, the place looked as if it had been trashed. We had all brought more clothes than we could possibly wear. It was like a jumble sale.

No one had much money at the time and our parents had packed some food to keep us going. It was mostly savoury rice and packet soup, tins of spam and corned beef. There was a small kitchen in the apartment, but no one used it. For the two weeks we were there the only thing in the fridge was a bottle of amyl nitrite.

We weren't being paid much for playing the Papagayo, but no one cared. We could drink as much as we liked in the bar, which seemed more than fair. On our first night we set up the gear, did a sound check, and went for a few drinks. If we hadn't been working there on a drink-as-much-as-you-like basis, we would never have been able to go near the place. It didn't matter what you had to drink, nothing was less than eight pounds. It was unbelievable, yet the place was packed with people getting through cocktails and champagne like they were going out of fashion. At 12.30 a.m., we went on and played the first set. They seemed to like us. A couple of hours later, we played the first set again, in a different order. Back at the bar, we had a few more drinks.

The next day, the owner of the club wanted to see us. It was a bit like being hauled in front of the headmaster. We shuffled into his office. He sat behind his desk, drawing on a hookah. The shades were drawn and the place was in semi-darkness, yet for some reason he was wearing sunglasses. He was not pleased. He had our bar bill from the night before. It came to just short of £1,500. It did seem like a lot, although later John Keeble worked out it was only around ten drinks each, which was moderate for us. From then on, we were told to stick to weak beer. We had a crisis meeting. Maybe we should just go home. Fuck him. Dagger advised against it. If we crossed the club owner, we were asking for trouble.

That night we went to the club feeling depressed. There wasn't much point in playing a fancy place on the Riviera if you couldn't afford a decent drink. Then one of the girls behind the bar slipped us some proper drinks. Things were looking up.

For the next couple of weeks we settled into a new routine. We would play our second set then head into the basement of the club to see a French mime act called Shaker. At around 5 a.m., we'd call it a night and head to the bakery for coffee and croissants. That's when I discovered pain au chocolat. Fantastic. At around 6 a.m., we'd get some sleep. The afternoons were spent on the beach, swimming and trying not to stare at the topless women. At some point I would go in search of something to eat. Most of the others didn't bother. Every night, John Keeble called at the local supermarket for a cheap bottle of wine and a couple of pots of yogurt. That was supper. After a few days, I lost my voice. I went to the doctor, who shone a light on my throat. The first thing he wanted to know was whether I had been swimming in the sea. I had. He pointed at a red button on his desk. 'Your throat is that colour,' he said. He gave me a jab of penicillin and advised me to stay out of the water. His lip curled in disgust. 'The Mediterranean is filthy,' he said. Apparently, it's all those fancy boats flushing their toilets straight into the sea.

While we were away, *Twentieth Century Box* aired. It was effectively a half-hour commercial for the band. Back in London, several record company executives were chasing us. They tried Brian Carr, our legal representative, who was polite but unhelpful. The band was out of the country, was about all he had to say. They tried Dagger. The calls were answered by his mum and dad, who knew less than Brian Carr. No one had mobile phones in 1980. We couldn't be contacted. Dagger, meanwhile, spoke to Carr. We knew what was going on in London. The deal we wanted could not be far away.

In St-Tropez, the set was going down well, but the local population was not sure what to make of us. One newspaper ran a picture of us drinking, under the headline, *They drink beer!* We did look odd. Although it was the height of summer, we strolled round town with our trousers tucked into knee-length leather boots, Sam Browne belts slung round our hips. Our Germanic name and odd dress sense had already resulted in some idle gossip in London about us being some kind of neo-Nazi group. During our stay in St-Tropez, we managed to offend the locals by posing for publicity shots in front of a local monument, dressed like storm troopers. The pictures were great, but the monument was a war memorial. We hadn't realized. It was asking for trouble. That night, out drinking, we were chased by thugs with baseball bats. It was terrifying. We got the message. We used a network of friendly barmen to spread the word that we were sorry for being such stupid arseholes. It seemed to do the trick. The heavies backed off.

With just a couple of days left in St-Tropez, the club treated us to a dinner in a restaurant up in the hills above the town. The view was spectacular. We were all knocking back the booze – me probably more than most. That night on stage I could barely stand. I did the whole set holding on to the mike stand. It was the only way I could stay upright. The funny thing was, everyone said it was the best set I'd done all week, which may – or may not – have been a compliment.

We all ended up drunkenly wandering along a jetty at the marina in the early hours. Simon Withers, unwisely, decided to dive in. It was about a foot deep. He gashed his head on an old bike that was rusting in the water. It could have been much worse. I was on the point of diving in after him and managed to stop myself just in time. That was one occasion when two (bleeding) heads would definitely not have been better than one.

We left St-Tropez in blistering heat. Steve Norman climbed into the van in his swimming trunks and a pair of flip-flops. The sun beat down as we began the journey north. When we reached Lyon, we stopped for petrol. It was a bit cooler already. We carried on. The temperature continued to drop. Steve started to shiver. His clothes were buried under an amplifier, the drum kit and a few lights.

South of Paris, we stopped for a rest. We were all starving. We were also broke. We sat watching people eat their meals, eyeing up their leftovers. We were so hungry we didn't care. After a couple of minutes, we spoke up. 'Excuse me, are you finished with that?' Then, while they watched in disgust, we slid their plates over and wolfed down the remains of their meals.

The only food left from the stuff we had brought from home was a tin of spam and a tin of corned beef. We had no knives or forks. John opened the corned beef. My stomach heaved. In the heat, the meat had turned almost to liquid. It wobbled. John, Martin and Steve dug around, using their fingers. The meat came out in soggy lumps. I went hungry.

I was driving as we approached Paris. I sailed past the exit for the ferry and ended up going round the ring road a second time. When I missed the turn-off a third time, there was so much shouting and name-calling in the back of the van that I braked and – at huge risk to us all – reversed at speed along the *periphérique*, while motorists swerved and swore and blasted their horns. That shut them up.

By the time we got back to London, interest in signing us had reached a mild frenzy. We arranged a gig, this time on HMS *Belfast*, a Second World War warship moored near Tower Bridge, on the Thames. I'm not quite sure how we pulled that one off. I suspect we lied to make ourselves sound more respectable. It was obvious from the expressions on the faces of the *Belfast*'s crew that they were expecting something more sedate, like a string quintet.

It was a bizarre venue. We were playing in a metal chamber, effectively. It felt like a furnace once the audience was in, and did strange things to the sound. The ceiling was so low I was worried about banging my head. It turned out to be the last gig we played as an unsigned band.

It was a good gig too. All the usual suspects from the Blitz showed up in their most outrageous gear. It was all about standing out from the crowd. Some people went to extremes to cause a stir. One guy helped himself to a rowing boat and came alongside the *Belfast*, where – with some difficulty – other guests hauled him on board. It was quite an entrance. The performance artist, Leigh Bowery, arrived in an outfit decorated with light bulbs. He spent the night plugged into the mains, a one-man light show in the corner.

In the end, we signed with Chrysalis. They were prepared to respect the fact we wanted to retain creative control. Chris Wright, the company's joint chairman, called us 'one of the most original and innovative bands to emerge in the UK over the last few years.' He said, 'Spandau Ballet are destined to become one of the major influential talents in the next few years.'

When the deal was finally agreed, we went into the boardroom and signed. There was no huge fanfare. It was all a bit flat. We had a glass of champagne, posed for a few photographs, and left. As with most things, the reality rarely matches the expectation. That afternoon, I went into the studio and laid down the vocal for our first single, 'To Cut A Long Story Short'.

Chapter Six

The London Dungeon was the setting for the 'To Cut A Long Story Short' video. We needed a location close to home because the budget was tight, around £5,000, which wasn't much. This was the new era of pop videos. Although the early promos were mostly shot on film, video technology – a cheaper option – was increasingly being used. We shot 'To Cut A Long Story Short' on video, which kept it within the budget, and gave it a raw quality. In a sense, I think the fact we didn't have much to spend worked to our advantage. We were a new band, and it was acceptable to experiment. We did the whole thing in a day. It was a simple shoot, the band miming to the track. We brought in a couple of girls from the Blitz to dance, and that was about it. I was incredibly nervous. The idea of performing to camera was new and strange. We all took it seriously. It *was* serious. It was our first video and we wanted it to be great. I was clutching a pair of binoculars, I've no idea why. I was just grateful to have something to hold; I didn't know what else to do with my hands. I could have done with a cigarette. We did include a couple of shots of people smoking, which the BBC made us cut.

There was a lot of tartan in the band at that point. Steve Norman was in a kilt. Gary Kemp was wearing tartan trousers. Martin Kemp had a skein of tartan slung across one shoulder. The influence came from a club in Greek Street called Le Kilt and run by the designer Chris Sullivan. Tartan was the next big thing. We captured the spirit of that and it caught on.

'To Cut A Long Story Short' was released on 1 November 1980, just a couple of weeks after we signed to Chrysalis. It charted in the lower reaches of the Top 100. Week by week, it steadily climbed. We were happy and so was the record company. No one expected a first single to shoot straight into the Top 10. In the Eighties, it was more about steady sales. Chrysalis would have been content with a Top 40 hit on the first single. It was about getting us on the map and raising the profile of the band.

Our new profile brought some negative comments, which were more to do with our floppy fringes and frilly shirts than our music. We had evolved a style that encouraged people to jump to the wrong conclusion. Scratch the surface, though, and what you had was five normal, *un*pretentious blokes. What we liked doing most was playing music and getting drunk. For all my bizarre dress sense and make-up, I was still mostly at home having a few pints with my mates in Dirty Dick's or the Percy Arms, in Islington.

The perception of us as bright young things meant we ended up on some unlikely guest lists. We weren't choosy. If there was free booze, we'd be there. Occasionally, it backfired, like the night we went to the opening of a high-brow art exhibition, in Clerkenwell.

I was dressed to kill in a tight leather jumpsuit and long, fur-trimmed boots. The jumpsuit was a Melissa Caplan design. Like most of her clothes, it was held together with poppers. In the Eighties, it was all poppers and Velcro. Zips were out. I was wearing the outfit for the first time and hadn't really thought about the implications of an all-in-one. When I went to the gents, I practically had to strip off just to relieve myself. As the night wore on, I realized the poppers weren't working very well. By the time I'd unfastened them a couple of times, they started coming undone by themselves. I'd be talking to someone and – ping! – they would burst open.

The gallery was packed. All the so-called smart set was there, most of them having trouble with their own poppers, one way or another. I had a few drinks and wandered round, wondering where all the good paintings were. It wasn't my idea of art. A couple came over. The woman gestured at the paintings. She chatted about the bold use of colour, the clever way the artist had experimented with texture, the *message* that came through his work. 'Isn't it wonderful?' she said. I looked around, confused. I said, 'Do you want an honest opinion?' She nodded, although that's probably the last thing she really wanted. I said, 'I'm not an expert, but I don't know what all the fuss is about. I've seen kids produce better work.' Her face fell. She shot a look at the bloke beside her, who was already looking round for someone else to talk to. I went on, 'I mean, this is . . . the biggest pile of shit.'

Of course, she was the organizer of the exhibition. The bloke with her was the artist.

Pretentious? Ha.

There was a huge air of mystery about Spandau Ballet. We were – or appeared to be – a band with no past, not one we were prepared to own up to at any rate. It seemed as if overnight success had landed in our laps, which undoubtedly put some people's backs up. In the beginning, I could see the sense in letting people believe we had come from nowhere. It gave us an edge, made us stand out from the crowd. As time wore on, though, it would have made sense to explain our roots. There was no shame in telling people we had done the circuit, played clubs like the Roxy. It would have lent us some kudos, and might just have made people feel warmer towards us. Instead, our strategy seemed to be to create an image of a band that was to some extent inaccessible and wrapped up in fashion. Some people loved that, but it put others off. I wish we'd been brave enough to come clean about our past. Maybe we could even have put a couple of the Makers tracks on the B-side of a single, let people know how we sounded in the early days.

The music press either loved us or hated us. Mostly, they hated us. There was no middle ground. Some writers dismissed us as pretentious and arrogant. We didn't mind. The last thing we wanted was for people to be blasé. Extreme reactions – good or bad – were to be encouraged, as far as we were concerned. Robert Elms, who had known us since the Blitz days, remained supportive. In *The Face* magazine in October 1980, he wrote, 'An incessantly booming drum sound couples with a powerful bass to produce a front line of a music made for dancing. In performance the rhythm section is always dominant, yet it is the voice of Tony Hadley which most embodies the Spandau Ballet style.'

We were happy to polarize the critics. We were brazen and opinionated. Yes, we had attitude, but we were young and hungry for success. We wanted to take over the world. Oh yes, and in those days, we also wore rather too much make-up.

Certain elements of the music press hated the fact we had done things our own way and landed a deal without their help. It pissed them off something rotten. From the outset, there was a lot of rubbish talked about us. Someone described Spandau Ballet as an 'immaculate conception', as if we had appeared, magically, out of the ether. Of course, nothing was further from the truth. We had tried everything we could think of, starting out at school as the Roots, reinventing ourselves as the Cut, the Makers and the Gentry, before finally emerging as Spandau Ballet – having played every dive that would have us along the way. There was nothing romantic about it, new or otherwise.

The first single gave the critics their chance to sound off. *Melody Maker* called it a 'forgettable piece of self-regarding fluff'. *New Musical Express* wrote us off as likely one-hit wonders. 'Top Five by Xmas and obscurity by the following yule-tide,' they predicted.

Sounds, though, loved the song. 'One of the most cutting drum tracks I've ever heard,' the reviewer wrote. 'Also distinctive is the lead vocal . . . a massively competent record by a band with, one suspects, plenty in reserve.'

I can see why there was a bit of a backlash from the critics. The notion that we had sprung up from nowhere was too far-fetched. It didn't ring true. We stuck to our guns on that, although I'm not altogether sure why. At the time we felt that having successfully re-invented ourselves we didn't want to remind people of our earlier, less successful attempts. Having said that, plenty of musicians start out in school bands. We decided to keep quiet about that, doing our best to bury our past rather than own up to it.

'To Cut A Long Story Short' was in the charts for something like five weeks before we got our first appearance on *Top Of The Pops*. By then, we were just outside the Top 50. Then, as now, *TOTP* was hugely influential. The week before we made our debut we sat at home watching the show. Adam Ant was so good we wondered how we could ever follow him.

On the day of the recording, we turned up at the BBC in

Wood Lane with our gear in the back of a van. We didn't have a road crew. One of our mates from the Blitz, Simon Withers, volunteered. He drove us to the studio. When we got there, it was raining. Simon peered through the windscreen at the drizzle. He was wearing a new pair of trousers and didn't want to get them wet. He made it clear he wasn't prepared to get out of the van. We started unloading the gear, which was in cardboard boxes, ourselves. Simon stayed put. Inside the studio, Iron Maiden's road crew was busy setting up their equipment. With as much dignity as we could muster, we hurried past their flight cases with our cardboard boxes, feeling like the school band we pretended we never were.

We'd all been fans of *TOTP* for years. It was THE show but being on it was a strange experience. On the one hand, everything was a lot smaller and less impressive than it looked on TV. We hung round in the studio and got in everyone's way. People kept yanking cables from under our feet and shouting at us to move. As far as I could tell, the cameras were metal gods. If you were in their path, they would just mow you down.

There was not the slightest hint of star treatment. Then again, we'd carted our own stuff in, so I don't suppose anyone was all that impressed. We were, though. That first appearance still ranks as one of my best memories. Appearing on the *Pops* was a dream come true. It was validation. After years of playing for a few quid here and there, we were on the most important music show in the world. It was what every band aspired to, and with good reason. It made or broke singles. If you went down well on *TOTP*, your record sales went up. It was that simple.

The atmosphere around the show was fantastic. It was all new to us and it showed. We hadn't even properly coordinated our clothes. John Keeble and I turned up wearing identical Willie Brown shirts. There was a short debate on who should change. In the end, neither of us did. Once he had put a gymslip on, you couldn't tell what he was wearing underneath. Steve Norman was wearing a mauve kilt and both Gary and Martin sported some tartan. During a break in rehearsals we trooped off to the canteen. There was a bloke, heavily made-up, in a costume that looked like it had been knocked together from a few egg boxes. To top it off, he was wearing a pair of rubber gloves, sprayed silver. No one gave him a second glance. He had strayed off the set of *Dr Who*. John, in his dress – sorry, gymslip – was tame by comparison. Back in the studio we mimed to the track and did our best to look convincing. TV was new to us and the art of miming was something we hadn't yet learned, but we managed.

In the bar afterwards you could hardly move for artists, crew and BBC staff. We were in the mood to celebrate. The following night an audience of more than ten million would tune in to *TOTP*. As we hoped, sales of 'To Cut A Long Story Short' began to rocket.

By Christmas, as *NME* had correctly predicted, the single was at Number 5 in the charts. It racked up sales of around 400,000 copies, which was phenomenal for a debut single. It was confirmation that we were on the right track, commercially. We had proved we could shift records in the kind of numbers no one had anticipated. For Chrysalis, it was a sign of things to come.

It was around this time, I think, that the issue of publishing arose.

Although both Gary and Steve had been writing in the early days, by now Gary was clearly the songwriter of the band. In my opinion, there was no question that he should receive the bulk of the royalties, but I felt we all put our stamp on the songs. At the time, I didn't know how other bands worked, but we operated as a collective. Later, I was to discover that other bands, such as U2 operated in a similar way. I'm not sure any of us was outstanding individually; we were much better together, and we knew it.

What emerged was a situation that saw a 50 per cent slice of Gary's publishing royalties go into Marbelow Limited, a company set up to handle the business side of things for the band. There was a six-way split, with each band member and our manager, Steve Dagger, receiving an equal share. As far as I was concerned that was my cut of the publishing royalties, and that's how it worked for the next seven or eight years, during which we made five albums. I never contemplated a day when that would change.

At the time we were happy with the way the split worked out. It seemed good and fair. No one complained. No one suggested we put anything in writing. It would have been unthinkable, unnecessary, to draw up a formal document. We trusted each other, so much so there was nothing in writing with our manager. By then, we had been together almost five years. We had shared some awful times and some good times. We had come to know each other well. Our backgrounds were similar. We knew each other's families. It wasn't as if we were dealing with strangers who might let us down, break their word. We were dealing with each other.

That was good enough.

A few years down the line, when the row blew up over publishing royalties, I was to learn – too late – that it was, in fact, far from good enough.

We had completed the album by the end of the year. The second single, 'The Freeze', came out in early '81, accompanied by a strange video. I was unshaven with my hair slicked back, wearing a vest, glasses, and a second-hand leather jacket I'd picked up in Belgium. A scarf knotted at the throat completed the look. John Keeble teamed his gymslip with a new shirt. A girl lay on a sofa in a cobweb shroud. It was around this time I started to wonder about the kind of people that came up with the concepts for our videos.

'The Freeze' made the Top 20, which was deemed respectable. While it was in the charts, we released the album.

Journeys To Glory more or less comprised the set we had been playing in the months leading up to the deal with Chrysalis. Under the terms of that deal, the packaging of the album was up to us. Graham Smith, our old mate from the Blitz, came up with a simple design. On the cover was a line drawing of a male torso. Robert Elms wrote the sleeve notes. The music press had a field day. The cover, coupled with a few words about sharp youth – plus the name of the band – proved our fascist leanings beyond all reasonable doubt. Allegedly. It's strange, but none of us had anticipated that calling ourselves Spandau Ballet would cause problems. It was a name, a bit of graffiti on a toilet wall, but people tried to read all kinds of deep meanings into it. Spandau is a suburb of Berlin. It's also the name of the prison where Nazi war criminals, including Rudolf Hess, were held after the war, which is what drew the most speculation. Was there some mysterious, unexplained link between the band and the German SS? Oh, please, leave it out.

No one guessed I'd be a singer, but I always had a good set of lungs.

At four years old there was nothing to suggest I'd turn into the kind of teenager who wore punk trousers and make-up.

My grandad, Bill Tee, and my nan, Rose Tee, with my mum, aged six.

My mum and dad always looked a million dollars. This is one of my favourite pictures, taken on holiday, in Europe, before I was born.

Me and my sister, Lee, dressed to the nines. I've just noticed how girly my shoes are!

Aged seven, practising my moody pop star look.

Aged ten, recovering from osteomyelitis – I had the time of my life in hospital.

Christmas at home with Lee and Steve. I loved a shirt and tie in those days!

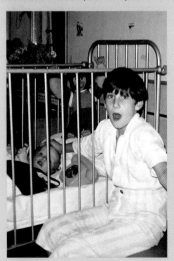

Performing at Pontin's, aged sixteen. I'd ditched the collar and tie in favour of drainpipes and Converse boots.

Headbands were an essential part of the New Romantic look. My sister, Lee, was as bad as me!

I jumped at the chance to model for a photo love story in a teen magazine. The rest of the band – trying hard to create a cool image – were less than impressed.

My grandad, Bill Tee, with all his grandsons.
The snappy dresser on the right is me.

My twenty-first birthday party —
that's little Nanny Hadley at the front.

This was the night me and my mates
segued from a Beatles number into
Monty Python's 'Lumberjack Song'
on stage at Pontin's . . . we
were very, very drunk.

I'm not sure what my musical
influence was at this point
— Village People?

Spandau Ballet on stage at
Heaven in London. This was
the look I adopted for the
'Freeze' video in 1981.

This front cover makes me smile.
Beefcake? More like Bela Lugosi!

In Japan with Steve Norman and
Martin Kemp. Once we'd signed
a record deal, limos became
a way of life.

BALLET
BEEFCAKE
Spandau, p26

We went to Compass Point in the Bahamas in 1982 to record the *True* album. When we had time off, the chances were we ended up in the pool – or playing it.

Left. Steve Jolley, one of the producers, on the left, and Gary Kemp going for a pot.

Below. Poolside: my best mate, Pete Hillier and (right) Nicky Sibley – who, in a certain light, is a dead ringer for me.

気さくなにーちゃん集団
スパンダー・バレエ

仲が良いケンプ兄弟(しかし似てらん兄弟ね)

女の子を トニー・ハドリーおじさん ピザの上に乗せてしまった〜!

Spandau were so big in Japan we even had our own comic strip.

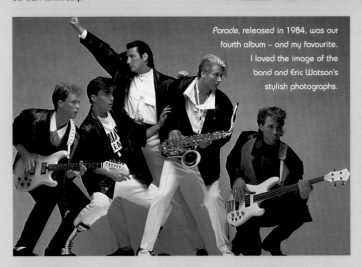

Parade, released in 1984, was our fourth album – and my favourite. I loved the image of the band and Eric Watson's stylish photographs.

I insisted on having the top down on our vintage wedding car – even though it was the middle of winter. Léonie was practically blue with cold by the time we got to the reception.

Outside St Mark's Church with my brother, Steve – one of my Best Men – on my wedding day, in February 1983.

I was over the moon when Tom, our first child, was born in 1984, just a year after Léonie and I were married.

What I actually told the reporter was that I don't like one-night stands, but I enjoy a couple of pints of lager – and this was the headline!

SUN EXCLUSIVE ON ROCK'S RAUNCHIEST BAND OF RAVERS

WILD WOMEN WHO BEG ME TO BED THEM

By Spandau's boozy Tony

With John Keeble, wearing his prized – and pricey – Gaultier jacket.

Everyone who was anyone appeared on Channel 4's *The Tube* in the eighties – Spandau was no exception.

It struck us as ridiculous but, with hindsight, I think the Spandau reference might have harmed us in the States, where some of the most powerful players in the record industry are Jewish. One US executive said he had worked out that our name was a euphemism for dancing on the graves of Jews killed in the Holocaust. There wasn't a shred of truth in that, but it showed how the minds of some executives worked (or didn't). Spandau Ballet was just a name. There were no hidden, sinister meanings. We just happened to like the sound of it.

According to *Melody Maker*, our image smacked of Hitler's master-race ideal. That was news to us. It was ludicrous. Their reviewer dismissed us as, 'nothing more than a bundle of fancy rags without a peg to hang them on.' The album, he wrote, represented, 'superficial music for superficial people.'

NME were equally unimpressed. 'An unremarkable affair by any standards,' was their verdict.

Sounds disagreed. 'This record oozes style, taste, cool and purity, reflecting perfectly the scene that spawned Spandau Ballet.'

We didn't really care. The album went straight to Number 7 in the charts.

Despite the success of the band, my feet were well and truly on the ground. I was still living at home. We all were. No one was mobbing us in the street. I didn't feel as if my life had changed, although I could sense that things were starting to shift. I remember being in a taxi one day with Gary and Martin, all of us dressed to the nines, and asking the driver to drop me in the West End so I could walk round to the BBC and see Léonie. They were appalled.

Martin said, 'You can't walk!'

I looked at him. 'Why not?'

He spluttered, 'You just . . . can't.'

I think the idea of the lead singer of Spandau Ballet walking down the road in full New Romantic gear was too much. I didn't care though; everyone at the BBC was well and truly used to me by then.

The third and final single off *Journeys To Glory* was 'Muscle-bound', slated for release in April. We went north to make the video. Although we were warned it would be cold, and told to bring warm clothing, no one did. We arrived at the location in the middle of a blizzard. The tour bus pulled up. We peered out of the windows. All we could see was snow, which was several feet deep, and still falling. No one moved. I hadn't brought a coat. John Keeble was wearing leather trousers, boxing boots, and a flimsy shirt, an outfit that was all right on the bus with the heater on, but not very practical in a snowdrift.

We were at Kirkstone Pass, the highest road pass in the Lake District, and a bleak spot at the best of times. It has a well-deserved reputation for being cold and grim – the pass is frequently impassable.

It was supposed to be a one-day shoot. With the band trapped inside the tour bus, the schedule was revised. Two days. Three, maximum. The one bit of good news was the discovery that Kirkstone Pass has a pub. It might have been the bleakest place on earth, but it was also opening time. During a lull in the blizzard, we all traipsed in. For the next couple of days, the pub was our base.

The video was on the scale of a short, surreal feature film with a budget to match, somewhere in the region of £15,000 – although by the time we'd finished the costs were more than double that. There were extras milling about, dwarves with painted faces and bright costumes, and various technical people with strange titles like Grip. I have watched this video several times since and still have no idea what it was about, which, bearing in mind how much it cost, is a worry.

With the hours ticking by, the director, Russell Mulcahy, was keen to make a start. 'Musclebound' was one of the most uncomfortable shoots we did. It was freezing and most of the time I was in flowing robes and headgear. Lawrence of Arabia meets Robin Hood. In one scene that lasted about two seconds, but took hours to shoot, John and I had no shirts on. It was madness. In between takes, we took bets on how long it would be before one of us turned blue and passed out. It was worse for the extras, though. Someone had the brilliant idea of burying them in the snow. As the camera rolled, disembodied hands, stiff with cold, poked up into the air. The shot was on screen for no more than a few seconds.

The plan was that all of us would be on horseback at some point. John objected. The director talked him round and, reluctantly, he got in the saddle, but he was far from happy. Horses, he argued, are dangerous, unpredictable beasts. As if to prove the point, Gary Kemp's horse threw him off. Although Gary wasn't hurt, John dismounted, unnerved. Nothing would persuade him to get back on. He ranted at Russell Mulcahy and anyone else prepared to listen. 'I don't like horses. They've got no brakes, no wing mirrors, *nothing*. They scare the *shit* out of me. We've got *cars* now, for fuck's sake.' Everyone shuffled about uncomfortably in the snow. He had a point. In the end, they came to a compromise. John agreed to film some horse sequences, as long as he didn't have to get on one. He and I talked about the 'Musclebound' video recently. After all this time, it still brings back bad memories.

Under the circumstances, and with the weather conditions worsening, the director decided it was unsafe for me to ride. I complained. Unlike John, I *wanted* to ride. I love horses. I'd had riding lessons at school – an option once the football season ended – and I was pretty good. The director overruled me. It was too dangerous. I refused to do anything until he gave in. In the end, in the interests of keeping the shoot within its budget, he decided he was willing to risk having me thrown headfirst into a snowdrift. He was probably tearing his hair out by then.

For two days we feasted on pub food prepared by a landlady who looked and sounded like the Monty Python character Mrs Cutout. She couldn't believe her luck. Her takings shot up. All day she produced scampi, chicken and sausage, all in a basket, and all with chips. We ate as much as she could cook. We drank a fair bit too. While we were away it was Steve Norman's birthday, so we probably drank a bit more than usual. On the way home, Steve was sick on the bus.

Once you start having a bit of success, everyone assumes your life changes. It doesn't. Often, what happens is the people around you change. We had been on TV a few times, had had a few hit records. People who didn't know us assumed that anyone who appeared on *Top Of The Pops* must be rich. Occasionally, someone would ask when I was buying my mum and dad a mansion. That made me smile. At that point I was still borrowing a few quid from my dad and my mates just so I could buy a drink at the pub. The truth was I earned more at IPC than I did in the early days of the band. Our first cheque from Chrysalis was for £50. It took a while to establish ourselves. Despite the success of 'To Cut A Long Story Short', we weren't selling enough records to pay for a stereotypical pop star lifestyle, and that was fine. No one, least of all us, expected to hit the jackpot straight away. The record company was content to give us room to develop.

Meanwhile, I was still living at home, spending time with Léonie, drinking with my mates. Nothing much had changed. My mum and dad made sure I kept my feet on the ground. I was never given special treatment at home.

My parents were always straightforward, down-to-earth people. They wanted me to do well but they never entirely lost their wariness about the whole idea of fame. Being a pop star didn't really count as a proper job. It was all a bit airy-fairy. My dad saw music and television as la-la land.

The fact that things were taking off for me never caused any friction with my brother, Steve, and sister, Lee. Just once, I remember Lee, who was an aspiring actress at the time, complaining to my mum that I'd had it easy. She must have only been about eighteen. My mum wouldn't have it. She knew how much effort had gone into getting the band off the ground, all the trailing round, setting up gigs in dingy pubs. We were not an overnight success, whatever anyone says. Success didn't fall into my lap.

It was in early '81 that the bottom threatened to drop out of my world.

I had been in Germany for a few days, on my first promotional trip with the band. That was a taste of things to come: a car to pick you up and take you to the airport, a couple of record company reps to ease you through the check-in process. It was the first time I'd flown business class. In Munich, more record company reps waited in the arrivals hall. We went to a TV station and did our bit. We were starting to discover that journalists, particularly European ones, were incredibly earnest. They always wanted to know about the deeper meaning of the song. Usually, there wasn't one.

That night, we ended up having dinner with the record company and drinking far too much beer. I can't remember the name of the hotel, but it had vibrating beds.

When I got home, I dumped my bag and went upstairs. My mum and sister followed. There was no sign of my dad. I assumed he was at work. In fact, he was in hospital.

While I was away, he had suffered a heart attack.

I went straight to the hospital to see him. Walking onto the ward to find my dad, pale and tired, hooked up to a machine that monitored the rhythm of his heart, was shocking. He gave me a smile. I said, 'Bloody hell, Dad, what have you done?'

For the next few minutes we chatted, both of us keeping things light. I don't think either of us wanted to let the other know how we were really feeling. I had only once seen my dad cry. I didn't think it would help to see his son break down.

I had learned a valuable lesson at IPC about keeping a stiff upper lip at times like this. My supervisor, Joe Kent, had a leg amputated, following a thrombosis. Although Joe was always pulling me up about all sorts of things, I respected him. While he was in hospital, the lads in the warehouse were merciless, cracking jokes about his leg at his expense. I couldn't handle it. Among the worst offenders were a couple of my mates, Paul and Chipper. One day, I lost it, grabbed a knife and went for Paul. When I realized what I was doing, I dropped the knife and ran off. Chipper came looking for me. He said, 'Don't you think we're all upset? It's not going to help Joe to have everyone feeling sorry for him. When he comes back to work, he won't expect anyone to treat him any differently.'

He was right. A few weeks later Joe was back, on crutches, his old self, still giving everyone a hard time.

I sat with my dad in hospital, chatting, telling him about

the Munich trip, trying not to think about the wires taped to his chest. It was only when I walked away that I bawled my eyes out.

Seeing your parents growing older is never easy. Even before my dad had his heart attack, things had started to change. It was almost imperceptible, but I sensed him slowing down. Our roles had started to shift. It was no longer clear cut who was taking care of who. On holiday, I had insisted on carrying the cases, heaving them onto the roof rack, taking the pressure off him, despite his protests. I didn't want to admit it, but I had noticed age creeping up on him.

At some point, no doubt my sons will do the same to me.

Chapter Seven

On the face of it, at least, things were going pretty well for the band.

It was less than a year since we had signed a recording deal with Chrysalis, and already Spandau Ballet had notched up three hit singles. All of a sudden we were a band people were talking about. We had achieved our dream. When it came to the second album, however, the dream began to turn sour for me. It was during the recording of *Diamond* in 1981 that I suffered a massive crisis of confidence. Suddenly, I wasn't sure I wanted to be in a band any more. Not this band, at any rate.

I came close to walking away from it all.

After the success of the debut album, *Journeys To Glory*, the pressure was on. In the summer of '81, before we even started recording the next album, we released our fourth single, 'Chant No. 1 (I Don't Need This Pressure On)', which was a huge hit. It was a different sound for us, with a horn section by the jazz-funk trio, Beggar and Co. It was also the first time Steve Norman played saxophone on a Spandau track. 'Chant No. 1' was shifting so many copies everyone thought it was on course to be our first Number 1. The day before the chart positions came through, we were at the Chrysalis offices, and champagne was already flowing. We got very drunk. Everyone was in high spirits and being a bit silly. At one point, John Keeble slid down the banister of the main staircase. As it turned out, our high jinks proved premature. While we were celebrating, another single was on its way up the charts, sneakily overtaking us. The chart positions came through the next day, as we were nursing hangovers. It was not the news we wanted to hear. We had stalled at Number 3, beaten to the top spot by Shakin' Stevens and 'Green Door'. Stevie Wonder was at Number 2 with 'Happy Birthday'.

Everyone assumed 'Chant No. 1' was representative of what was to come on *Diamond*. They were wrong.

Right from the beginning, I was unhappy with the album. I hated half the tracks. There was some pretty esoteric stuff, like 'Innocence And Science' and 'Missionary'. It felt as if we had lost all sense of direction. Worse, there was no one around to offer any guidance, although, in some respects, we only had ourselves to blame for that. In the days before landing a record deal, we all agreed it was critical to retain creative control. The idea of anyone – record company executive or otherwise – telling us how to do things was simply not on our agenda. Perhaps we were naïve, but we wanted to be able to experiment, musically. It was important to us to have the freedom to try – and fail if necessary.

I still believe in that, but now I understand the advantages of working with people who know what they're doing. In retrospect, what I needed was a mentor figure. I needed someone older and wiser who would inspire me. We thought we knew it all, but we actually knew remarkably little. Back then, I don't think that was something any of us appreciated, although now it seems obvious. One important lesson I learned from the *Diamond* experience was that having good people around is just as important as creative latitude. At the time, though, we were relatively new to the game. We wanted to do things our way. We did too. The irony was that leaving us so completely to our own devices meant there was actually no control of any kind.

Once again, we were working with Richard Burgess, who had produced the first album. That whole experience had been relatively pain-free. We had basically recorded the set we were playing at the time. I suppose I thought that making *Diamond* would be a similar experience. I was way off the mark. From the outset, *Diamond* felt like a disjointed affair. It was as if we couldn't quite find our rhythm. Perhaps that's why the album was recorded at six different London studios – Eden, Sarm East, Utopia, Air, Abbey Road and Jam. While we were working at Jam Studios in North London, I realized I was struggling. My confidence had completely vanished. The pressure was on and I was feeling it. I just wasn't getting the vocals right and the more I tried the worse it got. The bottom line was that I didn't think the album was very good. Once you lose faith in something it's hard to perform with any conviction and I just couldn't do it. It didn't help that I wasn't getting along with Gary Kemp at that point. It may have been that we were both just feeling the pressure, but our relationship was on thin ice. On top of that, I was feeling increasingly isolated within the band.

As Spandau Ballet had begun to take off, Gary and John Keeble had become best mates and would share a room when we were on the road. It was the same for Martin Kemp and Steve Norman, while I spent my time with my best mate from school, Pete Hillier. He was Gary's guitar tech at that point, and later became the band's stage manager. On the one hand there was the band. On the other there was me, still hanging out with my old mates. I was the only one who didn't play an instrument and I was beginning to feel that set me apart. Up until then, I'd always felt it was enough to sing. Suddenly, it was as if the others had formed some kind of cosy musicians' clique – and I wasn't part of it.

The irony is that anyone looking in from the outside would probably assume the lead singer of any band is the one in the spotlight, in the thick of it all, having a great time. During the *Diamond* era, I didn't feel like that at all. I felt like an outsider. It was painfully obvious – to me, anyway – that I didn't fit in. Consequently, I was not exactly brimming with confidence when I walked into Jam Studios to start work on *Diamond*.

Things came to a head on 'Paint Me Down'.

I just could not get the vocal right. The phrasing was wrong and I was struggling to sing in tune. As I sweated, the rest of the band watched from behind the glass that separated the studio from the control room. Everyone was willing me to get it right, which only made matters worse. Each time I messed up a line I sensed a collective rolling of the eyes. I hated it, every minute. I don't think anyone realized how miserable I was and how little it would take to tip me over the edge.

It was while I was wrestling with 'Paint Me Down' that Richard Burgess came up with what he thought was an inspired idea. He had heard – although precisely where from remains a mystery – that singers sometimes performed better lying down. He wanted to put me in a tent with a few candles to create a relaxed mood. It sounded like utter bollocks, but he was serious. I was too inexperienced and, by then, too desperate to argue.

It's hard to imagine singing in such bizarre circumstances, but somehow I did, although I felt like a complete prat in the process. I can remember lying in my tent in the middle of the studio, staring up at a microphone, in flickering candlelight, wondering what the fuck I was doing.

The 'vocal tent' was just about the last straw although, predictably, there was more to come.

When the band began laying down the backing vocals on 'Paint Me Down' it was clear to me they were flat. They sounded awful. Now it was my turn to watch in disbelief from the control room. I turned to Richard Burgess. 'They're out of tune,' I said.

I wanted to go back in and record my own backing vocals. He wouldn't have it. 'It will be fine,' he assured me.

At that point, I realized he and I were on an utterly different wavelength. The backing vocals sounded out of tune to me, yet he was happy. Nothing made sense to me any more.

Most of the time I'm easy-going. I love what I do and I want to do the best job I can. I also want to have a good time. I have a very simple take on my work. Music – singing – should be fun, not an ordeal, yet I was dreading going into the studio. Something was badly wrong. It takes a lot for me to lose my temper but when I do it's explosive and, inevitably, the moment arrived on *Diamond*. I don't even remember which track I was struggling with. I just remember losing it.

Again, the rest of the band was watching from the control room. It might have helped if they'd had the sense to leave the studio, or if the producer, aware that having them around was making things worse, had told them to leave, but that never happened. It was all, 'Come on, Tone . . . this is really important.' It was like being in a pressure cooker and the lid was about to come off.

Over the last few years I have produced a couple of bands, and so has John Keeble. We now know that a huge element of producing is about managing people. It's about respect and encouragement. When we were making *Diamond* I felt I was under intolerable pressure, which was never going to produce great results. Working in a studio can be claustrophobic, especially once things start going wrong, and the last thing a struggling performer needs is an audience. In the early days of Spandau Ballet we didn't understand that. Everyone wanted to be in the studio all the time, even when there was no reason to be there. There was a sense that turning up for every session was a sign of enthusiasm and commitment. No one told us it might be counter-productive. Looking back, I'd have preferred a bit of privacy – before I had a breakdown.

The day my temper finally snapped I grabbed a fire extinguisher and was about to hurl it through the control-room window. I was standing with a lump of metal in my hands, at absolute breaking point, and I thought, So this is how it feels to be the lead singer in a successful band. Wonderful. It was an ugly moment. In the end I dropped the fire extinguisher and walked out. I just wanted to get the fuck away.

I had no intention of coming back.

I don't think the others had the slightest idea how I was feeling. They knew I was struggling, but I don't think for one second they imagined I was close to jacking it all in. I hadn't actually spelled things out – and they hadn't asked – but the Spandau dream was in pieces, as far as I was concerned. If that was what being in a pop band was about, they could stick it. I was twenty-one years old and couldn't see the point of being so miserable. Life is just too short. For the next few days I stayed away from the studio. I'd reached the point where I couldn't keep it together any more. There was too much going on inside. I broke down and cried my heart out. It was like the floodgates had opened. I was in a real state.

I wasn't sure what it meant to have a breakdown, but that's what I thought was happening. I didn't want to speak to any of the others and I don't think they had the slightest clue I was ready to quit.

It was my mum and my girlfriend, Léonie, who persuaded me to give things another go. By then I had gone way past the point of thinking things through in a rational way. I just wanted out. There seemed no other option. The future was utterly bleak, as far as I could tell. Léonie and my mum saw things differently. Listening to them made me realize how much hard work it had taken to get this far. It was, surely, too good an opportunity to throw away. If I could just stick it out things might improve. I kept all this from the rest of the band, who carried on working on *Diamond* without me. As far as they were concerned, I was having a few days at home to clear my head. With some misgivings, I went back and finished the album. All that remained was to see what the record company thought of it.

Chrysalis had been happy to leave us alone during the making of *Diamond*, in the misguided belief they would get another seven or eight tracks in the vein of 'Chant No. 1'. They didn't, of course.

As the record company executives gathered at Air Studios in the heart of London's West End to hear the album for the first time in late 1981, expectations were high. We had already proved ourselves capable of making hit records, so there was a buzz of anticipation as everyone settled down. Before long, however, it became obvious that our audience was less than impressed. It was hard to see what the hit singles were, although, as far as I can remember, I think Gary was happy with the album. He had been keen to experiment with *Diamond*. When the album finished playing, no one said anything, probably because they couldn't think of anything to say. There was just a row of stony faces, which spoke volumes. Still, like it or not, we all had to try to make the album work.

The next single released from *Diamond* was 'Paint Me Down'. The video, shot early one morning on Primrose Hill in North London, saw us wearing chamois leather loincloths and streaked in paint. I had shaved my chest for the occasion. Gary thought it would look good to have one of us blindfold, tied to a tree. To everyone else's relief, Steve Norman (who knew an opportunity for a starring role when he saw one) volunteered.

Not surprisingly, one of the local residents, disturbed at the site of five near-naked blokes cavorting in public at sunrise, called the police. Two squad cars pulled up to investigate reports that some kind of satanic ritual was under way. While we explained it was nothing more sinister than a pop video shoot, in the background, Steve – still lashed to the tree trunk, blindfold – tried to wriggle free, as the rest of us scrambled to get our clothes on. The police told us to pack up and go home. We went back and finished the shoot a couple of days later. In another scene – filmed indoors, thankfully – I writhed naked on a bare mattress as paint splashed onto me from above. In a sequence filmed separately, paint ran down Paula Yates' bare back. I have no idea what it was all about. It was arty-farty nonsense. The BBC can't have liked it either, since they banned it. I'm still not sure why they felt it was unsuitable – unless they were trying to protect viewers from what, to me, was self-indulgent claptrap. In which case, I can see their point.

Before the single was released, we went in to *Top Of The Pops* and recorded the track for them. After the success of the first four singles everyone was reasonably confident another hit was on the cards. Unfortunately, it didn't happen. 'Paint Me Down' didn't even make the Top 20, and our *Top Of The Pops* recording never saw the light of day. It was sobering for all of us. However much I had hated the album, I wasn't prepared for the first single to flop.

In early '82 we released another track from the album, 'She Loved Like Diamond', in the hope that would turn things round. The video was shot in Bath, and this time we were fully clothed. The single stiffed anyway, only managing to reach Number 54 in the Top 100. It was a disaster. We were in Belgium when the news came through and it sent us into panic mode. It didn't take a genius to work out that if things carried on like this it could soon be game over for Spandau Ballet. I couldn't help thinking that having made a decision to stick with the band, the band might not have a future anyway, which had a certain irony.

We were in dire need of a hit single but nothing else on *Diamond* leaped out as an obvious contender. The only likely track was 'Instinction', which I hated – not because I thought the song was bad, but because of the production on the album version which I thought was abysmal. To this day, I cannot listen to the album version of that track. John Keeble reckons it is possibly the worst thing he has ever been associated with. He has a point.

'Instinction' was also our only hope.

This was the point at which I began to realize that our determination to keep creative control had backfired on us in a big way. Richard Burgess had come on board as producer primarily because he moved in the same social circles as us. We had run into him in the Blitz. There was no more to it than that, really. He wasn't even a producer; he was the drummer in a band called Landscape. In the course of making the first album, he and Gary Kemp had become good friends, and no one questioned whether he was right for the second album. He was Gary's mate and it was up to us to decide who we wanted to work with. That's the beauty of being in control. We knew best. Or so we thought. It never occurred to us to look around and see who else there was, who was making a splash in the industry. Not until after we had made *Diamond*, anyway.

Suddenly, we had two singles on our hands that had done nothing. To have the third single fail was not an option. We needed some help.

We turned to Trevor Horn.

I think at that point there was a real sense that our future as a band was hanging by a thread. Trevor Horn saved our necks. He was fast earning a name for himself as a gifted producer. Later, he would go on to produce some of the best-selling singles of the decade, including Frankie Goes To Hollywood's 'Relax', and Band Aid's 'Do They Know It's Christmas?'.

I loved working with Trevor. He had an innate sense of how to bring out the best in artists. Suddenly, I was working with a producer who actually listened to me. It was a real eye-opener. By the time we began working on 'Instinction' at Sarm East Studios my confidence was still in pieces. I was wary about going back into a studio, but I needn't have worried. Trevor Horn managed to bring out the best in all of us. He worked on our strengths. It didn't take long to appreciate that he was on our wavelength. I had always felt that as a singer, rather than a musician, I was never taken seriously. Suddenly, I was working with someone for whom the vocals were as important as any other aspect of the record. Inevitably, that rubbed off on me. During the making of *Diamond* I had struggled endlessly yet, with Trevor Horn's guidance, I managed to lay down the vocals on 'Instinction' with relative ease.

Working with him made me appreciate how important it was to have the right people around us. He was a gifted producer with a talented team around him, including Anne Dudley, who did an amazing job on the string arrangements. At the end of the process 'Instinction' was a different record. A hit record. I can remember feeling nervous before we re-worked 'Instinction'. There was a real sense that we couldn't afford it to flop. Once I heard the new version, though, I was confident it would be a hit. It jumped out of the speakers at you and I knew it would do the same thing on radio. It went to Number 10 in April 1982, which gave us the hit we needed and no doubt persuaded Chrysalis that we were worth another chance. I have no doubt that in the current climate, where there is no room for failure, we would have been dropped. In today's disposable industry, if you're not an instant hit you're out. Thankfully, during the Spandau era there was some margin for error. Anyone working in a creative medium needs a degree of freedom to make mistakes, particularly when they're starting out. Twenty years ago, there was a more tolerant attitude in the music business. No one really expected a band to have their biggest success with their first record. Or even their second. In our case, our biggest success came with the third album, *True*. Today if you make a rubbish album, it's unlikely there will be an opportunity to do another one. We were all smarting from the bad reviews *Diamond* had received. The music critics had scratched their heads in bewilderment and dismay. Dave Mc-Cullough, writing in *Sounds*, called side two a mess. 'The opener, "She Loved Like Diamond", is the worst tune I have ever clapped oversized ears on ... not so much pretentious (that would be all right!) as unlistenable. *Diamond* is a cold hotch-potch of a terribly sounding studio album.'

One thing was clear: from now on, we needed the right team around us. We were no longer dealing with demos. Now we all knew just how fragile success in the pop industry was and how much was at stake. It was a realization that shook us.

The release of *Diamond* saw our first tour, in 1982. I've always enjoyed touring. Once on stage, I feel as if I'm in my own world. While working in the studio used to intimidate me, performing live had the opposite effect. However nervous I may feel before a gig, going on stage is a huge adrenalin rush. In a sense, you're stepping into the unknown. Every crowd is different. Sometimes the air practically crackles with the energy coming off the audience. Occasionally, there's nothing there and it's up to you to work with the crowd to generate a buzz. In Germany, playing to a particularly reticent audience, I employed shock tactics to shake them up, bellowing, 'Everyone – on your feet – NOW!' For a split second I had the horrible feeling they were all going to stay put in their seats. Panic-stricken, I swung round and caught John Keeble's eye. It was obvious he was thinking the same thing. But, en masse, they all stood up. The atmosphere in the stadium suddenly picked up. I breathed a sigh of relief and made a mental note to think twice before barking orders in future. I might not get away with it a second time.

The Diamond tour represented a short foray into new and uncharted waters for us. We played some dates in Scotland, and earned favourable reviews. The show at the Ultratheque in Glasgow brought this from journalist Billy Sloan: 'Spandau's live show does everything. It kick-starts the senses with a succession of sublime bass lines, keyboard melodies and stunning vocals.'

We lined up some dates in Europe too. In Madrid, we played to a packed club. Before we went on, Martin – who was wearing dresses on stage at that point – decided he would 'faint' at the end of the set. Between them, Martin and Steve were constantly coming up with ways of generating headlines. By the time we came off stage, we were all drenched in sweat and gasping for air. There must have been about 500 people in the audience, tightly packed in, and the heat was unbearable. We could barely breathe. In the dressing room, we cracked open cold beers. A few minutes went by. Suddenly, someone said, 'Hang on, where's Martin?' We looked at each other. Martin had indeed 'fainted' on stage and was still there, waiting for someone to rescue him. Meanwhile, we'd all been so keen to get off and grab some air, we hadn't even noticed. When Pete Hillier and Nicky Sibley, our roadies, went to investigate, he was still flat out, his Crimplene dress hitched up a bit higher than usual, clutching his bass. They got him to his feet and dragged him off. It was pure *Spinal Tap*.

He appeared in the dressing room a few minutes later, well and truly pissed off. 'What happened to you lot?'

We all shrugged and muttered, 'Er, sorry, Mart, we just forgot . . .'

Fortunately, he did see the funny side.

There was a huge New Romantic movement in Portugal. We flew to Lisbon, then caught the train to Oporto for the first gig. It was my birthday. To celebrate, the band bought champagne and a chocolate bar in the shape of a 'T'.

In the early Eighties, Portugal was relatively unsophisticated. In Oporto, we had to wait until 5 p.m. to sound check because the power for the gig was coming from the factory next door to the venue. We couldn't start until they had knocked off for the day. After the sound check, we returned to the dressing room to find a small boy leaning through the open skylight, using a pole with a spike fastened on one end to spear the contents of the buffet table. There were expensive guitars in the room but he was after the small, dry cakes that made up the bulk of the refreshments. He was welcome to them.

Word reached us that our luggage had gone missing somewhere en route. All we had were the clothes we were standing up in, which were hardly suitable for a show in a country that took New Romanticism seriously. I was wearing jeans, which was enough to send the fashion police into apoplexy. The idea of going on stage so underdressed sent a wave of panic through the five of us. Luckily, I had my knee-length, fur-topped boots with me, which was something, but probably not enough. We improvised, ripping up bits of hotel sheets and serviettes to make headbands and scarves. We tried them on, feeling hopeful. They looked like bits of hotel sheets and serviettes. We wore them on stage that night anyway.

From Oporto, we headed south to Lisbon for another gig. That night we threw a belated birthday party back at the hotel. The manager wasn't having it. We sneaked girls in anyway, moving them from one room to another, in an attempt to confuse the staff. It was like a bedroom farce. Everyone ended up in Steve Norman's room, where we made such a racket the manager was banging on the door in no time. Steve answered looking bleary-eyed, claiming he'd just woken up. He didn't fool anyone. The manager, by now at the end of his tether, threatened to call the police. We didn't imagine for a second he meant it but, soon afterwards, we heard vehicles pulling up in front of the hotel, and raised voices. We hung over the balcony. Below us were military jeeps with machine-gun mounts on the back. John Keeble stumbled out into the night to have a word. We watched, impressed and slightly alarmed, as he argued, drunkenly, with men in army fatigues. It didn't make any difference. The girls were thrown out. We carried on celebrating. Quietly.

That same night, Martin phoned home. He chatted for no more than a couple of minutes but failed to replace the receiver properly at the end of the call. The next day when he checked out he was presented with a massive phone bill. It came to £230.

At least the luggage turned up.

Chapter Eight

Towards the end of '82 we spent six weeks at Compass Point Studios in Nassau in the Bahamas working on the third album – the so-called Pleasure Project. We all felt it made sense to record away from home where, free of everyday distractions, we could concentrate on the music. This was after an abortive start on the album at London's Air Studios, with Trevor Horn. After he had worked wonders with 'Instinction', he seemed like the best man for the job, but it didn't work out. We were used to getting our own way by then. So was Trevor. There was a clash over how things should be done. Before long, we agreed to go our separate ways. Trevor was up to his eyes in work anyway with bands like ABC and Frankie Goes To Hollywood.

We headed for Compass Point. Owned by Chris Blackwell, who had tried to sign us to his Island label in early 1980 several months before the Chrysalis deal, the studio had a good reputation. Talking Heads were recording there at the same time as us. An added bonus of Compass Point was its setting, on the edge of Love Beach, and just a short hop from Paradise Island, which was home to the local casino. In our down time we could lounge around the pool or on the nearby beach, and look forward to the odd game of blackjack. Things could hardly be better. The five of us were getting along, sharing an apartment, with no sign of the tensions that had surfaced during the making of *Diamond*. There was a renewed sense of optimism about the future.

It was the first time we worked with producers Tony Swain and Steve Jolley. Their work with the band Imagination, who had a major hit with 'Body Talk', had brought them to our attention and we worked well together. It was all remarkably laid-back. We would go into the studio, do our bit, then laze around the pool. Steve and Martin competed to see who could get the best sun tan. There were no rows, no one fell out. No one suggested I record my vocals in a tent. They were good times. There's some home-movie footage from that period which shows us larking about, having a laugh together.

It was great for me because I was able to go horse riding, which is one of my passions. I had my riding gear with me. When I appeared in full kit – jodhpurs, the lot – the others just fell about laughing. I was every inch the English country gentleman abroad.

Steve Norman decided to explore the undersea life around the island and got himself a snorkel and mask, flippers and – worryingly – a harpoon gun. One day the four of us were watching him from the shore when a shark appeared. As the fin cut through the water heading in his direction, we screamed and gestured at him to get out of the water. Steve, oblivious, waved back at us. Whether his harpoon gun would have been much use at that point is debatable. We continued jumping up and down like idiots until he finally got out of the water to see why we were getting so excited. It was a few days before he felt like getting the snorkel gear out again.

Those few weeks in the Bahamas making *True* marked a turning point for the band. The album would send us soaring to another level. The trip to Nassau signalled a major watershed for me too.

It was while I was away I discovered that I couldn't live without Léonie.

We had been apart for quite a lot of '82 and I had found the separations painful. In fact, they hurt like hell. There were times when I was away, in the early hours of the morning and with a few drinks inside me, I'd get the urge to call her to say how much I missed her. I would *have* to speak to her, even if it was 3 a.m. I've always been impulsive. Invariably, I'd be in a club pumping money into a payphone, and there'd be some girl hanging around. It would take me ages to get through. The phones had big, clunky dials that took for ever to connect. Often, you'd spend ages dialling the number, only to hear a foreign operator relaying a message you didn't understand before cutting you off. Even if you did get through, the delays on the line made it near enough impossible to have a normal conversation. I'd pour my heart out until I ran out of change. 'I love you, I miss you,' I'd say. In the background, there would be a fan saying, 'Tony, I love you, I *love* you!' It drove Léonie nuts. She knew I wasn't up to anything but she didn't want to be woken up night after night to hear some girl throwing herself at me. In the end she banned those late-night calls. So, while I'm not a big letter writer, I started writing long letters in Nassau.

Although the recording was going well, and the band was getting on, there were moments when I was down. I knew I had to make some big decisions.

I think we all sensed that *True* was going to be a big album and that things would take off. Gary had written the tracks and we'd rehearsed them before we'd arrived in Nassau. There was some really strong material and, with 'True', it felt as if we were changing direction. A big, soulful ballad was something new for us. We recorded the backing vocals for 'True' at

Compass Point, but I did the main vocals at Red Bus with Steve Jolley once we got back to London. It's quite a complicated song to sing in terms of phrasing and timing, and we soldiered on for ages before we felt we'd got it right. Although I liked the song, I never saw it as a single. No one was more surprised than me when it went on to become our biggest hit.

I didn't want my relationship with Léonie to be a casualty of the band's success. One day I went off by myself and sat on the beach staring out to sea, thinking about where I wanted my life to go. I knew the reputation of the pop industry for putting a strain on relationships. I felt I had a choice: I could leave things as they were, and risk us drifting apart, or I could make a commitment to her.

I knew that if I didn't marry her I would regret it for the rest of my life.

The band had returned from Nassau in November 1982, and, just before Christmas, I took Léonie to Frederick's in Islington for dinner. I'd bought a diamond engagement ring and, halfway through the evening, I took out this little box and asked her to marry me. Although we'd talked about getting married, she wasn't expecting me to pop the question that night and she got quite tearful. In fact, she was so churned up she couldn't eat her meal. To this day she is convinced I timed my proposal to put her off her food so that I could have it. It's not true, although I did manage to help her out. You can't let the lamb chops at Frederick's go to waste, they're too good.

If it was tricky breaking the news about getting married to both families, it was much worse telling the band.

We were rehearsing at Nomis, the West London studios owned by Simon Napier-Bell, who managed Wham! (Nomis spells Simon backwards). When I told the band about the wedding, it didn't go down well. Steve Dagger thought it was madness. So did the rest of the band. There was a massive bust-up.

Dagger shook his head. 'You won't be able to wear a wedding ring.'

I was livid. 'Don't fucking tell me I can't wear my wedding ring.'

They all seemed to think that by getting married I would jeopardize the success of Spandau Ballet. As far as they were concerned, the timing could not have been worse. Here we were, on the verge of releasing our third album, which, according to the record company, was going to be massive. If *True* was the hit everyone was predicting, the profile of the band would rocket. Having a married lead singer was bad for the image, apparently. It was ridiculous. As far as I was concerned, it would make no difference whatsoever.

I said, 'You'll all get an invitation to the wedding. It's up to you whether or not you come.'

I was seething. So were they. I think by then they knew me well enough to know nothing they could say would change my mind.

I was getting married and that was that.

I went to ask Léonie's dad, Neville, for his permission. I wanted to do it all properly. He was cool about it, although he must have had his reservations. For one thing, I was just twenty-two. For another, I came from a very different world.

Neville's background was military; he was a first-rate army officer, a major who had done a stint in the Parachute Regiment. The family had lived all over the world. Léonie had spent a big chunk of her life in Singapore. At home, there were servants. Before I came along, her boyfriends had been RAF pilots. I think her family had imagined she would marry an officer in the military, someone with a sensible haircut and a reliable job. I'm not sure they knew quite what to make of me, an oik from Islington. Plus, I didn't exactly have a conventional 'job'. In fairness, I probably wasn't what they would have chosen for their daughter. I know her mum was far from convinced. My parents weren't particularly happy either. The fact that Léonie was four years older than me concerned them. They wanted me to think long and hard before I took such a huge step. My sister Lee also had her doubts. I think everyone thought I was just too young.

The funny thing is that before I met Léonie, I would have agreed with them.

I can remember trying to talk some of my mates out of getting married for the exact same reason. When Bobby Watts announced he was going to marry Lynn Farrell, I was appalled. He was just eighteen. For a long time, I had this idea in my head that I wouldn't get married until I was thirty. I was adamant. That's fine, of course, until you meet someone and fall head over heels in love, at which point everything you once thought was reasonable flies out the window.

The date for the wedding was set for 19 February 1983, which gave us just a few weeks to get everything organized. Some of my relatives were alarmed at the speed it was all happening. They were convinced we were getting married in a hurry because Léonie was pregnant. She wasn't. It was just that the band was so busy that we didn't have much choice. That was practically our only free day.

As we began to plan the wedding, we also started looking for our first home. Although I had two albums under my belt, I didn't have much spare cash. Whatever anyone thinks, having a few records in the charts is no guarantee of prosperity. At that stage my earnings still didn't match what I'd been making at IPC. We started looking for a flat to rent. Léonie was working full-time, so I went to see a few on my own. Some were disgusting. I couldn't believe the state of them. Finally, we found a one-bedroom furnished flat in Highbury. It wasn't cheap. I think it was around £300 a month, which was a lot of money in 1983. We could barely afford it but, convinced the band was about to take off, we went ahead.

The décor was awful. Some bright spark had painted the kitchen black, presumably to hide the dirt. The bathroom was dingy. I told the landlady I planned to smarten it up a bit, then got my mate Doddy – Tony Dodds – round. Between us, we redecorated the whole place, tiled the bathroom, laid new carpet, put new worktops in the kitchen, and painted the staircase. I was pleased as punch. My landlady was furious. Under the terms of our rental agreement, decorating was forbidden. That was probably to stop tenants from doing stupid things like painting the kitchen black.

We had decided to get married in my local church, St Mark's, in Myddelton Square, Islington. St Mark's is an imposing nine-teenth-century building. Inside, the brick walls are bare. Apart from a huge stained-glass window above the altar, it's pretty austere. But it held memories for me. As a child, I had sung in the choir there. The reception was booked at the Bloomsbury Square Hotel, just a few minutes away. I wanted to do the whole thing with a bit of style, and splashed out on the wedding car. It was a vintage Rolls-Royce – a convertible – once owned by an Indian maharaja.

The weeks leading up to the wedding were hectic. Léonie

was away in Hong Kong with *My Music*, and there was promotion to do for our next single, 'Communication', due out the week before our big day.

Meanwhile, our first major UK tour was scheduled, and the title track from the album was generating excitement. The buzz around 'True' was huge. It was getting loads of radio play. I remember hearing the Radio 1 DJ Simon Bates play it for the first time on his morning show. He said, 'That is so good I'm going to play it again.' He was just one of the people who championed it.

I had no doubts about the wedding but, with Spandau tipped for major success, I wanted to make sure Léonie felt the same. Just a couple of weeks before the ceremony I sat down and spelled out that life with me was not likely to be easy. By most people's standards, we would not have a normal marriage. I remember saying that the likelihood was the band would be huge and, consequently, there would be a lot of pressure on the relationship. I wanted to make sure she knew what she was getting into, although, whatever we might have thought at the time, I don't think either of us was truly prepared for what was to come.

I loved Léonie, but I also loved the music business and I never wanted to have to choose between them. It would have been impossible. I honestly think that however much you love someone you also have to follow your dream. I've been singing for most of my life and I can't ever imagine giving it up. In fact, sometimes I'm at my happiest when I'm on stage. If the voice is kicking, the band's together, and the audience is having a good time nothing else matters. All the shit in your life goes away, and that's a good feeling. If I ever stopped singing I wouldn't be the same person. It's that simple. But being a musician is a selfish existence. It's about doing what I love, sometimes at the expense of everything else. I knew it was asking a lot of Léonie to tolerate lengthy separations and an erratic lifestyle. It's tough being the wife or girlfriend of a performer.

It's also almost impossible to go on the road with a wife and young children. With long spells apart you have to know that you can trust each other. I won't pretend that there aren't girls on the road. There are, not that I've ever been interested in one-night stands, either before I met Léonie or since, but in the Spandau days there was temptation everywhere. Beautiful girls telling you how brilliant you are. Meanwhile, you're lonely and missing being with someone. It's not easy for the other person to wait at home for the tour to end. If I put myself in Léonie's shoes, I know I would hate it. That's why I had to be sure she understood how much singing and performing meant to me, and that she would never ask me to choose between her and the business.

In twenty years she never did.

On the morning of the wedding, I woke up with my stomach in knots. It was a mixture of anticipation and nerves. I got into my morning suit and went to the pub for a couple of pints with my two best men, my brother, Steve, and my mate, Pete Hillier, and a few of the lads. I don't think my mum was too thrilled, but I was too wound up to hang around the house until it was time to leave for the church. That day was one of the best of my life. Léonie looked gorgeous. I remember turning to face her as she came down the aisle on the arm of her father, Neville. He looked so proud, and she looked beautiful. She was smiling, this big, happy smile. She looked a million dollars. My sister, Lee, and Léonie's sister, Gail, were bridesmaids.

I was so nervous as we exchanged vows, determined not to make a mess of them. That part of the service was incredibly moving. 'Do you, Léonie Helen, take Anthony Patrick . . .' Behind me, my mum was fighting back tears. I had no idea how affected she was by the sight of her eldest son getting married. I only discovered recently that she went home and sobbed her heart out that night.

As for me, I couldn't have been happier.

My family and friends were around me. The band was there. Léonie's brother, Neil, and my mate Michael 'Burt' Reynolds, both Royal Marines, were in their ceremonial blues. Waiting to whisk us from the church to the reception was the 1922 Rolls. It was a cold day, and there was an icy wind blowing, but I'd insisted on having the top down. Unfortunately, Léonie suffers with poor circulation and feels the cold. She wasn't keen on braving the elements in a lace dress, designed to look good rather than keep her warm, but she agreed, to keep me happy. It was only a five-minute trip from the church to the hotel, but it was fantastic. In fairness, it was bloody freezing as well.

We spent our wedding night at the Inn On The Park Hotel, which was fantastic and ridiculously expensive. The next morning I had a row in reception because I didn't have a credit card to pay the bill and they wouldn't let me write out three separate cheques. A queue of people waiting to check out formed behind me. In the end, an American guy who overheard what was going on, spoke up. 'Give him a break, he just got married.' The desk clerk caved in. I wrote out three separate cheques.

We went round to see my mum and dad to open wedding presents and had lunch at Manzi's fish restaurant in the West End. That marked the end of the honeymoon. The next morning I left for six weeks to tour with the band. For all everyone had been nervous about me getting married, it made no difference to Spandau Ballet. If anything, it turned out to be a good move – for everyone. The fans were just as keen. I swear women were more interested once I was wearing a wedding ring than when I was single, which never made sense. Meanwhile, I was much happier, more settled.

The True tour in 1983 changed things for good. We had twenty-three theatre dates scheduled in the UK, with a European leg booked for later in the year. We were also due to play Canada and the USA.

By the end of the UK dates we had our first Number 1 with 'True'. The news came through in Sheffield. The rule was that Steve Dagger called on a Tuesday morning to give us the chart position. The earlier the call, the better the news, basically. Just after 8 a.m., Gary Kemp and John Keeble, who were sharing a room, got the call to say we had a Number 1. They let themselves into my room with a passkey and woke me up by showering me with champagne. I'm not very good at getting up in the morning – actually, that's an understatement – but that did the trick. We were all in high spirits: at one point John careered along the hotel corridor on a room-service trolley, although that wasn't entirely out of the ordinary for him. In a way, though, it was all slightly flat. We had already had two hit singles off the True album: 'Lifeline', which reached Number 7, and 'Communication', which went to Number 12. Because of the way the record industry works, with daily feedback on sales, we were well aware that 'True' was likely to top the charts. It was selling 60,000 copies a day, which was phenomenal. When it entered the charts at Number 10 we were certain it would go all the way. It had such momentum the overwhelming feeling was, how can this *not* be a Number 1? It actually knocked David Bowie's 'Let's Dance' off the top spot, and stayed there for the next four weeks.

It was a major milestone for us and we wanted to celebrate. The problem was, the hotel we were in was quite depressing and not geared up for impromptu celebrations first thing in the morning. We managed to persuade them to rustle up scrambled eggs with smoked salmon washed down with champagne, which wasn't chilled, but we drank it anyway.

Then we got back on the tour bus for the short hop to Nottingham for that night's gig. After about twenty minutes on the road, we had to pull into a lay-by because Steve Norman had gone green. He was always the one who would get sick on trips. He couldn't travel backwards – which we suspected was a ploy to avoid jump seats on Lear jets and in limos – although it didn't seem to make any difference. Whether he faced forwards or backwards, he didn't travel well. So, there we were, celebrating our first Number 1, with the sax player throwing up at the side of the road.

Touring is like stepping into a different world, a safe, comfortable world, a million miles from reality. Once you're on the tour bus you leave everything else behind – which probably sounds selfish and irresponsible – but the fact is you need to be in a different frame of mind on the road. There has to be a degree of abandon in order to get up and perform each night. For the duration of the tour it's almost as if you operate in a parallel universe. Normal, everyday concerns go out the window. Home becomes a distant place. A different routine kicks in. Your working day starts with the sound check in the afternoon. The chances are you'll be up, unwinding after the gig, until the early hours. Lunchtime is about the earliest anyone is likely to surface. By most people's standards, it's all a bit back to front. Your mates are the band and the road crew. You're living and working together, drinking together. Those relationships become incredibly tight. Within that touring community, there is an extraordinary degree of trust and loyalty. Needless to say, it's not the kind of world that admits outsiders very easily. Day-to-day touring involves back-to-back shows most of the time. When Spandau was on the road, the only time wives and girlfriends appeared was when we were in one place for a few days. Generally speaking, they were pretty much excluded. You only have to watch *This Is Spinal Tap*, one of my favourite films, to see what happens when a wife or girlfriend joins the tour. Everything changes. There's a wonderful moment in the film when the lead singer's other half comes up with a new look for the band's stage show – masks based on each band member's star sign. Bewildered looks all round. Actually, I quite liked the idea of astrology masks. Maybe it's a Gemini thing.

I still love touring today. It's not something I could ever envisage giving up. Unless you've experienced it, it's hard to imagine the atmosphere, but a huge element of the appeal is being part of a tight-knit group, all working towards the same goal. I still get a kick out of arriving at a venue and seeing the crew load in the gear and get the place ready for that night's show. Even today, after twenty-three years in the business, the feeling remains the same. I've never imagined that one day I'd retire and stop performing. I enjoy it too much. I honestly believe I'm at my happiest when I'm on stage. I don't think that will ever change.

Although Léonie is used to me being away from home, over the years she has found it increasingly tough, I know. She has had to cope with being, effectively, a single parent for long periods. We both knew what we were letting ourselves in for, but I think she expected the touring would stop at some point, and that we would have more time at home together, like any normal couple. It hasn't turned out like that. In fact, in 2003 I was probably away from home more than ever. After a seven-week stint on the TV show, *Reborn In The USA*, I came home for a couple of days before leaving for a forty-five-date UK tour. I'm busier than ever, and I'm grateful for that. It means a lot to me to be able to earn a living doing what I love. How many people are that fortunate? On the downside, the separations are as frequent now as they ever were in the Spandau days.

I don't kid myself for a second that being married to me is easy.

Chapter Nine

It was during the True tour that we discovered the screaming fan phenomenon. They were there at every venue. At the Liverpool Empire two girls climbed a drainpipe to get to our dressing room. Suddenly there was a tapping on the window. We opened it to find a girl suspended in mid air. The dressing room was on the third floor. We dragged her – and the friend who was with her – to safety and gave her a cup of tea.

At first we'd only get screamed at by big gangs of fans. I suppose there was safety in numbers. As time went on, all it took was a lone girl to spot the tour bus and she would sprint down the middle of the road after us, screaming her head off. It was bizarre and it spilled over into every bit of our lives. One day, driving past Hackney Marshes, I stopped at the local bakery. When I came out of the shop four schoolgirls started screaming at me. The local shopkeepers came out to see what was going on. It sounded like someone was committing murder. I was standing there, panic-stricken, going, 'Please, just calm down.'

When John Keeble moved into his own place in Kentish Town, girls camped on the doorstep. He had to climb over them to get to the local shop. So did his girlfriend, Flea. The whole thing was mad.

When it came to playing London, the Hammersmith Odeon was the obvious venue. But, being Spandau Ballet, we never did the obvious. Instead, we decided to play the Albert Hall, the Festival Hall, and Sadler's Wells. We billed it as 'Spandau over London'. It was all part of fostering the sense that we were different from other pop groups. In some respects it was a smart move. We were perceived as innovative and imaginative. Off the wall. We set our own agenda. I suspect, however, that occasionally we might have benefited from being more conventional. Three ground-breaking venues, as well as a couple of nights at the Hammersmith Odeon, would have probably made more sense.

For me, the highlight of the True tour was playing the Albert Hall. It held special memories for me. Six years earlier, I had managed to engineer a backstage meeting with Frank Sinatra there.

Sinatra's London shows in 1977 were a huge event. He was a hero of mine and I was determined to see him. The fact I didn't have a ticket wasn't going to stop me. I was working in the warehouse at IPC at the time and we used address labels marked IPC Business Press. I trimmed one down and created my own laminated 'press pass'. As a seventeen-year-old warehouse worker I wouldn't have got near Sinatra. As Anthony Holden, a music journalist with *Melody Maker*, it was a different story.

On Sinatra's first night at the Albert Hall, I put on a suit, went to the stage door and showed my pass. I was in. Easy. I didn't have a seat, so I went up to the gods and scanned the stalls below. I spotted Roger Moore in the audience and, five rows back, an empty seat. Off I went. I flashed my pass at every security man. Anthony Holden, *Melody Maker*. No one challenged me. I had one of the best seats in the house, just a few feet away from Frank Sinatra.

The next day, I told my mum I would take her to see

Sinatra. She was worried I was about to pull some kind of stroke, but I promised I would get her a ticket. I managed to get her a seat in the gods from one of the touts, and off we went. I was in my suit again. At the theatre, she went in and I nipped round to the stage door. I showed my pass, and I was in. When I appeared in the gods my mum wanted to know how I'd got in. I showed her my pass. She was mortified. Below, I could see a couple of empty seats right at the side of the stage. I nodded at them. 'That's where we're going to sit,' I told my mum.

I took her arm and led her past all the security men. She was hanging on for dear life, convinced we'd be thrown out, but no one batted an eyelid. Having seen the show the night before, I knew how the set would end and where Sinatra would exit the stage. The door was about six feet away from where we were sitting. I leaned over and said, 'Mum, I'm just going to have a word with Frank Sinatra.' She clung to my arm. 'You can't!' As he disappeared through the door at the back of the stage, I followed. He stood a few feet away, surrounded by minders. I said, 'Excuse me, Mr Sinatra, can I just have a word?' There was a bit of a commotion and someone shoved me against the wall. Sinatra looked up. I said, 'I just wanted to say thanks very much. What a fantastic concert.'

He said, 'It's good to see some young people here.'

I said, 'I'm a big fan and so's my mum.'

'What do you do?' he replied. I decided against lying about working for *Melody Maker*. Sinatra was well known for his tricky relationship with the press.

I said, 'I'm a singer. I'm in a band, and one day I want to sing here.'

He said, 'Well, good luck to you son.' I went back to my seat. My mum couldn't believe it.

That would probably have been enough for most people, but not me. The next night I went back, ready to pull the *Melody Maker* stunt again, this time with my best mate, Pete Hillier. I didn't bother with a suit. I wore a pair of fluorescent punk trousers instead. We made it inside, but the security guys were onto us. They chased us all over the building. Finally, we were standing in the circle, next to one of the boxes, wondering if we'd got away with it, when a hand appeared and grabbed us. A man with silver hair stepped out. I recognized him from the night before. One of Sinatra's security team. He marched us out of the building. All the way, I pleaded with him not to hit us and gave him some sob story about being on the dole. He wasn't interested. He just wanted us out of there.

Several years later, at the start of the True tour, I was sitting in the back of a limo. There was something familiar about the minder, with his sharp suit and shock of silver hair, who faced me. I said, 'Mick, did you look after Sinatra when he was here six years ago?'

He said, 'Yeah, we always look after Mr Sinatra when he's in town.'

I couldn't believe it. I said, 'You're the sod who kicked me out of the Albert Hall!' It didn't ring any bells with him. He had thrown out too many people to remember one skinny kid in punk trousers. It seemed ironic that he was now looking after me.

The night Spandau Ballet played the Albert Hall was a special one for me in more ways than one. That night, the band stayed over the road at the Kensington Royal Garden Hotel. I celebrated with Léonie.

A few weeks later we discovered that she was pregnant with our first child.

Sadler's Wells also struck a chord because I had grown up

on the doorstep of the theatre, in Islington. Our old school, Dame Alice Owens, was over the road. It was the first time a pop band had played Sadler's Wells, and we felt as if we were breaking new ground. Looking back, it probably wasn't an ideal venue. It was too small, but it meant something special to all of us.

We played two nights at Sadler's Wells. The first night was filmed. The next night, we went in early so that the film crew could pick up some extra shots. We were all told to wear the same clothes, for continuity. Our style as a band was constantly evolving and the True tour was the era of suits and floppy fringes. I had a long black frock coat, in the style of Wyatt Earp. That second night, Steve Norman forgot all about continuity. He started with his jacket on. After a while, it came off. When it came to editing the video, none of the shots matched with the previous night. Throughout, he's got his jacket on in one shot, then off in the next. On, off, on, off.

But it was the Royal Festival Hall that caused the biggest headache. Like Sadler's Wells, it hardly fitted the bill as a typical pop venue. Far from it. I'm not sure the organizers knew what to expect. They were used to well-behaved audiences who stayed in their seats, and performers who were a lot quieter than us. To the alarm of the fire marshals, our audience pushed and shoved its way to the front of the stage. From our point of view, it was an entirely normal gig, but as far as the Royal Festival Hall marshals were concerned, things were spiralling out of control. It was tantamount to a riot. Word reached us midway through the set that, unless the audience moved away from the stage, the plug would be pulled for safety reasons and the gig would be over. It was all going horribly wrong.

We played on, although the crowd situation was precarious. The Festival Hall team was ready to halt the proceedings. I didn't see the point in fighting with them. They were genuinely concerned someone was going to get hurt. If we'd ignored their warnings and things had turned ugly we would have looked pretty stupid. By then, the fire brigade had turned up. I decided to ask the crush of fans at the front to move back, and Gary Kemp saw red. He said, 'What the fuck are you doing? This is *our* gig. I don't give a flying fuck about the fire marshals.'

When I came off stage, Gary and Martin were waiting for me. There was a huge row. I remember Steve Dagger stepping in to try to calm things down. Then Nicky Sibley, our old drum roadie, intervened. He told the pair of them to get a life. The next thing they were rounding on him and, unwisely, threatening to batter him. I was in the middle, holding them back. I wasn't worried about Nicky. He's a big bloke. A big, hard bloke. If things had got out of hand there wouldn't have been much left of Gary and Martin.

Despite that incident, the atmosphere between us all on the True tour was good. John and Gary were on a similar wavelength and had become close. Steve and Martin had established themselves as the jokers of the band. I liked all of them but still spent a lot of time with my old mates, Pete Hillier and Nicky Sibley. The tour marked the beginning of a solid, successful period for the band.

After the UK tour, we headed for the United States and Canada. Although we only had a few dates lined up in each country, the reception was amazing, particularly from the Canadian audiences. We played sell-out shows in Toronto, Vancouver and Montreal.

For reasons I never understood, that was the only time we toured there.

In Toronto, St John Ambulance staff worked flat out, pulling girls out of the crush at the front of the stage. Backstage, there were bodies everywhere. Mostly, girls who fainted recovered quickly, but one casualty of the crush ended up in hospital. Another girl was out cold long enough to be causing concern. I sat with Steve Norman talking to her, holding her hand, trying to bring her round. We were worried sick. The next thing, she opened her eyes, saw the pair of us leaning over her, and screamed. Then she passed out again. The guy from St John Ambulance said, 'I think you'd better go. You're not helping.'

When we got to Vancouver the weather was awful. It was raining hard on the night of the gig. Afterwards, we took refuge in the hotel bar. All of a sudden, there was an almighty bang. It sounded like a gun had gone off. The next thing, the glass roof of the bar collapsed and water poured in. We were on the first floor. Below us, the lobby was flooded. John Keeble and Gary Kemp huddled under umbrellas, indoors, as firemen tramped in and out. Amazingly, no one was hurt, but it was mayhem.

We were starting to get used to the fact that wherever we played, there were girls. I've never understood the appeal of groupies. The idea of someone you've only just met throwing herself at you turns me off. Not all the band members agreed. Sometimes you'd see the same girls turn up in different cities. I bumped into one girl in Stockholm, who later appeared in the same hotel as us in Dortmund. She had been on the road with the rock group Saxon and, by all accounts, was on very good terms with them. Somewhere on her travels she'd picked up the clap. Word went round to stay well away. That night she turned her attentions to one of the guys in the Michael Schenker band. Either he was the only person who hadn't heard or he wasn't choosy. As he left the bar with her at the end of the night, I waited for one of his band mates to tell him. No one did, poor sod.

Although we met some lovely girls, I never felt like putting my marriage at risk with a one-night stand with a stranger. It wasn't worth it.

When we were away from home, I always made sure I was too drunk to get up to anything. As a strategy, it served me well. On a promotional trip to Montreux in Switzerland, we were coming to the end of a day of back-to-back interviews when Steve Dagger told us there was one more. A Greek journalist wanted to speak to us. No one wanted to do it, until Dagger mentioned that the reporter was gorgeous. John Keeble and I immediately volunteered. It was the longest interview of the day. The longest interview *ever*. She was absolutely beautiful and there was a bit of harmless flirting going on. That night, the same girl turned up at a party at the hotel. I got very drunk, went to bed and passed out. Later, she was knocking on my door, calling my name. Inside, I was unconscious. Gary Kemp saw her in the corridor and told her she was wasting her time. Nothing wakes me after I've had a few drinks.

Sometimes, it was hard to steer clear of girls while we were on the road. In San Francisco in 1983, we were all in a club when two girls started chatting to us. They were good-looking, sexy – and dead saucy. They had trouble written all over them in big letters. When I decided to head back to the hotel, they insisted on giving me a lift, despite my protests. I wasn't sure I wanted a free ride.

I said, 'No, really, girls, I'll be fine. I'll get a cab.'

They wouldn't have it, though, so the three of us ended up in the car, with me sandwiched between them.

On the way back, all I could think about was how I was

going to escape at the other end. I suspected I might have my work cut out. Meanwhile, they kept up a constant barrage of compliments about my 'cute' accent.

When we pulled up outside the hotel one of the girls drawled, 'Hey, can we come up to your room?'

I said, 'No, sorry, girls.'

Neither of them budged so I added, 'Actually, I'm sharing a room,' which was true. For some reason, I was doubling up that night with Jess Bailey, our keyboard player. I hoped that would put them off, but I was wrong.

'Oh, that's OK. We can show your friend a good time too.'

I said, 'Look, girls, you're lovely and I really like you, but I have to go.'

Thankfully, they released me. The next morning, no one could believe I'd actually turned the pair of them down.

Some of the girls we ran into looked like they'd been around. I don't judge anyone, but I find the whole groupie scene a bit seedy. I suspect I'm in a minority, although there was an incident in Canada that brought home the perils of casual sex.

After the show in Toronto, I was in the bar with Pete Hillier and Nicky Sibley. Both were on our crew and both had been good friends of mine for years. We were having a few drinks when a girl came over. She was good-looking, intelligent – I thought – an artist. She seemed about as far removed from your average groupie as possible. Eventually, I went to my room, leaving the three of them there. A bit later, Pete and Nicky, who were sharing a room, went to bed. In the middle of the night there was a tapping on their door. They ignored it. The tapping became louder, more urgent. Pete got out of bed to find the girl they'd left in the bar standing in the corridor. She had wrongly assumed that the pair of us were sharing a room.

In fact, I was fast asleep somewhere else. She pushed past Pete and climbed into bed with Nicky. Annoyed at being woken up – and probably a bit worse the wear for alcohol – Pete went back to bed. Casual sex was nothing unusual on the road. A girl willing to get into bed with a band member, or one of the crew, was normal. Pete was not concerned. The girl started telling Nicky she could hardly believe they were in bed together, that they were going to make love. Nicky – who is a good foot shorter than me and a lot heavier – could hardly believe it either. He thought he was dreaming.

After they'd had sex, she went to the bathroom. Nicky padded along behind her, naked. When she flicked on the light switch she got the shock of her life. She screamed the place down. 'You're not Tony!' Now, with the best will in the world, Nicky was not me. Then again, he'd never claimed to be. Even in the dark it's hard to imagine anyone confusing the pair of us. To put it mildly, she was extremely unhappy. Nicky took a more philosophical what's-done-is-done view.

Looking back, I'm surprised we didn't get into serious trouble more times than we actually did.

In the US, we played a handful of gigs, a couple on the west coast in Los Angeles and San Francisco, and one in Minnesota near the Great Lakes. I'm not sure any of us knew what to expect of Minneapolis, but it turned out to be a memorable trip, for a couple of reasons.

First impressions, however, were not good. When we arrived at the venue to sound check we were appalled to see tables and chairs arranged in front of the stage. It looked like a cabaret club and we had visions of people tucking into a three-course meal while we went through our set to a bit of polite applause now and then. We were all furious. I thought we'd made a big mistake, that we'd been confused with another band, a middle-of-the-road covers band, maybe. As it turned out, it was one of the best gigs we ever did. The audience went wild. Girls jumped on the tables and, from there, scrambled onto the stage. It's one of the very few occasions the stage was overrun. It was fantastic, and not a prawn cocktail in sight.

In Minneapolis, John and Gary spent an afternoon at the Walker Art Institute wandering round the Hockney exhibition. They came back fired up with ideas. That was the inspiration for the next album, *Parade*.

Although the North American trip was short, it made us realize there was a market for us there. The strange thing was, after such a promising start, we never really went back. I've spoken at length with John Keeble about this since and neither of us understands why the band failed so miserably in the US. It was like so much of the Spandau story. It didn't quite add up. We never went to South America or Thailand. We never played festivals. We were always veering off down the less obvious route, feeling smart because we managed to be out of step with conventional thinking. But there were times when doing the conventional thing, following a tried and trusted path, was exactly what we needed. The only way we were going to crack America was by playing there. A lot. Looking back, it's obvious we needed to tour extensively. The option never came up. I think that even at the time we knew that we needed to deliver a clear message to the American market about the band and our music. We had desperately wanted a hit in the States before 'True', and we'd tried to get 'Communication' away, without success. The feeling was that if 'True' was our first major hit in the US it would paint the wrong picture. It wasn't typical of our music as a whole – if anything, it was atypical – and there was a danger it could pigeonhole us in the eyes of the American market as five blokes in suits singing a ballad. The scale of the success of 'True' elsewhere in the world meant that, inevitably, it was released in the US and went to Number 4 in the charts. It was a huge hit. But, as we'd feared, the record-buying public in America saw us as white soul balladeers. No one was in the least bit interested in the heritage of the band. In a perverse way, the scale of the success of 'True' damaged our chances in the States. The fact was, we had proved ourselves capable of balancing a ballad like 'True' with electro-pop and funk, but we couldn't quite get the US market to understand that. We needed to spend months touring, letting them hear the whole repertoire, but we never did. We should have toured extensively all around the world, capitalizing on the success of 'True'. It reached Number 1 in twenty-one countries, which is extraordinary, yet we didn't seem to use it as a foundation for the future. Our lack of success in the US led to us falling out with our record label a couple of years down the line.

The strange thing is that even during 1983, which marked a turning point for Spandau Ballet, we weren't working at full tilt. We still had time off. We had time to go flat hunting and buy cars. I'm busier now than I was then.

Every now and then I'd wonder whether the band was heading in the right direction. A couple of times I suggested we bring in a more experienced manager. It wasn't about ditching Steve Dagger. I just thought it made sense to have someone working with us who knew more about the business than we did. We were all – Steve included – as inexperienced as each other, learning (or not) as we went along. It wouldn't have hurt to have someone with more commercial know-how on our side. No one else saw it that way. They were wary of bringing in outsiders. The others didn't want someone in a suit handling things, even if it made sound financial sense. We stuck with Steve.

In August, '83 we released 'Gold', our fourth single from the album. It was a great track and I'm convinced it could have been a second Number 1 for us if it hadn't been for a decision by *Top Of The Pops*. We were under no illusions about the extent to which an appearance on the show could affect record sales. Consequently, if *TOTP* summoned us, we were always there. The sole exception was for 'Gold', which climbed to Number 2 while we were out of the country doing promotional work. *TOTP* asked us to appear that week and we turned them down, not because we were arrogant or complacent – we were working in Norway and would have had to shelve other commitments to return to the UK. Still, it wasn't as if we didn't have a fallback. I had gone to Spain with Gary to shoot the *Gold* video. Sadie Frost made a guest appearance, in gold make-up and a short skirt, although I didn't really know her. She was just the girl in the video. Steve, John and Martin stayed at home. As far as they were concerned, it was a case of, 'You're doing your bits in Kensington . . .' I don't think they were impressed. Actually, they were lucky not to come to Spain. It was a nightmare shoot. The director walked out and we ended up working crazy hours to complete it. When we got to the last scene, where I had to place a jigsaw piece on Sadie's bare shoulder, I had fallen asleep. It was the early hours of the morning and we'd worked through the night. Someone had to wake me up to shoot the scene. I was wiped out.

Anyway, the idea was that the video would play when we couldn't. But when we couldn't make *TOTP*, they decided not to run it.

I'm sure that's what cost 'Gold' the Number 1 slot.

We were finally starting to make some money, and we felt secure enough to start spending it. There was a sense that we had arrived, I suppose. It was a relief, bearing in mind the awfulness of the year before, in the wake of *Diamond*, and a couple of flops. Up until then our lifestyles hadn't really changed in any dramatic way. We had become famous but not rich.

With the True tour behind us, we felt secure enough to buy places of our own.

I had another reason to buy a place. I was about to become a father. I had always wanted kids, but it was a bit of a shock to both of us when Léonie discovered she was pregnant with Thomas. We had assumed it would be a while before the first baby came along. Neither of us was in any hurry. If a year had gone by, it would have made no difference. Instead, just three months after the wedding, she was pregnant. I think she was concerned about breaking the news to me. On the face of it, the timing was less than ideal. My career was taking off, and the chances were I'd be spending more time away from home. Also, the money was not yet rolling in. Still, I was delighted at the news. The woman I loved was having our baby.

Léonie made a beautiful mum-to-be. I remember she came to Paris to see us when we were playing there. I hadn't seen her for three weeks, which was a bloody long time. When she arrived, she was glowing. She looked amazing. I remember she wanted a hamburger and asked for it well done. It arrived cooked the French way. I cut into it. It was practically raw inside. I sent it back. A few minutes later, it reappeared, still pink inside. I called the waiter. 'Look,' I said, 'my wife is pregnant. She cannot eat this. Now, please, *burn* the fucker.'

The first property we bought was a two-bedroom flat in John Spencer Square, in Islington. It cost £47,500 and it was in a modern, purpose-built block, with a garden. Ideal for a couple expecting their first child.

By the time we actually moved in, the baby was almost due. Léonie went off to stay with her parents for a week while I blitzed the place with a gang of mates. We decorated the whole flat, and fitted a new kitchen, all in the space of a couple of days. Within days of Léonie coming back, she woke in the early hours of the morning with contractions. She nudged me. 'It's time,' she whispered. I was awake at once. 'Right. I'll just have a quick shower.' Léonie said, 'There's no time. Get dressed.' She was breathing hard, counting between contractions. I started scrabbling about in the wardrobe. I said, 'OK. Where's my suit?' Léonie looked at me, astounded. She was battling to keep her breathing even. She said, 'What are you doing?'

'I'm looking for my suit. I want to be smart when the baby comes.' I rifled through my clothes. I was twenty-three years old, and I had no idea.

Léonie said, 'How long do you think all this is going to take?'

I thought for a moment. 'Well, once the waters have broken, it's not going to take that long.'

She said, 'It could take hours. *Hours.* Now will you just *get dressed.* Put on a T-shirt and jeans.'

I started fumbling around on the top of the wardrobe. Léonie was gripping the edge of the bed, panting. '*Now* what are you doing?'

I said, 'I'm just looking for the camera, the Polaroid. I'm sure it's up here somewhere.'

'For fuck's sake, *I'm having a baby.*' She was shouting by now. I threw on some clothes and we left for the hospital.

As we drove towards King's Cross, Léonie was increasingly tense. I was trying to keep one eye on her and one on the road, which probably wasn't a good idea. I was going a bit faster than usual and the pavement had been widened since I'd last driven down there. I smacked into the kerb and the car tipped up on its side. I think Léonie was relieved when we finally arrived at the hospital.

Once there, she was hooked up to a drip and given pethidine to help control the pain. Then the waiting began. Hours went by. I asked the nurse how much longer it was likely to take. It seemed we were in for a long wait. I nipped out to the pub for a cigarette and a pint but instantly regretted it. If she had the baby while I was out, I would never forgive myself. I rushed back to the ward. Nothing had changed. Several more hours went by before Thomas finally arrived.

It's an extraordinary thing to see your child born. I was completely overwhelmed. I felt euphoric, but I cried too. I wanted to be strong for Léonie, but I couldn't hold back the tears. We had a healthy, strong boy. The strange thing is, you have nine months to get used to the idea that you're going to have a baby, but when it happens it still knocks you sideways. I don't think you can prepare for how it's going to make you feel. It was an intense, emotional experience. Nothing else in my life had felt anything like it.

By then Léonie was exhausted, but she was also ecstatic. We were laughing and crying at the same time.

Within a few hours, visitors started arriving. John Bowles, an old family friend, was first to appear, followed by Léonie's boss at the BBC, Bobby Jay, then my mum and dad.

I don't know if having a child changed me. It must have done, I suppose. All I do know is that when you have children your whole *life* changes. Everything revolves around the baby. As soon as we had Thomas, I couldn't imagine life without him. He became the focus of attention wherever we went, which is how it should be.

The hardest thing was being away from home. I was never very good at being apart from Léonie anyway, but now it was worse. It was tough for her too, but she was a brilliant mum. For long periods, she had to cope on her own, but it never got her down. I was the one, sitting in a hotel room, missing home, feeling depressed. I would call Léonie and she'd hold the phone to Thomas so I could speak to him, not that he knew what I was saying. All I could hear was a bit of gurgling, which was good enough. For me, that was a conversation with my son. As he got older, he understood what it meant when his daddy was on the phone, and his face would light up.

At times I'd have given anything just to be able to get home for a few hours. As time wore on, that was exactly what I would do. If there was a break in the schedule I'd hop on a plane and come home, even if it was just for a night. I was loving married life.

It didn't take Léonie long to work out that when she took me on, she also took on my mates. They were forever dropping in, uninvited. One morning, the police turned up to question me. Actually, it was an old school pal, Mark Corker, who'd joined the force, winding me up. Léonie took it in her stride. Just as well. The next surprise was courtesy of a couple of mates on their way to the Royal Tournament. Léonie let them into the flat one morning while I was still in bed. They burst into the bedroom, in full army kit, like a pair of commandos. I was fast asleep and normally it takes a lot to wake me. These two managed, no bother. I came round to find one on either side of the bed aiming a rifle at my head. It was their idea of a practical joke. We ended up having a couple of pints in the Salmon and Compasses at the top of Chapel Market in Islington.

The rifles, wrapped in blankets, came with us.

We had all bought ourselves smart cars, worthy of pop stars. Well, the others had. John Keeble got himself a Triumph Spitfire, which he soon traded up to a Lotus Europa. Steve went for a Lotus too. I think Martin and Gary each had a Porsche.

I had a wife and a small child. I needed something more practical. I decided on a second-hand Rover. It was yellow with mustard velour seats and it never really ran that well. I don't know why I bought it, to be honest. I couldn't wait to get rid of it. Next, I bought an Opel Manta GTE. It was a huge gold thing – and marked the start of my love affair with gold cars – and a bit smarter than the Rover. I felt like I was going in the right direction. It cost £6,700 and it was the first new car I'd owned. Other than the Rover, all I'd ever owned was a clapped-out Vauxhall Viva that went to the breaker's yard after it blew up. The Opel was something else. I was so excited about it I drove Léonie mad. Every night I'd open up the manual and spend hours reading the specifications. It must have bored her to tears.

Before long, and with not many miles on the clock, I started having problems with it and it was in and out of the garage. By the time I'd done 14,000 miles I'd had enough. I decided to get rid of it. Despite the fact it had caused me nothing but trouble, Pete Hillier decided he wanted to buy it. I did my best to put him off, but he was convinced it would be fine and, to be honest, it was. Funny that. Meanwhile, I bought a beautiful Jaguar XJ6. Cobalt blue with leather seats. It was my pride and joy. By this time, we were living on North Hill in Highgate and one night – stupidly – I decided not to put the car in the drive. It was winter and the roads were icy. In the early hours of the morning there was an almighty bang. Léonie woke up and jumped out of bed. As usual, I was in a deep sleep and didn't stir. Outside, a seven-ton van had skewed across the road at an angle. Léonie thought the driver had lost control and run into a lamp post. All she was worried about was whether he was hurt. While she was trying to wake me, the van started up, the driver reversed and disappeared, at which point she began to suspect it wasn't the lamp post he'd hit, but the Jag. She was shaking me, trying to get me out of bed and I was saying, 'Look, if he's hit the car, there's nothing we can do. Let's just leave it until the morning.' In the end, I looked out the window and decided there was nothing much to worry about. 'I think the back end might be a bit smashed,' I said, before going back to bed.

Léonie was all for calling the police. She'd had a good look at the van and reckoned it wouldn't be that difficult to spot: it had a giant yellow chicken on the side. Chicken or no chicken, I wasn't convinced the police would scramble a patrol car in pursuit, so in the end we went back to sleep.

The next morning I went out to inspect the damage. My car was concertinaed. It had been hit so hard it had shunted the car in front, which was on top of the car in front of that. The fourth car in the line had its bonnet in the boot of the next one. My beloved car was about half its original length. There was no way I could drive it. I wasn't even sure I could get into it. I can't tell you how upset I was.

A few months later, I got a call from Pete Hillier about the Opel, which had given him miles of trouble-free motoring. He wanted to know why I'd sold him a car I was still paying off. I had no idea what he was talking about. I'd bought the Opel outright with a banker's draft. According to Pete, I had several loan payments outstanding. It turned out that the guy I'd bought it from had a scam going at the garage, which involved falsifying hire purchase agreements against customers who'd paid with cash or a banker's draft. In the end, the Fraud Squad was involved.

I don't know why, but me and cars spell trouble.

It was while we were living in John Spencer Square that I first started having problems with my back. I had always had a few aches and pains, probably because of my height, but suddenly it became much more serious.

One morning I was in the bathroom cleaning my teeth when a stabbing pain pierced the base of my spine. I leaned on the washbasin as pain shot through me. I lost all feeling in my legs and sank to the floor. It took me a few minutes to pull myself together. Once I did, I wondered if I'd jarred my back during the night, or if I'd just experienced a particularly nasty form of cramp. I stood up. Pain shot through me again and I collapsed. This became a daily ritual. Afterwards, I'd feel fine for the rest of the day. Naturally, Léonie was worried. Every time I brushed my teeth I collapsed. It wasn't normal. This went on for months before I went to the doctor. He referred me to a specialist. When I explained my symptoms, he was mystified. He took X-rays and arranged for me to go back a couple of days later for the results. When I walked into his consulting rooms in Harley Street, he had the look of a worried man. He showed me the X-rays. A shadow was visible on the base of the spine. I said, 'What does that mean?'

He said, 'I'm sure it's fine.'

I said, 'Do you think it's cancer? If you do, just tell me.'

He said, 'I don't want you to worry. We'll do more X-rays to be sure.'

I went away wondering if there was something seriously wrong, but decided there was no point in worrying until the second set of X-rays came through. When they did, the shadow had disappeared. My consultant could find nothing wrong with my back.

I went home, relieved. The next morning I got up to clean my teeth and collapsed. I went to see a second specialist, this time at Guy's Hospital. He examined me and took more X-rays. He could find nothing wrong. He guessed it might be a trapped nerve, which might right itself eventually. It did get better, although it didn't clear up altogether.

Later, on a trip to Japan, I finally sorted it out. I went to the bathhouse in the hotel for a steam and a relaxing massage. Now I know a bit more about Japanese bathing rituals, I suspect a relaxing massage is a contradiction in terms. I was sitting in my trunks, with a towel round my waist, being coyly British, when the masseuse walked in. She took one look at me and told me to get undressed. 'Everything off.' The Japanese aren't quite as reserved as we are. She pointed at a stool. I sat with my hands in my lap while she sloshed buckets of water over me and gave me a rub down. Every inch of flesh was exposed and scrubbed. I was dying with embarrassment. Then she bundled me into the steam cabinet. It was a torture device. Sweat poured off me. I was burning up. I could only stand it for a couple of minutes. I hammered on the side. 'Get me out!' So far, I don't think I was making a very good impression.

I ended up face down on a slab. She took one look at my back and said, 'You have a lot of problems with your back.'

I said, 'If you can sort them out, I'll be happy.' I didn't think for a second she would.

She kneeled on me, pounded and pummelled my back, pulled me in every direction. I could hear strange, crunching sounds. Afterwards, I felt fantastic. She had managed to do more than two back specialists.

The trapped nerve, or whatever it was, never bothered me again.

Chapter Ten

We had decided to record the fourth album, *Parade*, in Munich. There was a real energy about the band at that time and a strong, collective spirit. We'd had our first Number 1, and a successful tour was behind us; we had proved ourselves. I think there was a genuine sense of surprise among those critics who'd written us off as little more than clothes horses that we were capable of playing and performing live to such a level. There is no doubt we improved hugely during the True tour. The experience had given us an edge, and being on the road had made us closer. We all recognized that going away together to Compass Point to record *True* had worked. We wanted to give *Parade* the same treatment, but we felt we needed an urban setting. We looked at a few options in Europe, including Abba's Polar Studios in Stockholm, but decided Sweden was too cold. Finally, we decided on Musicland, in Munich. Actually, Germany was cold too, but Musicland had a superb track record. Led Zeppelin had recorded there, as had Queen. Importantly, we liked the look of Munich. Tony Swain and Steve Jolley, who'd done a great job producing the *True* album, were on board again for *Parade*.

In early '84 we set off for Munich, stopping at Frankfurt en route, and calling in at Dr Muller's. By this time we had travelled extensively in Europe, frequently catching connecting flights in Frankfurt. On each visit, we would make an appointment with the airport doctor. Dr Muller's was actually a sex shop, and we'd never seen anything like it. We'd go in out of curiosity and marvel at the goods on display. On the face of it, most of the stock seemed to have little to do with enhancing pleasure. Mostly, the goods appeared to be instruments of torture. At that point we were clearly a lot more naïve than we imagined. Dr Muller's certainly opened our eyes. In fact, it made our eyes water. Needless to say, we never bought anything.

We spent about six weeks working on *Parade* in Munich, and it was a brilliant time. There was a confidence about what we were doing and we were all pulling in the same direction. I was happy with my voice, the standard of playing was getting better and better, and the newly rehearsed songs Gary had written had shaped up extremely well too. *Parade* is still my favourite Spandau album. At that point, the band was a fantastically stable ship.

We were staying in the Arabella Haus hotel, and the studio was in the basement. It couldn't have been more convenient. We'd fall out of bed and go downstairs to the studio, the so-called bunker. There were times when I'd work on the vocals with Steve Jolley in Union Studios across town. We'd jump in a cab with the tapes and lay down extra vocals and backing, while Tony Swain was busy with the others at Musicland. It worked pretty well. In each studio there was always someone on hand to look after us. Thinking back, we were probably one of the least demanding bands around. No one asked for bowls of Smarties with the orange ones taken out, or chilled Cristal champagne. In fact, we never touched alcohol while we were recording. We were disciplined. Let's face it, we weren't Led Zeppelin.

Still, the studios provided people – interesting, unusual

people – who could probably have done a lot more than relay whatever the lunch special of the day was, if necessary. At Union, Helmut was on hand, a well-groomed fifty-something with a blue rinse and a coy manner. Every day he would greet Steve Jolley and I with a very slow, seductive, 'Hellooooo, how are you? What can I get for you today?' All delivered with a bit of eyelash fluttering. We were convinced he had a crush on one of us, although we never found out which one.

At Musicland, there was Stefan. He had managed to avoid conscription by drinking vinegar for three weeks, making himself so ill in the process he was declared unfit for military training. Every morning he turned up with a couple of porn movies, which we would half watch over dinner. I don't know what it is about German porn movies, but they never struck me as erotic. There seemed to be an awful lot of slapping of bare bottoms, as I recall. Bizarre. Not surprisingly, we added a new word to our German vocabulary. *Langsam*. It means, slowly.

There was also Dr Death, the studio drug dealer. Spandau's drug use was sporadic. There was cocaine around from time to time, but it was never part of the culture of the band. I never touched drugs, mainly because I'd promised my nan I wouldn't. Sometimes the others went wild. They'd buy five grams and do the lot in one session. A lot of the time I wasn't even aware it was happening. They knew I wasn't into it, so they'd keep it from me. It never actually bothered me. I found it fascinating to watch pop stars on their hands and knees snorting lines of coke off a toilet seat. Although I enjoyed watching the ritual, I never felt tempted to try it.

The first time I saw cocaine was when we went on a promotional trip to Paris in 1981. We had an amazing meal and ended up in someone's suite for drinks. There was champagne on ice, and lines of coke chopped and ready on a marble table. I wouldn't like to say who was responsible for the white powder. At the time, no one thought to ask. Since I don't really like champagne, or take drugs, it wasn't my night.

One of our record company reps in Europe was a huge fan of cocaine. She made no secret of it. She came with us when we went to do a TV show. I went into the make-up department and chopped a couple of lines of face powder onto a mirror, then went to find her. I said, 'I might be able to get hold of some coke.' Her face lit up.

Later, I gave her a twenty-mark bill and said, 'Two lines, in the make-up room. It's yours.'

Off she went and snorted both lines, straight up. I was falling about. It didn't take long for the penny to drop. Her hand flew up to her nose. She screamed at me, 'You *bastard*.' I took off. She chased me all round the studio. Luckily, once she calmed down, she saw the funny side. I said, 'I hope you've learned your lesson—'

John Keeble interrupted. 'Always taste it first.'

I found the ritual surrounding cocaine fascinating. In San Remo a few years later we were all in high spirits, having picked up a triple platinum disc for 'Through The Barricades'. The Duran Duran boys were around, and we decided to make a night of it. We all ended up in someone's hotel room. Out came the white powder, which was chopped into lines on our precious disc. I just watched in amazement as various people went for it.

A few months earlier, we had been in Ibiza, playing the Ku Club for a TV show. There was a lot of Ecstasy around. Everyone was egging me on to try some. I remember saying, 'I can have just as good a night with a few drinks as you can with your stupid drugs.' A few hours later I was wandering round with a bottle of wine in each hand, blind drunk. I staggered up to the others, who were all stone-cold sober after drinking water for most of the night. 'I can enjoy myself just as much with a few drinks,' I said, swaying about unsteadily. No one said anything.

Queen were in Ibiza at the same time, appearing on the same TV show as us. After the recording, I met up with Freddie and the others – plus a few assorted ladies – for dinner. The girl sitting next to me was lovely, but she'd taken a couple of tabs of Ecstasy and seemed a bit out of it. I thought she was mad messing around with drugs and I started giving her a lecture, which seemed to go in one ear and out the other. I decided to leave her to it. Towards the end of the meal, Roger Taylor caught my eye across the table, and nodded in her direction. He was shaking with laughter. Her dress, a 1950s number with a springy underskirt, had popped up. It was vertical. Her stockings and suspenders were on full view. She was so off her face, she hadn't noticed. I popped her skirt back down. We carried on eating.

Evenings in Munich revolved around Doris's Bar, a traditional bier keller in the precinct a short walk from the hotel. It took us a while to get to know people, but once we did we were made welcome. Some nights we'd end up mixing with the British guys working for British Aerospace on a new fighter plane. It was a good vibe. There were a couple of great clubs in Munich too. The P1 was the posh one, but the Sugar Shack was at the heart of the city's rock 'n' roll scene. It was *the* place to go. All the girls had big hair, practically glued into place with hairspray. They were a brazen lot, and they were scary. So many bands had spent time in Munich recording that there was a thriving groupie scene. You got the feeling that some of those Sugar Shack girls knew an awful lot of musicians intimately.

Meanwhile, Léonie was at home looking after Tom. Although we were in touch every day, I missed being with them. Léonie actually seemed to cope an awful lot better than I did.

While we were in Munich we got to know the city – and some of the people – pretty well, although, predictably, we weren't always models of good behaviour. One day John Keeble and Steve Norman hired a rowing boat in the Englischer Garten, which, in some respects, is a bit like Hyde Park, with a lake and little islands dotted around. The nude sunbathing and beer gardens, though, make it a bit different. It was a fine day, and there were lots of people out, enjoying the sunshine and being on the water. Even when they're enjoying themselves, the Germans tend to show restraint, which is more than can be said for John and Steve. With several litres of beer inside them, the simple act of rowing was proving difficult. Eventually, a good 500 yards from dry land, they managed to turn the boat over. Fortunately, they were in shallow water, so they waded through silt and sludge back to dry land, leaving the boat behind, and ignoring the boat keeper who was screaming at them.

Unbelievably, they stripped off their shirts, squelched their way down Leopoldstrasse, and hailed a cab back to the hotel. Dripping wet. I mean, *soaking*. I hope they gave the driver a decent tip.

All my memories around that time are happy. We were established, earning money, enjoying success and having a good time together. *Parade* was well received. It was probably the happiest period for the band.

We emerged with a different look from the *Parade* period. Eric Watson's photography for the album was stylish. His portraits were among the best pictures I think we ever had done. We had moved on from the suits of the *True* era. The new styling – which included leather jackets and lace-up boxing boots – was a departure from what had been a relatively staid look, and it worked. We liked what we had become. The first single off the album, 'Only When You Leave', went to Number 3 in June '84. A few months later, 'I'll Fly For You' went to Number 9. In October '84, 'Highly Strung' reached Number 15.

The videos for 'I'll Fly For You' and 'Highly Strung' were like glossy, three-minute movies, shot on 35mm film. Simon Mills directed both of them. We shot 'I'll Fly For You' in New Orleans. John, Steve and I appeared in a fictitious courtroom scene – the first time we faced a judge together. Martin was there too. Only Gary was missing. Actually, for all it was made up, it was a lot more plausible than our genuine court appearance a few years later.

We filmed the 'Highly Strung' video in Hong Kong. The night we arrived, we all went out for dinner. Band and crew sat round a huge table. At the centre of the lazy Susan was duck baked in clay. I think we were expecting some kind of crispy duck dish. It wasn't to be. When we broke open the pot, we found a bird that hadn't been plucked or cleaned. Its head lolled on the plate. A pair of webbed feet stuck in the air. It was a baked duck, nothing more, nothing less. Most people lost their appetites. I tucked in. It wasn't bad, actually.

I'm rarely squeamish when it comes to food. I don't mind if things arrive with the head still attached. In fact, in the case of fish, I prefer it like that. I like the whole thing on the plate, so I can do the autopsy myself. It must be the frustrated surgeon in me. In the Philippines a couple of years ago, while other people were leaving the table on some pretext or other because they couldn't face eating anything, I was tucking into jellyfish and pigeons' heads. The only thing I won't go near is aspic.

When I was trying to get my solo career off the ground, I visited Hong Kong with Steve Dagger. During one lunch with some record company executives we were faced with a selection of dishes, most of them unfamiliar.

I dipped a chopstick into one of the bowls. A chicken's foot, pale and insipid, bobbed to the surface. More followed. One of our hosts explained that the feet had been boiled, left to go cold and sautéed in soy sauce. He gave me a knowing smile. 'Not many Western people try them.'

That was enough of a challenge for me. I bit into one. It was cold. The bones had been removed and the texture had an odd, rubbery feel. It wasn't great to be honest, but I didn't want to offend my hosts. I said, 'Actually, that's really quite nice.' I glanced across the table at Dagger, who was looking queasy. 'Go on, Steve, try one – they're good.'

That's just one of many occasions when I'm sure he could have cheerfully throttled me.

With 'Round and Round' scheduled for a December release, we decided we needed to generate some publicity. The Chrysalis press office lined up interviews with the *Sun* for Steve Norman, Martin Kemp and myself. The three of us trooped down to the record company offices to meet the *Sun* reporter. We knew we had to come up with three big stories to raise the profile of the band.

The Chrysalis offices were partitioned, but the walls didn't reach as far as the ceiling, which meant there was no such thing as a private conversation. Martin was first to go in. Steve and I sat outside, listening. He didn't give too much away. I went in next. The reporter wanted to know what it was like being on the road.

'Oh, it's great,' I said.

She said, 'Yeah, but all the girls. I know you're married but I'm sure you must shag around.'

'Actually, I don't.'

'What about drugs? You must have done a line of coke . . .'

'Actually, I've never done drugs. I don't touch them.'

She started to lose her patience. The old sex, drugs and rock 'n' roll image was hardly falling into place.

She said, 'So what exactly do you do?'

I said, 'Well . . . I like a drink.'

'Oh, do you? How much do you like to drink?'

I considered this. My drinking at that point was spectacular. 'Quite a lot actually. Sometimes I get absolutely slaughtered, and I love it.'

I did, too. If we had back-to-back shows on tour, I was usually pretty well behaved. I'd go to bed early and save my voice. Whenever we had a couple of days off, though, I'd go mad. Jack Daniel's was my drink. I'd go straight to the bar and order a bottle. Our tour manager, John Martin – 'the blob' – dreaded those nights. He used to beg me not to go out drinking, but if there was a day off coming up nothing would keep me in. He always got one of the minders to stick like glue to stop me from getting into trouble. Every one of them put me to bed at some stage.

If we were working it was a different story. Usually. But things went slightly awry when we appeared on a TV show in Germany to promote *Parade*. Ultravox, another Chrysalis band, were doing the same show and, the night before, we all met up and started working our way through every kind of schnapps in the hotel bar. Liam McCoy from the record company wasn't drinking, but shots kept appearing in front of him anyway. He ended up with eight lined up. I drank them. The next trip to the toilets found me in the Ladies by mistake, being screamed at by two busty – and extremely irate – Fräuleins. I was very drunk.

Russell, the minder, put me to bed.

The next afternoon we went to the TV studio to rehearse and sound check, not that there was any sound to check, since we were miming. We were clear by 4 p.m. The show was going out live that night. We were on at 11.45 p.m. It was a bad idea to let us loose with seven hours to kill. We went for an early dinner with Ultravox, although no one ate much. We did have an awful lot to drink though. Seven hours later, completely spanked, we were back at the TV studio. It was just as well we were miming. I could barely stand up, never mind sing. We were all in a similar state. On stage, Gary fell over and couldn't get back up.

Our A&R man in Germany, a skinny guy with a mullet, drainpipe trousers and cowboy boots, underestimated us. He talked about rock 'n' roll as if it had nothing to do with Spandau Ballet. In his view we were a pop group, which made us inferior, a million miles removed from 'real' bands. We called him Keith Richards. Keith never took us seriously, which was a mistake. He'd shrug and say, 'I like you boys but, hey – you know, rock 'n' roll.' It pissed us off something rotten.

This particular night we were miming our four numbers on an unremarkable hired kit, although Martin's zebra-print bass was a bit special – it was the pride and joy of the guy we had hired the gear from.

At the end of the last song, we smashed the kit to pieces.

Steve Norman was whacking the stage with the sax. I looked round to see Gary with his guitar over his head and John about to throw a high hat pedal. There was nothing else left of the drum kit. It was mayhem. The audience loved it. We wandered off, happy. None of it had been planned. We were all just drunk. When we got to the dressing room, the minders were keeping the hire company boss at bay. I suspect he'd have liked to beat the shit out of us. Keith Richards was apoplectic. We said, 'How rock 'n' roll's *that!*' You'd have thought he'd have been pleased, but he looked ready to kill us.

We went back to the hotel, leaving him to pick up the pieces, literally.

Russell put me to bed, again. John, Steve, Martin and Nicky Sibley, our drum roadie, went looking for a late bar. They ended up in a dark, dingy dive where the drinks cost a fortune. Halfway through their first round, a pair of curtains opened and a naked girl appeared. A man, also naked, followed. They started having sex on a stage the size of a kitchen table a few feet away from John and the others. A waitress (topless) appeared with another round of drinks. There was something fishy about her German accent. It turned out she was from Leicester. The sound of moaning came from the direction of the stage. John shook his head. He was not happy. He glanced over at the couple. From where he was sitting, the girl wasn't even attractive. He said, 'Can you please get them to stop? They're putting us off our drinks.'

Steve was last to face the *Sun* journalist. He had clearly taken seriously his brief to give her something juicy. Martin and I could hardly believe what we were hearing as he started relaying a story about having sex with two girls in the back of a limo. Then he confessed to having sex in a lift. At the time he was going out with my sister-in-law, Gail. The two of them were pretty serious. I wondered how she was going to react when she saw the *Sun*. When Steve finally emerged he was looking pleased with himself. Martin and I rounded on him. 'What the hell was that about? They're going to slaughter you,' I said. 'What's Gail going to say?'

Steve said, 'It's OK, I didn't tell her much.'

My mouth fell open. 'Steve, you told her *every*thing. And it's all crap.'

The day before the story was due to appear we were in a disused warehouse in South London making the video for 'Round and Round'. It was one of those typical video shoots where you spend a lot of time sitting about. I seem to remember throwing a box of matches into a carton of fireworks at one point to relieve the boredom and everyone diving for cover as rockets went off all over the building. That night we got someone to go out and buy the early edition of the *Sun*. All day we'd been winding Steve up. 'Gail's going to go mad. Your mum's going to go mad . . .' He was starting to get nervous, but he stuck to his guns. 'I didn't say that much,' he insisted.

When the early edition arrived, we all pored over it. We were crying with laughter. It was full of quotes from Steve about having it off in the back of the limo, having it off in a lift. He was horrified.

The next day, his mum was on the phone to mine. Crying. Mind you, my mum wasn't that pleased with me. My interview appeared under the headline, *My life on the road, by boozy Tony from Spandau*. I couldn't complain. It was all completely true. Léonie took it in her stride.

Still, it could have been much worse for Steve. I don't think Gail ever did see the story.

In November '84, just a few days before the Parade tour kicked off in the UK, we went into the studio to record the Band Aid single, 'Do They Know It's Christmas?'. We got involved after Bob Geldof bumped into Gary and Steve in the King's Road and told them he wanted to make a record to raise money for the famine victims in Ethiopia. We were happy to do it, although we had no sense of how massive the record would be, or what it would lead to. Nobody knew.

The night before the recording we appeared on *Peter's Pop Show* in Germany with Duran Duran. It turned into a heavy night. Everyone was wasted. Our tour manager, John Martin, passed out in a toilet and we had to climb over the top of the door to get him out. The press loved to paint Spandau Ballet and Duran Duran as bitter rivals. In fact, although there was competition between us, we actually all got along very well. We first met the band years earlier at the Rum Runner, a club in Birmingham, after we'd played a gig in the Botanical Gardens nearby. This was in the early days of Spandau Ballet, when we were a newly signed band, and they were on the verge of signing to EMI. They had their first big hit with 'Planet Earth' in 1981. Subsequently, we saw a lot of each other, as our careers ran virtually in parallel. And, despite what the press might have thought, there were never any slanging matches.

The night before the Live Aid recording, in Germany, we all had a major session and no one got much sleep. The next day, we rolled up at the airport to fly back to London. No one looked very well. Roger Taylor, Duran's drummer, and John Keeble were wearing the same jacket. They tossed, Roger lost, and he had to take his off.

When we landed at Heathrow, we heard there were fans waiting, plus photographers and camera crews. We all looked like shit. There was a mad scramble for the toilet, where everyone tried to make themselves look half decent. This was the era of big hair, and the air was thick with the smell of hairspray. I swear that Spandau Ballet and Duran Duran made a major contribution to the hole in the ozone layer. The Cure didn't help either.

There were cars waiting to take us off to Sarm West, Trevor Horn's studio. At that point we didn't even know what we were singing. Geldof and Midge Ure had written the song, Phil Collins had laid down the drum track and, as far as I remember, Sting had done some harmonies. The studio was packed with an unusual mix of people, Status Quo, Bono, Bananarama, the Boomtown Rats and Culture Club among them.

It was a fantastic atmosphere. Léonie was there with Thomas. Paula Yates was there with Fifi.

I can remember Bob Geldof gathering all the singers in the studio control room and running through everyone's lines. No one wanted to go first. Bob said, 'Go on, Hadley, you'll go first, won't you?' I went in, did two takes, and that was it. Everyone sang on the chorus. What I remember was that there were no egos in evidence. No one complaining that someone had more lines than them, or better lines, or whatever. It was done in the right spirit. There was a documentary crew filming the whole thing. At one point they interviewed Steve Norman about the plight of the Ethiopians. Steve, hung-over, and not entirely clued-up, said something along the lines of, 'I'd like to say hi to everyone in Ethiopia. Sorry we haven't got out there this year, but we'll try and get over as soon as we can . . .'

We were crying with laughter.

The single went straight to Number 1, with unprecedented sales. That was when we all understood the scale of it. Band Aid hit a nerve. People were touched, they wanted to do something to ease the famine in Ethiopia. 'Do They Know It's

Christmas?' sold more than three million copies. It was the biggest-selling UK single ever until 1997 when Elton John's tribute to Diana, Princess of Wales, 'Candle In The Wind', overtook it.

I'm so glad I was part of the whole Live Aid experience. I don't think any of us ever imagined our dream of being a successful pop band would lead to being part of something that would have such a major and lasting impact. Live Aid changed the way people felt about famine, and changed the way we raise money for charity. So many of the major fund-raising events that followed – such as Comic Relief – were influenced by Live Aid.

Chapter Eleven

We knew we were doing well when, in 1984, we were advised to spend a year out of the UK for tax reasons. When we began the Parade tour towards the end of that year, the plan was to take the show around the world and then complete our twelve months out of the country in Dublin.

Our schedule at that stage had gone into overdrive. We spent seven weeks touring Europe, during which we had two days off, one of which we spent flying from one country to another for a TV interview. I think the crew spent just three nights in hotels during that entire period. The rest of the time they were on the road, sleeping on the tour bus, and working flat out to keep pace with an itinerary that had us playing all over Europe, from Norway down to southern Spain.

In the UK we played six nights in a row at Wembley Arena and broke the house record. It was during that tour that we made some crazy trips to fulfil engagements. One night we played Tokyo, then jumped on a plane for our next show . . . which happened to be in Dortmund. We flew via New York, where we had a two-hour stopover, boarded a flight to Frankfurt (quick visit to Dr Muller's) then connected to Dortmund, arriving just in time to go straight from the airport to the sound check. The whole trip took around twenty-six hours. It was madness, but the tour was a big success. We were playing bigger venues than ever and the audiences were amazing. We were having a laugh too, both off stage and on.

As the tour wore on, we all started to pick up on Steve Norman's backing vocals on 'Always In The Back Of My Mind'. For some reason, he sang like a (bad) East End pub singer on that track. Everyone noticed, including the crew. Night after night, they would be crying with laughter. Steve, meanwhile, was oblivious.

One night, in the middle of the song, all our monitors were simultaneously switched off. All we could hear were Steve's vocals. Steve, still getting his usual mix, carried on singing his heart out. *Always In The Back Of My Mind-ah!* It was the funniest thing. We all fell apart. The entire crew was at the monitor desk, in bits. Only Steve, blissfully unaware, kept going. (You could always count on Steve to lift the band with his unique sense of humour.)

As the tour progressed at breakneck speed, we started to feel run down and ill. In Rotterdam, on the eve of a massive gig, I lost my voice. A few nights before, we were in Germany doing some promotional TV interviews. I was feeling awful but the record company had arranged to take us out for dinner, which wasn't something you could just duck out of. I suspected I wasn't well enough to go, but Steve Dagger felt it was important to make an effort. Halfway through the meal I'd had it. I left and went back to the hotel. I was burning up and sweat was running off me. I couldn't open the windows and the room felt like an inferno. The next morning I woke up feeling worse than ever and went straight to see a local specialist. He diagnosed an acute respiratory infection. At this point I was still croaking about being well enough to sing that night. He was blunt. 'Forget it,' he said.

Later, we did a TV show in Munich, by which time I was

feeling like death. Afterwards, we caught a flight to Amsterdam ready for the gig at the Ahoy in Rotterdam. I couldn't speak. I could just about manage to croak, but even that was painful. I kept telling everyone I'd be all right, although it was probably obvious to everyone else that the chances of me singing that night were slim.

Meanwhile, we carried on as if the gig was going to happen. The band went to the stadium to sound check, and I waited for our insurers to fly out a specialist from the UK for a second opinion. He confirmed what the Dutch specialist had said. There was no way I could sing that night. It was hardly surprising. By then I couldn't even speak. He gave me an injection of antibiotics and told me to rest. I was devastated.

By this time there were 10,000 people in the Ahoy. The rest of the band was sitting in the back lounge of the tour bus, rolling joints, waiting to hear whether the show was on or off. Our rider of beer, champagne and Jack Daniel's was already inside the venue. John Martin, the tour manager, appeared. 'The gig's off,' he said.

John Keeble told me recently that everyone's first concern was the rider. John Martin went to the dressing room to recover it. It probably sounds heartless, but I'd have been the same. Then everyone lit up a joint.

Back at the hotel, I was practically in tears. I felt I'd let everyone down and I didn't feel much like facing them. We all went to the hotel bar where I croaked an apology. They were fantastic. I think we were all aware of how easily illness could lay any one of us low. By then, John was battling with blisters on his hands. Three weeks into the tour, they were totally trashed. Steve's lips were raw from playing the sax. Martin had calluses on his fingers from playing the bass. Only Gary was unscathed. It was a punishing schedule on Parade, and we were all aware of the fragile nature of it all, how easily illness or injury could mean an abrupt end to the tour.

Which is exactly what happened a few months down the line.

That night in Rotterdam, I had a couple of drinks and went to bed. Thankfully, the antibiotics began to work straight away. We had a couple of days off, which gave me a chance to recover. The infection cleared up and my voice was fine. We rescheduled the Ahoy and, amazingly, almost all the original ticket holders turned up. There were hardly any returns. The Dutch fans were incredibly kind.

In all the time I've been singing I've only ever had to cancel four gigs. I've been lucky with my voice. Most of the time it holds up, even when I'm touring and it starts to feel tired. The first time I pulled the plug on a gig was in December 1978 when the Makers were due to play at the Brecknock pub. That was John Keeble's local and he'd worked hard to get the gig. I don't think he ever forgave me. There was one night at the Papagayo in St-Tropez in 1980 and a couple of years ago in Preston, where I was booked for a PA. I felt dreadful, but went anyway, kidding myself I'd be all right. The truth was I was about as ill as I'd been in Rotterdam. I managed the first song, but halfway through the second I had to stop. I remember standing there, barely able to speak let alone sing, trying to apologize in this scratchy voice, before leaving. It was terrible. You feel completely mortified, as if you're letting everyone down. Actually, in the main, people seem to understand.

On the Parade tour, we ended up in Italy. The band was huge there – in Rome, we outsold Madonna and Michael Jackson – and the fans were crazy. Hundreds of girls camped outside the hotel. If one of us so much as poked a head out of the window, screams went up. We couldn't walk down the road without being chased. We had police escorts wherever we went. Even so, fans ran after us, hammering on the side of the cars. It was mental. In the early days of Spandau there had been death threats in Italy against the band. As far as I remember, they started around about the time of the 'Paint Me Down' video. All that bare flesh probably made us look even more debauched than we were, which can't have gone down well in a strict Catholic country.

The Italian authorities took the death threats seriously. Every time we went there, we had the deputy head of the anti-terrorist squad, Agostino, assigned to us for protection. By the time we got to the Barricades tour in 1986 he was heading up the unit. Agostino was a slim, smooth, don't-mess-with-me kind of guy. His car had reinforced glass and armour plating. One day I climbed into the back seat and sat on something uncomfortable. It was a gun. In the boot, where other people keep a spare petrol can, he carried stun grenades and other assorted weapons. He was heavy duty. He became a good friend to the band. If we were running late he'd leap out of the car, waving a police badge in one hand and a gun in the other, stop the traffic and wave us through. It came in handy, especially if we were on our way somewhere important, like Sabatini's, one of the best restaurants in Rome. You could lose your table if you turned up late there.

During the Parade tour, our families joined us in Rome for a few days. All the mums and dads were there. They stayed in the Leonardo da Vinci, a smart hotel in the heart of the city. It was a brilliant time. We were living in a different world then, moving in circles we still hadn't got used to. Our parents could barely believe it. John's mum, Doris, was so impressed she took a picture of the minibar in their room. After a couple of days, his dad let slip they'd been making their bed in the morning before going out for the day. John had a word with them about that. The fact is, staying in a luxury hotel was a new experience for everyone, including us. We were all still getting used to it.

Alfie Weaver, who handled security for us, took care of our folks on that trip. They were whisked from place to place in limousines, taken to all the tourist attractions, and ate in the best restaurants. They had the time of their lives. It was a world apart from what they were used to. After a couple of days, Doris Keeble confided to my mum that she was finding all the rich food a bit much. She said, 'This is lovely, Jo, but I'm dying for a Big Mac.'

As we played in front of an audience of 16,000 at the Nettuna Stadia that night, our parents – almost bursting with pride – watched. They were our guests of honour: Sheila and Tony Norman, Doris and Stan Keeble, Eileen and Frank Kemp, and my mum and dad, Pat and Jo. Our success meant a huge amount to them, but they remained the same grounded, decent people throughout the lifetime of Spandau Ballet. I don't suppose it was easy to accept that their sons wanted to be pop stars, not in the beginning anyway, but somehow they did. My dad was an electrical engineer. John's dad ran a tile warehouse. Frank Kemp was in the print trade. Tony Norman was a cabbie. Their sons shared a dream that must have struck them as crazy. At times, our parents must have thought we were mad and, quite possibly, heading for huge disappointment. If they did, they kept it to themselves and gave us every encouragement. I'm still grateful for that.

That night, the noise from the crowd was deafening. A sound pressure monitor recorded the loudest screams ever heard in the venue. It was extraordinary. Afterwards, we had a party at the hotel. Outside, a media posse and loads of kids formed a crush, trying to get a look at what was going on. If they'd managed to, they'd have found a family party – a knees-up – in full swing, with our folks in the thick of it.

The band *was* a family then. We had something special, a camaraderie rarely seen. Everyone who worked with us noticed.

Alfie Weaver told me he'd never seen anything like it.

We had some of our best times in Italy, although it took us a while to adjust to the Italian way, which varied depending on which bit of the country you happened to be in. When we visited Bari in the south, we discovered everything moved at its own, slower pace. Time became meaningless. We were booked to appear on a TV show and given a call time to be at the studio. We arrived. Hours went by. We sat in our dressing room with only small dry cakes for company getting more and more annoyed. The head of our record company in Italy was with us. He shrugged. 'It's Italy, it's fucked up,' he offered, as if that explained anything.

Leee John and Imagination were appearing on the same show. They were due on before us, but there was no sign of them. They finally appeared, having been relaxing on the beach. I said, 'What's going on?'

Leee had some advice: 'Just go with the flow. Learn to chill out – go to the beach, have lunch. Don't take any notice of the call times. No one else does.'

I took him at his word. I'd never been very good at timekeeping, but I've been a lot worse since then. I caught up with Leee again on the *Reborn In The USA* tour last year. We're about as bad as each other when it comes to timekeeping.

After Europe, we headed to Australia, which was amazing. After seven weeks of non-stop touring, we arrived in Sydney with time on our hands. The first ten days was a break. It was fantastic, a chance for everyone to rest and get well. By then, we all had bags under our eyes and were feeling very run down. We needed some down time. We had three weeks of gigs booked, including five nights at the Sydney Entertainment Centre, which were sold out. The reception we got down under was extraordinary. Wherever we went there were lavish parties thrown for us. Léonie and Thomas, who was just coming up to his first birthday, flew out and we spent three weeks together. It was a magical time. Thomas took his first steps during that trip. I have good memories of that whole period.

The parties in Australia became legendary. We would walk into a room and there would be forty or fifty gorgeous models, each one keen to talk to Spandau Ballet. Léonie saw, first-hand, what it was like. One night, as I was talking to a girl, she slid her hand inside my shirt. Shirley Lewis, one of our backing singers, came storming over. 'Get your hand out of his shirt! That's his *wife* over there.' The girl backed off. On the other side of the room, I caught Léonie's eye. She shrugged. She knew better than anyone that girls threw themselves at us, wherever we played. I can't pretend it's not flattering to have beautiful women around, flirting with you, but it didn't go further than that for me.

We arrived in Melbourne to find a music journalist from the UK waiting for us. Paul Simper had heard all about the after-show parties. He wanted to see for himself what was going on. That night he came to the gig. Afterwards, we all went back to the hotel together. We had taken over the entire seventeenth floor. The lift opened and we stepped out. There were minders posted along the corridor. The smell of weed hung in the air. I nodded towards the suite where the party was being held and told him to go on ahead. I went to my room. A minute later, there was a knock at the door. Paul stood there. He said, 'Er, can I wait, and go with you?' He had walked into the suite and found himself in the midst of forty beautiful girls. Apart from the barman, he was the only man in the room. He turned tail and ran. 'It's too scary,' he said.

After Melbourne, we headed back to Sydney for a few days. More parties followed. At a barbecue one night I got chatting to a girl about her car, which happened to be parked outside. Actually, it was her husband's car. He was a police officer and he wasn't at the party. If he had been, I don't suppose he would have been too thrilled at the idea of his wife, who'd had a few by then, driving his motor home. He would have been even less thrilled at the idea of me getting behind the wheel. I was drunk but, when she said I could go for a spin, my eyes lit up. I love driving. She was drunk too, which probably explains why she was happy to hand over the keys. When I think back, it was crazy. I could have killed both of us. Or someone else. I never drink and drive now. Then, I was still young and stupid, and in the mood to show off. I gave the minders the slip and drove, too fast, over Sydney Harbour Bridge. I came unstuck with a handbrake turn at the end. Not realizing there was a sharp bend coming up, I smacked into the central reservation. The car went up on its side and juddered to a stop next to a police car. The cop got out and came to take a look at our bashed and dented wheel rims.

He leaned into the car. I was shaking. So was she. I said, 'I'm really sorry, I'm not familiar with the road. I'm from England.'

He peered at me. 'Is this your car?'

I said, 'No, it's hers.' Her husband's, actually, one of your colleagues, in fact.

He said, 'Have you got a driver's licence?' I hadn't. 'Insurance?' No. He frowned. 'Have you been drinking?'

'Just a couple,' I said.

He shook his head. 'Do yourself a favour – go home. And let your friend drive.'

She was as drunk as I was, but we swapped places anyway and left before he changed his mind. Back at the party, we examined the damage. The driver's side of the car was in a bad way. She'd have some explaining to do when she got home.

Everywhere we stayed, there were girls outside the hotel. Not that there was any chance of them getting anywhere near us because our minders were both intimidating and efficient. We hadn't taken our usual minders to Australia because it was too expensive. Instead, we hired a local firm to handle security. They were an interesting bunch. One day a group of us went for lunch at the home of the boss. He had a fantastic house. He also had an extraordinary collection of firearms. It was a small arsenal. There were guns in every room, mostly mounted on the walls. He explained that some of his people were currently in Angola. I don't think they were minding pop stars. It seemed odd that there was no alarm system on the property, but it turned out there was no need for one. A pack of ferocious Rottweilers roaming the grounds was all the security he needed.

At home, we had an interesting collection of minders. Alfie Weaver, our head of security, was brilliant, but I'm not sure about some of the others.

We had Rick the Thick, a beefy bodybuilder, who went on a room-service binge when we were staying at Jury's Hotel in Dublin. We only found out when he started boasting about how you could order all the food and drink you wanted in your room – and it was free.

John Keeble said, 'How do you work that out?'

Rick said, 'I've done it loads of times. I've never had to pay.'

We looked at each other. John said, 'What are you talking about, you idiot? That's *room service*. It goes on the *bill*.'

There was Dynamite George – whose club in North London had blown up – and Neil, who remains a bit of a mystery. I got on well with him, although I never quite worked out what made him tick. He was one of the first people I knew to swap his diary for a personal organizer. He was always making notes. I assumed he was jotting down vital scraps of information to do with schedules and security arrangements. One day I looked over his shoulder. Under Monday's entry he had written . . . Monday. Neil was with us in Seville. We spent the night in a club, drinking and flamenco dancing. It was Neil's job to get us out safely at the end of the evening. He led us in a swaying crocodile along a narrow corridor with a low ceiling. Everyone stumbled on blindly, muttering and bumping into each other. It was too dark to see where we were going. We ended up in a cellar. The exit was back the way we had just come. There was a lot more muttering. Once Neil stopped working for us, he sold his story to a national newspaper.

There was no mention of the Seville incident.

Oh, and there was Mori. We were watching *Police 5* one day and a mug shot popped up we thought was a dead ringer for him.

They were certainly a mixed bunch, but they all got me out of trouble at some point, for which I'm grateful.

The Australian minders were nothing like the ones we'd left at home. They were a lot bigger for a start. And a lot more serious. They taught us a few moves, just in case we needed to defend ourselves. It wasn't actually necessary, because there was no chance of anyone getting within about ten feet of us, as we found out when a fight broke out one night at a club in Sydney. Our agent, Iain Hill, got into a row with a local. A big, angry local. The next thing, they started hitting each other. A very drunk John Keeble stepped in to calm things down. Straight away, he wished he hadn't. He was in no condition to do anything. Just as he was wondering how to get himself out of trouble, the bloke who'd punched Iain disappeared. Joe, our minder, had appeared from nowhere and shoved him out of the way with such force he practically took off. *Whoooosh.* He landed about ten feet away. It happened so fast that John didn't even see the blow. Joe went up to the bloke and had a quiet word, something along the lines of, 'Don't fuck with these people.' That was enough. He, and all his mates, left at once.

It was rare that our minders had to prove themselves but, once or twice, they got us out of serious trouble. In Japan, at the start of the Parade tour we were in a club called Tokyo's. It was very hip, lots of pop stars and models posing, looking cool. We were all drinking heavily, as usual. John Keeble went to the toilet and, finding a queue, decided he couldn't wait. He peed in the sink instead. In Japan, there are rigid codes of behaviour. Peeing in the sink is practically a capital offence. It is a sign of massive disrespect. Worse, the man washing his hands in the next sink along happened to be the owner of the club. To put it mildly, all hell broke loose. It was only the prompt intervention of our security boss, Alfie Weaver, and one of the minders, Russell, that got JK out of there in one piece. He was banned for life, which was mild under the circumstances.

I also got into trouble one night in Tokyo's. Actually, the trouble started before I even got there. I had the address written down in Japanese on a piece of paper, but I couldn't for the life of me find a cab driver who would take me. A cab would pull up, I'd try to explain where I wanted to go and, before I got to the end of the sentence, the driver would accelerate off again. In the end I made it but by then I was in a foul mood. Russell, my minder, was doing his best to calm me down. He wasn't having much luck.

Inside, we bumped into Mike Allen from our record company, trying to get served at the bar, which was crowded. Suddenly, another bloke came along and pushed him out of the way. I might add that this guy was a six-foot-plus, American square-jawed model. Mike Allen was a lot smaller. I saw red. I went over and said, 'Who are you fucking pushing?' The next thing, we were squaring up to each other. I was saying, 'If you want a fight let's have it now, outside.' I even offered him the first punch. It didn't get that far. Russell came steaming in and pulled us apart.

After Australia, the plan was to play some dates in Western Springs, in New Zealand, but a few weeks before we were due to arrive the shows were pulled. Apparently, there had been some trouble in the area – rioting is probably too strong for it – and the promoter had become nervous.

We all had round-the-world air tickets, and were due to meet up again in Los Angeles, for the next date of the world tour. In the meantime, we had a few days to ourselves.

I had heard that Queen were in New Zealand, so I decided to go and visit them before heading off to LA. Queen are one of my favourite bands. I always thought Freddie Mercury was amazing, one of the best singers ever, and a lovely bloke. We knew each other quite well by then. The first time I met Queen was backstage after one of their shows at the NEC in Birmingham. By then Spandau had had a few hits, but I was still in awe of Freddie and the others. They had been among my idols when I was growing up. Freddie invited Léonie and me to the after-show party at the Metropole Hotel. When we arrived, there was a strip show under way. Freddie beckoned us over and tapped the seat next to him.

'Come and sit beside me, dear,' he said. He was talking to me. I sat down and the two of us chatted for ages about music. Léonie left us to it.

Later, she told me she'd felt well and truly blown out.

She said, 'I was thinking, Bloody hell, I've lost him – to Freddie Mercury!'

Because Spandau had just cancelled gigs in New Zealand, Steve Dagger wasn't too happy about me showing up there. Before I left Sydney he warned me to keep a low profile. I wasn't sure I could. To this day, I find it hard to maintain a low profile. Even in the most remote corners of the world, I seem to run into someone who knows me. Back in 1985, when Spandau was at its height, the chances of me staying out of sight were slim.

Dagger sent Mark, one of the minders, with me to keep me out of trouble. It was a nice thought, but unlikely to make any difference.

Queen were due to play an open-air gig in front of 40,000 people. On the day of the show I met up with the band and went with them to the sound check. Backstage, the Queen dressing room was an eye-opener. All kinds of food and drink, even bowls of Smarties (minus the orange ones).

Afterwards, I went back to the hotel with Freddie and we ended up in the bar. I never usually drink vodka, but Freddie's tipple was Stolichnaya and, between us, we polished off a bottle. We went to his room and worked our way through a bottle of port. By this time, we were both wrecked. Freddie was due on stage in a few hours. Suddenly, he had an idea. With all that vodka and port inside him, it seemed like a very good idea. He decided I should make a guest appearance on stage with him and the rest of the guys from Queen at the gig. Thanks to my own vodka and port cocktail, I was all for it. Freddie said, 'We'll do a duet. Do you know the words to "Jailhouse Rock"?' I said, 'No.' He said, 'Neither do I. We'll make them up.'

Freddie rang round Brian May, Roger Taylor and John Deacon to see how they felt about me appearing with them that night. Miraculously, bearing in mind they were sober, they agreed. I couldn't believe my luck. I was in New Zealand and I was going on stage with Queen. Fantastic. Me and Freddie did a bit of work on 'Jailhouse Rock', but it was obvious neither of us had a grasp of the lyrics. In the end, we gave up. I grabbed some sleep, then we left for the stadium.

Meanwhile, Steve Dagger had left numerous messages for me at the hotel. It was the following day before I picked them up. They all said more or less the same thing: keep a low profile.

That night, oblivious, I watched Queen from the side of the stage. There had been little time since our vodka and port session to sober up. Freddie was very drunk. At one point he rushed up, grinning, and said, 'Hadley, you bastard – I'm still pissed!' Even so, he looked – and sounded – good to me. Then again, I was also pissed.

When the moment came for me to join him on stage, Freddie gave me a huge build-up. 'Please welcome on stage . . . TONY HADLEY!' On I went, as Queen struck up the opening of 'Jailhouse Rock'. I still didn't know the words, but I'd scribbled a few lines on my hand, not that it made much difference. The whole version was utterly garbled. At one point I was on my knees, playing air guitar with Brian May.

It was one of the best moments of my life.

That night, back at the hotel, I went to Freddie's suite to

see if he fancied the after-show party, but he was already in bed, propped up on satin pillows. 'No, darling,' he said. 'I've had more than enough for one night.'

The next day, I picked up a string of messages from Dagger. He wanted me to call him. Urgently.

Still on a high from the previous night, I called him. 'What's the problem?'

He said, 'You have *got* to keep a low profile in New Zealand, we've had to cancel gigs there. I'm serious. I know what you're like—'

I said, 'Ah. There's a bit of a problem.' Silence. 'I've just been on stage doing "Jailhouse Rock" with Queen in front of 40,000 people . . .'

When he spoke again, his voice had gone up a couple of registers. 'Fuck off,' he said. The line went dead.

I don't know why Dagger was in such a state. There were never any repercussions from my unscheduled appearance with Queen in NZ.

I met up with Martin and Gary in Hawaii and we flew on to California to continue the tour. Steve Norman was doing his own thing. So was John Keeble. He had treated his mum and dad to a holiday on the west coast and had gone on ahead to meet them.

We had four dates in the US, followed by a few days off, during which the plan was to return to Europe ready for another twenty-one dates in Italy and Spain. But, during the third show in America, disaster struck.

We were all on a high by the time we reached the States. The first show, at the Irvine Meadows Amphitheater, Orange County, to an audience of around 5,000 people, was fantastic. We had reached the point where we were playing so well together. We were very sure of what we were doing and it showed. When we came off stage I was on an absolute high. I can remember knocking back neat Jack Daniel's with Steve and Martin. In the space of forty-five minutes, the three of us had finished the bottle. We stayed up drinking until 5 a.m. The next night we played the first of two shows at the Universal Amphitheater, Los Angeles. There was a posse of executives from the record company there, and it was another great show.

During the Parade tour Steve and I had developed a routine where he would climb on to my shoulders during 'Always In The Back Of My Mind'. It probably wasn't wise. Once or twice I wobbled and almost dropped him, but we always got away with it. Steve had also taken to sliding across the stage on his knees with the sax. It looked like an awkward manoeuvre and we all warned him to be careful. The second night we played at the Universal Amphitheater he went skidding from one side of the stage to the other on his knees as usual. Afterwards he was limping when he came to the bar. He seemed OK. We just thought he'd taken a knock. No one had any idea just how badly hurt he was. The next morning we were due to move on to San Francisco, so we all left our luggage outside our rooms for collection. When we got up, the bags were still there. That's when we found out we weren't going anywhere. Steve had damaged his knee. The gig was off.

We hung round in LA that day, waiting for news. It was a bit depressing. I think we sensed it wasn't just one gig at stake but that the rest of the tour could be in jeopardy. Everyone went out and spent ridiculous amounts of money to take their minds off the thought of going home. John Keeble splashed out $1,300 on a Gaultier jacket, which was a heavy-duty purchase in 1985.

The tour was off. After a day of loafing about, we flew back to London. Steve followed a week later, hobbling back into

Heathrow on crutches. What we never discussed, as a band, was whether there was any way of salvaging the remaining dates. There was no debate about whether Steve could have played sitting down. In retrospect, that's exactly what should have happened. Instead, the tour was over, and that was that. It was one of the stupidest things we did.

Chapter Twelve

The timing was awkward because we were just a few months into our tax year, which meant we could only spend a limited amount of time in the UK. We had always intended to base ourselves in Dublin for the rest of that year in exile, but suddenly we had to bring all our plans forward. Meanwhile, we had to stay away from the UK.

I decided to take Léonie – now pregnant with our second child – and Thomas to Jersey, while things were sorted out. I took my mum and dad along too, and we stayed in a hotel right on the cliff overlooking the sea. It was beautiful. Tom was just a toddler. There's video footage of him teetering about, unsteady on his feet, having a whale of a time. Steve Norman and Gail, Léonie's sister, came out and joined us. It was a good couple of weeks.

We had all agreed that Dublin was the best option as a base for the remainder of the tax year. It seemed an obvious choice, mainly because no one wanted to be a million miles away from London. The idea was to be able to get back in a hurry if we needed to, although on the one occasion I put that to the test it was more difficult than I imagined. I hated the idea of being apart from Léonie for months on end. The plan was that she and Thomas would come to Dublin too and, for a while, that worked. But there were complications during her second pregnancy, which stemmed from having spent too long in labour during her first.

I had a morbid fear something would go wrong while she was with me in Dublin. Early on in the pregnancy, she had collapsed while she was out shopping and been rushed to hospital. I wanted her with me, but I also wanted her to be within reach of the medical staff we knew and trusted. That meant returning to London.

It didn't seem like much of a hardship to spend a few months in Dublin. I was used to being on the road, used to separations. How hard could it be? In fact, it was far more difficult than I imagined. Living in a strange city is not the same as being on tour. Touring has a structure, a routine. Although we were rehearsing the *Through The Barricades* album, we were not in tour mode. There was no real structure to our daily lives.

That period taught me that I'm not very good at being by myself. It's the only time I have ever lived alone, and I wouldn't want to repeat the experience. I need people around me. Although the others were around, we didn't spend every waking moment together. Martin had the flat above me, but his girlfriend Shirlie Holliman, who was a backing singer in Wham!, was there a lot of the time. Steve had Gail. John and Gary shared a place. I spent a lot of time alone in my flat, watching videos, drinking. Sometimes, I'd be slumped in front of the television until transmission ended and the screen became white noise. It was a lonely time. I was living in Donnybrook, a couple of miles from the centre of Dublin, in a modern flat – luxurious, by most people's standards – but I hated it. It was utterly soulless. Other than my clothes, I had no personal belongings around me, which was probably a mistake. The flat was functional, but it never felt like home. At least I did have my privacy, unlike Steve Norman. His flat overlooked the street where fans would hang about, hoping for a glimpse of him. It drove him mad. He used to crawl across the floor to change channels on the TV, to keep out of sight. We probably all went a bit mad during those few months.

One thing that kept me going was the prospect of another baby. I was determined to be there for the birth of our second child. Two days before Léonie was due to be induced I went home. We were still living in the flat at John Spencer Square in Islington, and I remember my mother-in-law, Helen, opening the door. The first thing she said to me was, 'Has no one been able to get hold of you?'

I said, 'No, why? What's the matter?'

'Everything's fine,' she said. 'Léonie's fine. The baby's fine.'

I was too late. Léonie had gone into labour and given birth while I was on my way. I had missed the birth of my daughter by just a few hours.

In my frustration, I turned the air blue. I think my mother-in-law was a bit shocked. She'd never heard me use such foul language. I was just upset.

I raced off to the Middlesex Hospital in a bit of a state. Léonie was exhausted, but we had a beautiful baby girl. My frustration at missing the birth evaporated. There was this helpless little thing with a shock of black hair. Our daughter. I felt incredibly protective. I think there is a special bond between fathers and daughters. It was there between my dad and my sister Lee, and it's there for me with Toni. As I held her in my arms I had no doubt how precious my family was to me. The last thing I wanted to do was go back to Dublin, despite the tax implications. Being apart from my wife and children was killing me. It didn't seem worth it. I told Léonie I would stay in

London, but she persuaded me to think again. With two young children, we couldn't stay in our flat much longer. It wasn't practical. My year in exile would give us the means to buy a house.

It made sense, but I was reluctant to leave. I couldn't see beyond the separation, which had already been difficult enough. Now, with a new baby, it was going to be even harder. Léonie showed enormous strength. Unlike me, she was considering our long-term future. I was just miserable and missing home. We talked things over. Two days later I returned to Dublin.

It was almost four weeks before I saw my family again. In all, I was out of the country for eighteen months during that period. I would never do another tax year, no matter what.

The biggest irony is, the tax year didn't make us rich anyway. We had these fantastical notions of a mansion in the country and an Aston Martin. We never came anywhere near that.

We used the time in Dublin to work on the *Barricades* album. Gary was writing and we were rehearsing in an old, disused theatre in Dun Laoghaire, a few miles along the coast. It wasn't the most comfortable place to work. It was so cold Martin used to rehearse with his coat on and a couple of Calor gas heaters turned up full around him.

We needed to find a producer for that album and it probably wasn't an option to work with Steve Jolley and Tony Swain again. They'd done a brilliant job on *True* and *Parade*, but I suspect using the same producers would not have worked as well a third time. For some reason, Gary Langan's name came up. He was Trevor Horn's engineer, and had been involved with 'Instinction' a few years before. I'm not sure why he was deemed the right person to produce the next album, but Steve Dagger was certainly keen to have him on board. We clinched the deal over dinner at a Chinese restaurant in Dublin. Gary Langan turned up with his girlfriend, who was also his manager. She was a lovely girl but always seemed to look a little orange, which we found out later was to do with spending too much time on sun beds. Hence the nickname we came up with for her, the orange dragon.

I remember insisting on ordering for everyone that night. There were eight of us at the table and I went way over the top with food. We got to the point where there wasn't room for any more dishes on the table. It was heaving with food, and still waiters kept appearing with more, mostly crab claws. It was mad. The bill came to just over £600, which wasn't bad going for 1985 in Dublin.

We all tended to rattle around in Dublin, not sure what to do with our time. Because Gary and John were sharing a place, they hung out together a lot, mainly watching cricket, smoking dope and playing with the Subbuteo set and Scalextric they'd bought the day after they got there.

When we weren't rehearsing I was a bit lost. I've always been used to having lots of people around. When I was growing up, all my mates would congregate at my mum and dad's place. There was always someone to keep you company. In Dublin, I had too much time on my hands. I got into the habit of buying a litre bottle of Liebfraumilch and drinking it at home on my own. We'd always been a big drinking band, but it was a new thing to drink on my own. I think I got depressed because I started drinking myself into oblivion. It was all too easy to use booze to block out the fact I didn't want to be there. Alcohol became a comfort blanket during those months. Worryingly, I was barely conscious of how much I was drinking. It just crept up on me.

When we did go out, we'd go mad. We got to know the owner of an Indian restaurant, where the food was terrific, and whenever we went in, he would plonk a bottle of brandy on the table. We'd drink the lot. We became regulars at a club called the Pink Elephant. It was normal for us to stay out until five or six in the morning, drinking.

While we were in Dublin, we were invited to see Bruce Springsteen play at Slane Castle. We flew in by helicopter and, before we even got there, we were horribly drunk. We had been knocking back champagne and beer since breakfast. I could hardly stand. I had spilled beer on my white suit. It wasn't a good look. I remember John and Martin going off to do an interview with MTV. They were so pissed they couldn't remember the name of our first album. It was 10.45 a.m.

Unbelievably, Lord Mountcharles of Slane Castle invited Steve Norman and I back for dinner a few weeks later. It was incredibly grand. We ate in a huge, gothic hall, me and Léonie, Steve and Gail, and a few others. The drink was flowing. I think his Lordship took a shine to Gail and Steve was not happy about it. As the evening wore on, he was getting more and more wound up. I overheard him tell his Lordship to fuck off at one point, which was a sign of things to come. A bit later, I went to the toilet. When I came back, there were two empty seats at the table and an embarrassed silence, punctuated by the odd grunting sound. On the floor, Steve was grappling with his Lordship. It was the most bizarre thing. We left shortly afterwards.

That night, I drove us back to Dublin, although I was in no fit state to be behind the wheel. I was seeing double. The only way I could focus was by closing one eye. I drove all the way like that. I'm pleased to say my days of drinking and driving are well and truly behind me.

We weren't the only band in Dublin at that point. Frankie Goes To Hollywood were also there, recording, and so were Def Leppard. Musically, we were hardly in the same sphere, but it didn't matter. We got along. The first time the Spandau boys saw *This Is Spinal Tap* was with Joe Elliot, Def Leppard's singer, and the rest of the band, during that Dublin trip. We thought it was hysterical but I wasn't sure how much to laugh; Joe and the boys seemed less amused.

The papers had made out that there was some kind of ill-feeling between the Frankies and us, but that was rubbish. It probably stemmed from the fact we were such different bands in terms of style and music. The Frankies wore leather shorts and singlets. Their first single, 'Relax', was banned by the BBC in 1983, because the lyrics were deemed too dirty. On the face of it, we had nothing in common, although my image during 'The Freeze' era – tight vest and cravat – wouldn't have been out of place in the Frankies. In any case, we all got on. They were an interesting band. Holly Johnson and Paul Rutherford always struck me as refined, while the others were just heavy-duty party animals. Nash, the guitarist, and Ped, the drummer, were huge drinkers. They would order nine pints at once – four each, plus a floater just in case they ran out. During the week they were in the studio and at the weekend they'd be in Dublin having a good time. That was the theory, anyway, but their weekends eventually began on a Thursday and ended on a Tuesday. They always made sure they had one full day in the studio.

We came back to London from Dublin for Live Aid on 13 July 1985. The scale of it was colossal, with bands on stage in London and Philadelphia simultaneously. We were part of a line-up that included the Who, Elton John, Paul McCartney, U2, Bryan Ferry, David Bowie and Queen, playing to an audience of 80,000 in Wembley Stadium. Among the artists at the JFK Stadium in the States were Eric Clapton, Bob Dylan, Tina Turner, Madonna, Duran Duran, and a re-formed Led Zeppelin – Jimmy Page, Robert Plant, John Paul Jones – with Phil Collins on drums in place of the late John Bonham. Phil managed to play at both venues.

Bringing together so many major artists was extraordinary in itself. The whole thing was ground-breaking. John Keeble describes Live Aid as our generation's Woodstock, and I think he's right. On the day, it felt like we were part of something phenomenal, something meaningful that people would look back on.

With a billion people watching on television, the eyes of the world really were on you.

Status Quo was the first band on in London. I watched from the side of the stage with the Radio 1 DJ Janice Long as they kicked things off with 'Rockin' All Over The World'. It sent a shiver down my spine. The atmosphere in the stadium was charged.

We were on about an hour later. I'd decided to wear leather, which wasn't wise as it was an extremely hot day. I had leather trousers on and a heavy, reversible leather jacket, purple on one side, black on the other. I was just about dying in the heat. The sweat was pouring off me. No one could understand why I was wearing such an unsuitable outfit. Nearly twenty years on, people still ask why I wore leather in a heat wave. It's a good question.

I was so nervous that day. My heart was beating much too fast. All I could think of was the scale of it all. Spandau had never played Wembley Stadium, so that alone was momentous.

I can remember thinking I wanted everything to be perfect, that we would never play to a bigger audience than this. Before we went on I was thinking, I want to take all of it in. In fact, I remember very little about being on stage that day, apart from the microphone flying out of my hand at one point. I still don't know how that happened. We played for around twenty minutes and I think we did five songs, but I can't remember what they were. I know we did 'True' and 'We Are Virgin', which we had been rehearsing in Ireland for the *Barricades* album. It was the only new song in any fit state to be performed by then. As far as the other tracks go, my mind is a blank.

The whole experience was strange. Although it was a long day, once we were on stage, everything happened so fast there was no time to take it in. We went on, played, then we were off. Twenty minutes, over in a flash.

Afterwards, I watched the rest of the show with Léonie from the Royal Box.

Although we all understood that Live Aid was enormous, it was difficult to step back and put it into perspective. For those of us taking part, the atmosphere within Wembley Stadium was overwhelming. I had no sense of how it felt outside although it seems that, in many respects, normal life was suspended that day. Once we came off stage, John Keeble decided to go home for a few hours and that gave him a different perspective. The roads were empty. There was virtually no one about. Almost everyone was off the streets, at home, in pubs, wherever, watching Live Aid.

At the end of the show, when we all came off after 'Do They Know It's Christmas?' no one really knew what to do next. Although it was an incredible day, everyone appeared to be emotionally drained. There was a party that night at Legend's in London's West End – now the Embassy Club – but no one was in the mood. People were drifting about, looking exhausted. Spandau had a huge reputation for boozing, but we weren't up for it that night. I think I lasted about an hour, if that. I was knackered.

A couple of days later we headed back to Dublin to carry on rehearsing the *Barricades* album.

It was during this period that we fell out with our record company, Chrysalis, although to this day I'm not sure exactly what the dispute was about. That's partly because no one sat down and explained in any detail to us, the band, what was happening. And partly because we never asked. The day-to-day running of our legal affairs was of little concern to us.

I was content to leave the finer points of the fall-out to our management and legal representatives. I trusted the team working on our behalf. At that stage, we were all in the dark to some extent. And content to be in the dark. Our job was to get on with the next record. We had no desire to be embroiled in a court case. That was for management. So, there was a massive dispute rumbling on in the background, which I think was triggered by the fact we had failed to break America – a critical market for us and every other band. There was a sense that being on the Chrysalis label hadn't worked for us in the US, and we wanted out.

I know that the relationship between Steve Dagger, our manager, and Chris Wright, the Chrysalis chairman, had disintegrated. As far as I could see, Steve was just trying to get the best deal for the band. Things were so bad that when a case of champagne arrived, courtesy of the record company, it went straight back. The note, from us to them, read, 'Piss off'. Our working relationship had pretty much run its course.

While the Chrysalis deal unravelled in the background, we returned to Musicland in Munich to record our fifth album. We decided to mix it in Miraval, in the south of France, and not because the technical facilities were excellent. Miraval had a vineyard, and wine from the estate was part of the package. We could hardly believe it. I remember we checked at least five times that there was a drink-as-much-as-you-want clause in the deal. That's what swung it. Léonie came down with Thomas and Toni. It felt like there was plenty to celebrate. The tax year was over. We could go home. I could hardly wait. I wanted things to be back to normal. We were on the brink of a new record deal. Financially, I felt secure.

I decided to splash out and buy my dad a new car. It was the least I could do, having smashed up both his Hillman Hunters, first the green one, then the orange one. I got away with the green one, since it was about to fall apart anyway, but the orange one was a different story. It was his pride and joy. I drove it into a crash barrier when someone pulled out in front of me. The passenger side was a bit of a mess. When I told Dad, he hit the roof. Still, at least it wasn't a write-off. Anyway, I bought him a brand-new Rover, with leather seats and a walnut dash, and had it delivered. It was gold, of course. He looked a bit uneasy when I said I had something to show him – outside. He probably thought I'd smashed up another Hillman Hunter. When I gave him the keys to the Rover, he was lost for words, which was unusual for my dad. It was my way of thanking both him and my mum for being there for me. And for letting me off with wrecking two of their cars.

Once Through The Barricades was finished, the DJ Simon Bates joined us at Miraval to record interviews for Radio 1. I think there was a lot of curiosity about the album, mainly because we had been away for such a long time. More than a year had gone by since the previous single, 'Round and Round'. There was a lot riding on what came next. It not only had to be good, it had to be a hit. We had high expectations. Musically, *Barricades* was a departure for us – particularly the title track – very different to the other albums. We hoped it would prove to be the album that would finally crack the American market.

By this time, Léonie and I had moved into a beautiful five-bedroom Georgian house in Highgate, North London. The Pink House was our dream home. It cost a fortune – £280,000 – and we reckoned we needed to spend several thousand pounds more on improvements to get it the way we wanted it. I had taken out a mortgage of £140,000, which was huge in 1986 with interest rates hovering around 13 per cent but, at that stage, things were going so well with the band I was confident I could afford it.

In May 1986 we went to Paris to sign a new record deal with CBS. I can remember feeling buoyed at the prospect of the CBS deal, believing – wrongly as it turned out – that signing with an American record company would finally bring us the success we wanted in the US.

The signing process was long, drawn-out and tedious. Our lawyers huddled in one room, the CBS lawyers were in another, with the band in between. CBS presented a draft of the deal to Brian Carr, our legal representative. He went through it with us, and requested changes to various clauses. The document went back and forth for hours. Every amendment meant retyping the entire page. It was tortuous, especially for the girl sitting at a typewriter doing the changes. The whole process took forever but the pay-off was an amazing deal. I thought the CBS relationship would signal major changes for us. It didn't. We just didn't sell enough records. The first single released from

Barricades was 'Fight For Ourselves', released to coincide with a dispute between our new record company and a chain of record shops. By now, eighteen months had gone between singles, which is a long time in pop. We managed Top 20, which hardly squared with our hopes of global success.

We were counting on the next single, the title track from the album, to give us a huge hit.

To this day I believe the track, 'Through The Barricades', is the best thing we've ever done. I think it's the best song Gary wrote. The first time I heard it I knew it was special; we all did. When we recorded it there was a lot of pressure to get it right. I remember working on the vocals in the studio at Musicland, as Gary and the others watched from the control room. It was incredibly off-putting, everyone going on about the sentiment of the song, and how important it was. I understood all about the sentiment of the song, and I knew its significance to us as a band. As soon as I started singing, Gary cut in and stopped me. I started again. A couple of lines in the same thing happened. If it wasn't Gary, it was someone else trying to stick an oar in. Stop start. Stop start. This carried on until I lost patience. Finally, I said, 'Look, I'll go away and learn the song in my own way and when I'm ready to sing it, I'll tell you. But I do *not* want everyone in the studio.'

In the end, it was just me, and producer Gary Langan. I think it's the best recording we ever did. Almost twenty years on, it remains an outstanding track for me – lyrically, melodically and structurally. Everyone's performance was the best it could be. For me, 'Through The Barricades' is Spandau Ballet at its best. In the years that followed nothing else came close.

And just for the record, I'm very pleased with the way the vocals turned out.

We were confident it would be a huge hit. When it peaked

at Number 6 in November '86, we were all disappointed. It deserved to be a bigger hit.

As for the US, I just don't think the audience understood 'Barricades'. They heard this haunting song, almost six minutes long, and they were confused. It was too much of a departure. Were we a pop band, a soul band or a folk group? The American market likes to know exactly what it's dealing with, but with tracks ranging from 'How Many Lies' to 'Through The Barricades', it was almost impossible to put a label on us. We were banking on CBS to make a crucial difference in the US, but nothing actually changed.

Sometimes, you just have to do the obvious, and we were never very good at that. We worked hard at being different, often for the sake of it. Looking back, we probably shouldn't have bothered. There's a lot to be said for finding a formula that works and sticking with it. As a band, we never understood that. You have a hit record, you make another one just like it. It was obvious. Instead, we would go out of our way to pursue something new, but not necessarily better. We were too clever – or stupid – for our own good at times.

Even so, we remained positive. Our profile was good and we had another huge tour coming up. Through The Barricades – Across The Borders was our most ambitious tour. In the UK, we sold out six dates (again) at Wembley Arena before taking the show to Europe.

The only thing I hated about touring was the excessive amount of rehearsing we did beforehand. We would spend weeks in a rehearsal studio running through the set. Mostly, we based ourselves at Nomis, in West London. There was a clear difference of opinion within the band about how much time we needed to spend rehearsing. By the mid-Eighties we had spent a lot of time playing and recording together and we knew what we were doing. A few days in rehearsal nailed it as far as John Keeble and I were concerned. It was one thing to learn the songs, another to become too polished. We wanted to keep an edge to the live performance. The others disagreed. They wanted lengthy rehearsal periods, on the grounds that practice makes perfect. I sometimes wonder what we did with all that time. There seemed to be an awful lot of hanging about. It was extremely wasteful. Costly, too. We had a permanent road crew of three, who set up the equipment, then hung around for weeks on end. Other than changing the odd guitar string, there was little for them to do. Thinking back, they must have been bored rigid too. Several weeks later, by which time we were well and truly sick of the sound of ourselves, we would finally call a halt.

It was during one of these lengthy rehearsal sessions at Nomis that we decided a bit of light relief was in order. Gary and Martin's birthdays – which fall just a few days apart – were the perfect excuse. We arranged a joint celebration in the shape of a fat-a-gram – a very large stripper, in other words. The woman who arrived was huge and, thankfully, a good sport. The plan was to surprise Gary and Martin. When an enormous woman wearing only a pair of panties and high heels walked in to Studio B and smothered them in bare flesh, they were surprised all right. Our entire road crew turned out to watch, as did all the Nomis staff, and everyone else who happened to be rehearsing that day. The studio was packed.

Someone took photographs of the birthday boys grinning happily with the fat-a-gram lady between them, a huge breast slung over each of their shoulders. It was quite a sight. I never found out what happened to those pictures.

On another occasion we were working in Studio A and Status Quo were in Studio B, also rehearsing for a tour. The

Quo boys are brilliant, rock 'n' roll through and through. Although we were huge drinkers, we had an unwritten rule that we didn't drink while we were working. Quo had a different outlook. Their studio was awash with booze. There were bottles of wine everywhere, and it had definitely taken its toll. Rick Parfitt and Francis Rossi turned up in our studio, seeming a bit worse for wear, joking that they couldn't remember half their songs. Gary happily obliged with a quick rendition of 'Caroline'. Rick Parfitt brightened. 'My God,' he said, 'he's found the elusive fourth chord.'

They sent the roadies for more supplies of wine.

Chapter Thirteen

The scale of the Barricades tour in 1986 was impressive. We had more people on the road than ever before. More trucks carrying bigger, more complicated sets. An extra crew bus. It was a case of, How did we get by with just thirty people on the last tour? Let's have sixty. By the time we got to Italy, I think we were nudging ninety people. We had the best of everything. It cost an absolute fortune.

We went out of our way to create a ground-breaking show. Patrick Woodroffe, known for his innovative lighting and set design, came up with a lighting rig that tilted during 'Through The Barricades', transforming the set. The effect was breathtaking. It was the centrepiece of the show. The only drawback was that this huge, costly piece of kit was too big for many of the venues on the itinerary. On some nights it sat in the truck, redundant, while we played.

John Keeble had an eight-foot-tall drum riser. Underneath was a bar, complete with optics and a dartboard. At the beginning of 'Through The Barricades', when he had nothing to do, he would disappear for a Jack Daniel's and Coke and a game of darts, returning when needed.

We hired one of the most expensive sound engineers in the business, Lars Brogaard, who had worked with Rod Stewart. It was spend, spend, spend. We were behaving as if we were a much bigger band than we actually were, although it was an amazing experience for us. In terms of performance, I think we were at our best on that tour.

The tour took us all over Italy, where we had seventeen dates scheduled. As usual, we had an eventful time. My mate, Gary Hersham, an estate agent, came out to Milan for a few days. He had no idea what he was letting himself in for. Within hours of stepping off the plane, we were chased by hordes of girls. That night we went to a club, and were led past screaming fans into the roped off VIP area. Above us, two members of the road crew hung from the balcony, waving at us, wasted. He couldn't believe it. We were invited to some glitzy film bash in Milan. That was the night I met Roger Moore. I arrived with a bottle of wine in each hand and made my way round the room saying hello to people I didn't know. I fell over at one point. When I looked up Roger Moore was looking down at me. I said, 'Hello, Rog, how's it going?' Thankfully, he saw the funny side.

Russell the minder put me to bed.

In Italy, I got alcohol poisoning (once) and had guns pulled on me (twice). I don't recommend either. Most of the time, we had Agostino with us, by then head of the country's anti-terrorist unit, which was just as well. He got us out of a few scrapes.

In Rome, we played two sell-out shows at the Campo Sportivo, 15,000 people a night. We celebrated on the second night with an alcohol-fuelled dinner. I'd started on gin and tonics, moved on to lager, white wine, red wine and liqueurs. By the end of the night, there was a bottle of sambuca and a bottle of grappa on the table. A couple of Italy's top film producers happened to be eating in the same restaurant. They came over to say hello. Steve Dagger introduced them. When they got to me, I greeted them with a cheery, 'Top on, top off,' and smashed a walnut on my forehead. I sat grinning, with bits of shell embedded in my skin, which was bleeding. They excused themselves. I don't suppose they wanted to hang around to find out what I did for an encore.

After dinner, still with the remnants of the walnut in my forehead, we headed off for Zelda's, a club known for having a girl on a high wire suspended over the dance floor. On the way, influenced by large amounts of grappa, I decided to do a stunt roll over the bonnet of a silver Porsche that was cruising towards us. It was meant to be a *Starsky and Hutch*-type manoeuvre but, from the point of view of the driver, it probably felt more like some big bloke throwing himself across the bonnet. He stopped the car and jumped out. I was in the gutter at the side of the road by this time, laughing; he wasn't amused. He pointed a gun at me and started screaming. I recognized a couple of Italian swear words. Luckily, Agostino stepped in, gun drawn. '*Polizia*,' he said. Then, showing off his grasp of English, he added, 'Fuck off.' That sorted it. Inside Zelda's, I started on Jack Daniel's. I was horribly drunk by now and I needed to get to the toilet, which was down a flight of stairs. I knew I'd never make it. I swayed about on the top step and signalled to the people below that I was going to dive. Then I threw myself off and landed safely, caught by the crowd. It must have been me that started crowd surfing, then.

I'm not sure who put me to bed that night. Russell, probably. I was in a bad way. Usually, after a heavy session, I pass out, but this time I couldn't sleep. I had alcohol poisoning. I was sick as a dog. My heart thumped. I shook from head to toe. It was the worst feeling. For a couple of days I couldn't eat. The only thing I could keep down was water.

I was drinking an outrageous amount of alcohol at this point, but so was everyone else. It was just part of being a pop star. I never worried about it because, mostly, I was having too good a time. Also, I never got a hangover. I'd turn up the morning after a heavy session, all bright and breezy, while everyone else was wearing their shades and feeling awful. It drove them mad. Whenever I needed to lay off the booze, I did. When it came to performing, I was disciplined. I never went crazy if we had a show the next day, because I knew I had to save my voice. It wasn't unusual for me to have an early night while the others were out caning it.

We were due to play in Sicily and had been warned to keep our wits about us. Everyone was aware of the Mafia connection. Before we got there, we had a few days in Sardinia. There had been a few mutterings about mob-related kidnappings, but we weren't too concerned. Predictably, when we least expected it, we found ourselves up to our eyes in trouble. We'd gone out to eat with Viv Cook, who was looking after us. Word got round that we were in the restaurant, and a crowd appeared outside, banging on the windows. We left through the kitchen at the back and ran out into a narrow alley. At the end, we bumped into a couple of guys in plain clothes with guns drawn. They were standing next to an unmarked car. They waved the guns. 'In the car. In the car!' We weren't really thinking straight at this point. We didn't even know who – or what – they were. Police? Kidnappers? We were going to get in the car anyway. But as we did they barred Viv's way. We all backed off. Either we all got in or nobody did. One of them pointed his gun at John. It was all getting out of hand. I don't speak Italian, but I was gesturing and trying to calm the situation. We were all terrified. I stepped in front of John. The gun that was pointing at him was now pressed against my forehead. Its owner held up his ID. 'Polizia.' Thank God for that. We all piled in the car, Viv included, and made it back to the hotel. There were a few repercussions. We weren't happy about the police methods, which were heavy-handed and had left us shit scared. The authorities were full of apologies. We tried not to get into any more trouble during our stay in Sardinia.

Even having Agostino around was no guarantee that the local police would fall into line. In Lecce, in the far south of the country, we were playing in a football stadium. The police, fearing a riot, wouldn't let the fans onto the pitch in front of the stage. We came on to find a line of cops in front of the stage, facing the crowd, their rifles pointing at the sky. It was madness. We appealed to Agostino but he shrugged, saying, 'Here, I can't do anything. I'd advise you to accept it.' He frowned at the armed cops spread out in the stadium. 'I have no jurisdiction,' he said. 'This is Africa.'

If they wouldn't let the fans come to us, I decided to go to them. Halfway through the fourth number, I jumped off the stage, crossed the police line and headed towards the audience. The fans reacted well, but the police weren't happy. Neither was the rest of the band. The further away from the stage I got, the more of a delay there was between their playing and my singing. By the time they were on the second chorus, I was still on the first verse, oblivious of course. This was in the days before in-ear monitors were invented.

It was only as I strolled back to the stage, crossing the police line again – who looked daggers at me – that I realized how big a drop there was from the stage to the pitch. I couldn't get back up. Nicky Sibley, a big bloke, thankfully, came to my rescue, heaving me back up. I was singing unaccompanied by then. The band, having finished a good twenty seconds earlier, was waiting for me to catch up. Captain Chaos strikes again.

It's not hard to see why *This Is Spinal Tap* is my favourite film.

I almost came unstuck at the last show in Italy, in Treviso. Before the show, Pete Hillier, by this time our stage manager, and Mikkel Brogaard, the carpenter, warned me that there was a gap at the end of the stage. In it, they had constructed a trough to hold the monitors. The whole thing was suspended on chains. It wasn't strong. Pete said, 'Whatever you do, don't jump into the trough. It won't take your weight.'

Of course, during the show, I got completely carried away and leapt into the trough. As Pete had predicted, it collapsed. I dropped six feet. A monitor landed on top of me. I surfaced from the pit in agony, clutching several broken ribs, still singing 'I'll Fly For You'. I've always been accident prone on stage. At Wembley, on the same tour, I fell down the stairs – also during 'I'll Fly For You' – messing up my big entrance and landing in a heap on the stage. No one was surprised. A lot of the time I wanted to be cool but I didn't quite pull it off. Clumsiness got the better of me.

I went on stage one night in a pair of new 'pixie' boots. It was a fair bet they'd pinch my feet so I asked our wardrobe man, Alan Keyes – the so-called travelling iron – to stand by at the side of the stage in case I needed to do a quick change. Five numbers in, my feet were killing me. I was crippled. I mouthed at him to bring my other boots. A couple of minutes later he waved them at me. I disappeared behind the PA stack and lay down, still singing. Alan dashed on stage, pulled off my boots, and slipped the new (old) ones on. The relief was fantastic. As I got to my feet I caught sight of various members of the crew, doubled up.

Barricades proved to be a good tour. We had a wealth of material to choose from and, by then, we had been together for ten years. The set was tight, we were a strong unit, and we were confident playing live. Musically, and in terms of production, those were among the best shows we did, although not every gig was a success. In Sweden, just 200 people turned up for one of the gigs. It hardly seemed worth bothering with our state-of-the-art lighting rig. Thinking back, I'm not sure we were able to get it into that particular venue anyway. When Gary heard how many tickets we'd sold he blew a fuse, laying in to everyone. It was the promoter's fault, it was security's fault; the whole fucking world was to blame. Actually, it was *our* fault; the audience reflected our (lack of) popularity in that town at that time.

That's sometimes how it is and you just have to take it on the chin.

The strange thing was, no one thought to ask if we could afford to be so excessive on the Barricades tour. I assumed the scale of it all was a sign of how well we were doing. In fact, I suspect record sales were below expectations. I still have no idea how many albums Spandau Ballet sold. That seemed to be classified information, which can't have been a good sign. I remember someone bandying about the figure of twenty million, but if that was true we'd all have made a lot more than we did. Subsequently I worked out that during the Spandau Ballet era, my average earnings were around £40,000 a year, which was good, but hardly in the league of the super rich. Considering the scale of the band, it doesn't seem very much. We were living beyond our means on the Barricades tour, although we didn't know it. It was costing around £80,000 a week just to be on the road, which was phenomenal. When it was over, there was little to show for it. While we were congratulating ourselves on a great tour, the figures weren't adding up. We hardly made anything.

Now, when I tour, I have a manager and tour manager

scrutinizing every penny we spend. They have to. The tour has to make money. It's that simple. With Spandau Ballet, that never seemed to be a concern. I never heard anyone say, Do we really need this? And it never occurred to me to ask. I look back now and curse myself for being so trusting and naïve.

I'm a real Jack Daniel's man. I love all the bourbons . . . Scotch . . . Irish whiskey . . . brandy . . . wine . . . beer . . . grappa . . . Limoncello. Pretty much anything that's around, really. *Ethanol.*

Spandau was always a big drinking band. That often came as a shock to people. Our silly shirts and hairspray made people think we were a bunch of softies. The truth was we could drink almost anyone under the table.

Gary Farrow, who worked with Elton John, could not believe how much we put away. He said, 'If I drank as much as them I'd be dead.'

Actually, it's a wonder one of us isn't.

Just after we signed with CBS in 1986 we were at a party in Montreux. I decided to go for a walk and get some air. I didn't want to stroll round the block, though. I wanted to climb on the balcony and go from one to the next, all the way round the building. It seemed like a good idea at the time. Before anyone knew what was going on, I was perched on the ledge of the balcony outside my room. Two floors up. John and Gary spotted me lurching about and dragged me back inside. It's just as well. I would have killed myself.

On that same trip we ran into the Beastie Boys. They'd heard we liked a drink. They did too and they thought it would be a laugh to challenge us to a drinking competition. Last man standing, kind of. I think our appearance made them think we'd be a pushover. It's always worth remembering that appearances can be deceptive. We met up in the CBS hospitality tent. Beastie Boys, Spandau Ballet, nice to meet you. What's your tipple? Jack Daniel's all round, thanks very much. We started knocking them back. The Beasties did their best to keep up. We were still warming up when one of them turned green and puked on the carpet. They all looked embarrassed and left.

We had a few good sessions on that trip. At the end of it, I was due to fly to Munich with John and Gary. The night before we were due to leave we went to bed after the sun came up. I was dead to the world. When I failed to show in reception a couple of hours later, John and Gary asked a hotel porter to wake me while they went for a coffee. A few minutes later, they checked back with the concierge. The porter admitted defeat. He shook his head. 'I have phoned Mr Hadley, I have knocked on Mr Hadley's door . . .' He paused. 'I have even knocked on Mr Hadley, but he won't wake up.'

They took a passkey and let themselves into my room. According to John, it looked like my suitcases had exploded, spraying clothes everywhere. In the middle of it, I lay splayed out on the bed, fast asleep. He and Gary picked their way through the wreckage, dragged me out of bed, hauled me into the bathroom, and left me under the shower. I don't remember any of this. I was still dead to the world.

Fifteen minutes later, they came looking for me again. I was back in bed, sopping wet, unconscious. John shouted in my ear, 'We're going *now*!' There were probably a few expletives in there as well. I shot up and started opening the drawers of the bedside cabinet. I'm not sure how I thought that was going to help, but at least I was moving. They left me to it.

By now, two cars had arrived to get us to the airport – a Rolls-Royce, which was for us, and some kind of hatchback for the bags. We were spoiled in those days.

John and Gary took the Rolls and left. They'd given up on me by then. Just as they were about to board the flight, I arrived at the gate, dishevelled and out of breath. I'm still not sure how I made it. I have no recollection of the journey. I felt rough though, I don't mind saying.

It's no secret that I like a drink, but I'd started going off the rails in Dublin. It got to the point where I just didn't know what I was doing. It wasn't such a lark any more. I was having blackouts. At the wedding of Bob Geldof and Paula Yates in 1986, I was wasted.

I was drinking straight Jack Daniel's all day and was horribly drunk. At one point I fell over Geldof's uncle and ended up sprawled across a table. I was so wrecked I didn't know what was going on. One of our minders managed to get me into a limo. Before Léonie could get in, I'd sneaked out the other side and was staggering back to the party. A couple of minders got hold of me and bundled me back to the car. This time I stayed put and went home.

The next morning I had to get Léonie to fill in the gaps. I couldn't remember any of it. I got really upset. I was in a bad way and I was the last person to see it. Everyone around me had worked it out a long while before, including Alfie Weaver, who ran the security firm that looked after us. He had pulled Léonie aside and said he was seriously worried about me. I wasn't just having a few drinks, enjoying myself; I was permanently off my face, as far as he could tell. I had been going too wild for too long.

I don't know how I managed it, but somehow I finally decided to pull myself together and rein it in. I laid off the hard stuff and calmed right down.

I've actually given up drinking on a couple of occasions. A

few years ago, when I was doing the BBC series *Down To Earth*, I laid off alcohol for five weeks. It drove everyone nuts. I became razor sharp, picking at everything, pulling people up about every tiny detail. Dave Williams, my tour manager, couldn't stand it. In the end, he practically begged me to have a drink.

It was while we were busy recording our sixth album, *Heart Like A Sky*, in 1988, that I had some kind of breakdown, although it had nothing to do with alcohol. Somewhere between the last album and this one, things had changed. It had been two years since we'd recorded together and the unity of the band was crumbling. Perhaps we'd allowed too much time to elapse between albums. Even though Barricades had been a fantastic time, there was a noticeable distance between us by the time we got together for recording again. Our approach to *Heart Like A Sky* was also entirely different to the previous five albums. We were working with the kind of technology in the studio we didn't fully understand, which I really didn't enjoy. I don't deny I was feeling the pressure while we were recording the album.

For weeks I had been unable to sleep, mainly because I was too scared to let myself drift off. I lay in the dark convinced that if I went to sleep I wouldn't wake up in the morning. The tension around my chest told me I was about to have a heart attack. I was suffering from acute hypertension. It was terrifying. Each day I felt worse than the one before.

One morning, on my way to Air Studios, in London, I started to feel increasingly anxious and panic-stricken. It was a beautiful sunny day, but my mood was grim. As I drew close to Oxford Circus, I felt a growing tightness in my chest. It was a familiar sensation. My hands were cold and clammy. I wiped them on my jeans. Seconds later, they were damp again. I pressed on. Sweat ran down the back of my neck. I felt awful. When I finally walked into the studio, Steve Norman took one look at me and said, 'You look terrible.' The colour had drained from my face. I shook my head. 'I feel terrible.' The others were staring at me. I must have looked like death. Steve said, 'Why don't you go home?' It was clear I was in no fit state to work. There was no point in sticking around. I said, 'Yeah, I think I will.'

Once I got home, I went upstairs, sat on the bed, and cried. The album was weak. I had no faith in the songs, my confidence had gone, and I had no idea where we were going as a band. I felt like I was on the verge of a breakdown. It was like *Diamond* all over again.

Except that this time, to make matters worse, I had other worries. I was struggling to meet the mortgage repayments on the Pink House. Two years after moving in, I was wondering if we could actually afford to stay there.

For the next few days I stayed at home. The thought of going back to the studio made me feel ill. I couldn't face the others. I was a mess, unable to break the pattern of sleepless nights. Something had to give and, as far as I could see, it had to be the band. I didn't want to be part of it any more, although I was loath to throw in the towel in the middle of an album. Still, there was no way I could carry on as I was. I needed help. Gary Kemp suggested acupuncture. I had no idea what to expect, but I made an appointment. For the next few months I had regular sessions. It was bizarre, but it worked. I began to feel calmer. The hypertension eased. I started to fall asleep at night, without worrying about whether I'd wake up in the morning.

There was no mystery about why I was feeling so bad.

Heart Like A Sky took its toll on all of us. It was the beginning of the end, as far as I was concerned.

Although the band was still together, things were approaching meltdown. The *Barricades* era, when we were touring and spending time together, was over; two years on, it was clear that the five of us just didn't get along as well as we used to. It no longer felt like we were a unit, each with a contribution to make.

With the new album came a new way of working. In the past we had set up the gear and played. It was simple and it worked. Everyone was involved. There was room to play around, take time to fine-tune and improve the tracks. Our success stemmed from five individuals working well together. Spandau Ballet was an ensemble. The previous albums had demonstrated what we could do as a collective. If it worked – and usually it did – great. If not, that was also OK.

Gary wrote the words and melody for the songs as far as I was aware. As a band, we would start rehearsing, fleshing things out. It's exactly what we did on *Barricades*, spending weeks in a freezing theatre at Dun Laoghaire, with Martin hunched round heaters in his coat. The process was familiar to all of us because it was what we had always done, going back to the days when we were unsigned.

In the end, I felt the songs were the fruit of all of our efforts.

Suddenly, we had the advent of new technology. It seemed that recording was no longer so much about playing as programming. I don't think any of us had a problem with technological innovation. It's just that, at the time, it was new and no one really knew what they were doing. Programming, in itself, wasn't going to produce a better album. I don't actually believe it was about using new techniques anyway. I think Gary thought he could do it more or less by himself. Not that he ever said as much.

As a result there was a sense of detachment about *Heart Like A Sky*. It was Gary Kemp in tandem with the producer, Gary Langan, saying, This is how it's going to be. The rest of us weren't all that involved and it showed. It was like working in a vacuum and it sucked the life out of the band, sucked the life out of the songs. The whole process became difficult and unsatisfactory. Ultimately, the record had no soul.

Even before we got into the studio there were disagreements. The first was about where to record. It made sense to me to go away together, which is how we had worked on *True*, *Parade* and *Through The Barricades*. Too much time had elapsed between albums. We had started to drift apart. The camaraderie had gone. With the band at odds, it was unlikely we would produce good work. We had managed to pull things round before. In the wake of *Diamond* we had gone to Compass Point and come up with 'True'. We could do it again. Martin and Gary wanted to stay in London. Steve wasn't sure.

I was dead against staying at home. There were too many distractions. We all had places of our own now and were busy decorating and buying furniture. I had a family. I had visions of us drifting in and out of the studio, less committed than we should be. I argued that we had consistently produced our best work by getting away from London. Gary and Martin stood firm. The band was split. The decision lay with Steve Norman. He opted to stay at home.

It was a mistake.

I'm convinced that, had we gone away together to make that album, we'd still be on speaking terms now.

We argued about what to call the album. John Keeble suggested *Home*, since we were recording in London. It neatly summed up where we were in our lives. John felt everyone could relate to the idea of home. It was simple, but meaningful. I thought it was a brilliant idea. Martin objected. 'It makes me think of slippers and a pipe,' he said.

John shook his head. 'I don't know what your home's like, but mine's nothing like that,' he said.

Gary had a better idea: *Heart Like A Sky*. It was more . . . esoteric. We were, after all, Spandau Ballet. An album title the entire world would understand was too obvious. Thinking back, that was probably the problem. Why be obvious when you can be clever? Or stupid? to quote Spinal Tap. Predictably, we went down the esoteric road.

A few months later, I listened, fascinated, as Gary explained the thinking behind *Heart Like A Sky* to a music journalist from Germany, babbling on – very intellectually, I might add – about the heart being infinite in its love and grandness, just like the sky. I hope that clears up any confusion.

As with *Diamond*, we traipsed from one studio to another; in all, we recorded at Westside, Townhouse, Air, Olympic and Mayfair. We were all over the place. There was no cohesion. The album took for ever and, in the process, relationships deteriorated. Since the early days, John had always been close to Gary, but that was no longer the case. John was as thrown as I was by what was happening. His passion was playing. He was used to going into the studio and making a noise. He loved the blood, sweat and tears of it all. For him, music was, and is, a visceral experience. On *Heart Like A Sky*, playing was secondary. It was a case of, 'Let's just go through another eighty-two snare drum sounds and see if we can find a good one . . .' It drove him mad.

More than once, I lost it during vocal sessions. Gary would be on my case, telling me how to sing. It was wearing me down. I needed him to shut the fuck up and leave me to it. It was horrible. When it came to recording the vocals for 'Empty Spaces', probably the best song on the album, the pressure intensified. Gary hovered in the control room. The song was about his split with his girlfriend, Lee, and meant a lot to him. I understood the significance. There was no chance of getting through the recording uninterrupted. Before we started, Gary Langan left the control room and came into the studio. Gary Kemp was in tow. He'd had an idea. Perhaps we could carve up the vocals between us. I could do the first verse and he could take the second. I stared at him. Gary Langan was nodding. He thought it could work. I wondered what planet he was on.

I shook my head. 'I'm just about to record a vocal. I'm the lead singer of this fucking band. Now fuck *off*.' I was furious. I knew I had to deliver a great vocal. I did two takes, dropped in on a couple of lines, and walked out.

Perhaps Gary would have liked to be the lead singer of Spandau Ballet. He wasn't though.

There were more problems when I went in to lay down the vocals on 'Windy Town'. Gary Kemp had faxed the lyrics through to Olympic. I looked at them. They were shite. I turned to Gary Langan and said, 'I can't sing this. It's just not right.' It was the first time I'd ever had an issue with lyrics.

Gary Langan called Gary Kemp. He took the tactful approach. 'Tone's not very happy with some of the lines—' There was a small explosion on the other end of the line. A sound like machine-gun fire reached me. Rat-a-tat-a-tat-tat. Gary Langan held the receiver away from his ear. I took it from him. 'Gary. *Gary.* Will you shut the fuck *up* and *listen*.' Silence. 'These lyrics aren't up to scratch. You know you're better than this.' Pause. He said, 'Yeah, OK, I'll have a look at them.'

A while later, the fax machine spewed out the new lyrics for 'Windy Town'. Even with the rewrite, a couple of lines still made me wince.

It's not easy being the songwriter. Coming up with new tunes is a stressful business. We all understand the pressure to deliver. It would have made sense to share the load, but Gary never seemed to want that. As a band, we always supported him. Even if he presented the bare bones of a song, we had the imagination to see where it could go. We produced our best work through mutual support. No one told Gary how to write. No one pulled the songs apart. In the early days of the band, Steve Norman used to write. Before long, he took a back seat to Gary. Clearly, Steve could have taken some of the weight. It might have given us more material. During the Dublin period, both Steve and I did some writing. The idea was to ease the pressure on Gary. I brought two songs to rehearsals, but he – and the rest of the band – brushed my efforts aside as if I'd committed a mortal sin by stepping onto hallowed ground. I'm not saying that my first ever efforts were necessarily good enough, but a bit of bloody support for trying wouldn't have gone amiss.

At one point, when we were working on *Heart Like A Sky*, Steve Dagger turned up at Olympic Studios to talk about the album credits. On all five previous albums, the producers were credited alongside the band. Dagger explained that Gary Kemp wanted a separate production credit on *Heart Like A Sky*. There was an almighty row. It was out of order. I could not understand what was going on. It felt like, as a band, we were constantly being undermined. For years, we had worked *together*. There was a genuine sense of one for all and all for one and that's what made it work. Now, that had gone out of the window. The writing was on the wall. I objected to a separate production credit for Gary Kemp. John Keeble objected. Dagger wanted us to go along with it for an easy life. He rode roughshod over our views and made it clear he was right behind Gary. He told us to get on and finish the record. Squabbling over a credit would only delay things even more. In the end, we caved in on the credit, but all it did was cause resentment, and things dragged on anyway. I really wish we had told Steve Dagger where to stick the credit at that stage.

By now, it was hard to know who was in charge. Months went by and still the album wasn't finished. It was all taking far too long but no one actually did anything about it.

In the end, we spent £600,000 – an obscene amount of money – making a dire album.

For years, we had hung out together. Our families were close. We were all in long-term relationships and our girlfriends/ wives got along. In 1988, it all became unstuck. At the beginning of the year, Gary broke up with his long-term girlfriend, Lee Andrews. She had been with him since the early days. Lee was a down-to-earth girl from the Angel, Islington. She had always been a good influence. If Gary showed signs of taking his feet off the ground, Lee would bring him back to earth. Suddenly, she was gone. While everyone was still coming to terms with the split, wondering if they might patch things up, a new girl was on the scene. Sadie Frost was no stranger to Spandau Ballet. She had been around for a while. In 1983 she was in the 'Gold' video and, more recently, in 1986, 'Fight For Ourselves'. Within a few months, Gary married her. It happened so fast, it was alarming. In 1988, John Keeble, who'd been with his girlfriend Flea for eight years, was planning a summer wedding. Gary beat him to it.

Steve Norman had been going out with Gail, my sister-in-law, for years. They broke up too. Steve became a different person. He had always been the joker, the guy to lift you if you were low. Suddenly, he wanted to be the serious one in the band. Being serious had always been more Gary's thing. It was as if Steve wanted to prove his worth, which was never in any doubt, anyway. I think it was more to do with how he felt about himself than how we saw him. Perhaps it was also about wanting to compete with Gary.

In the early days, they were both writing and playing guitar but as time wore on Steve went in a different direction, playing sax and percussion, which was something no one else was doing. There's no doubt he was a gifted musician, and his influence in terms of Spandau is clear. If he had a problem, it was that he never wanted to concentrate on any one thing for long. If he had, I think he could have been brilliant. By the time we were making *Heart Like A Sky*, Steve had a bee in his bonnet about being taken seriously as a musician. He always was. It was another sign that, suddenly, everything was unstable.

We got together for a photo shoot before the first single off the album – 'Raw' – was released. Things between us were on a knife-edge by then. I was feeling low anyway. That whole period was about the unhappiest I remember. Gary made some derogatory comment, probably about whatever I was wearing, and I didn't have the energy to fight back. There was a long history of Gary having a go at me for what he saw as my lack of style. I don't mind admitting I'm not the most fashion-conscious person in the world. I'm colour blind, for a start, which doesn't help, but clothes never seemed such a big deal.

I always understood that image played a part but, for me, music came first. Always.

At the shoot that day, Steve Norman took Gary on and had a right old go. He could see I really wasn't very well. The photographer, our old mate from school, Neil Matthews, watched, horrified. It was clear the band was about to implode. You just have to look at the shots from that session to see the hostility written all over our faces.

We shot the video, which was inspired by the Mickey Rourke film, *Angel Heart*, and featured movie sound effects, at an old power station in South London. For the next two videos, 'Be Free With Your Love' and 'Crashed Into Love', we went to LA. The atmosphere around those was slightly more chilled, just because we were in LA and enjoying some sunshine, I suspect.

Late one night, Martin, John and I sat in the jacuzzi at the hotel drinking, bemoaning the state of the band. I was depressed about the album. With the exception of one or two tracks, I thought it was dire. All that messing about with technology had produced a bland and soulless collection of songs. Martin let slip that Gary was about to stop paying 50 per cent of the publishing royalties into Marbelow, the band's company, which was the existing arrangement. It was one more nail in the coffin. Having shut us out during the making of *Heart Like A Sky*, it came as no surprise that Gary planned to keep the publishing royalties on the album to himself. I told Martin I didn't care. *Heart Like A Sky was* different to the other albums. He could stick the royalties up his arse.

What I didn't appreciate at the time was that Gary was planning to keep *all* the publishing royalties on *every* song that we'd ever recorded.

In September '88, we released 'Raw'. Eighteen months had elapsed since the previous single, 'How Many Lies'. 'Raw' scraped into the Top 50. Almost a year later, the second single from the album went on sale. 'Be Free With Your Love' reached Number 42. The third – and last – single from *Heart Like A Sky*, 'Crashed Into Love', failed to chart.

Our records weren't shifting in anything like the quantities they once did. CBS were no doubt wringing their hands. We went to Europe to promote the album. Relationships were strained. In Germany, a journalist wanted to interview me and Gary together. Neither of us wanted to do it. I suggested he do it on his own. He said, 'You won't even do an interview with me now.'

I said, 'What's the point? I won't agree with anything you say, and you won't agree with anything I say.'

Steve Dagger persuaded the pair of us.

In the end, we did the interview together. Gary remained sullen and silent throughout. It was a complete waste of time.

There was still plenty of interest in the band, but we were no longer the solid five-piece we had once been. Gary and Martin were busy working on their film, *The Krays*. On a couple of occasions they weren't available and John, Steve and I performed with a couple of stand-ins. Kevin Miller covered for Martin on bass and, for Gary, Simon Baisley came in on guitar. Both became good friends of mine, and still are today. That summed up the extent to which things had changed. At one time, it would have been unthinkable for Spandau Ballet to play with two members missing from the line-up.

We decided to tour, to see if that would go some way towards repairing the bruised spirit of the band. In the past, going on the road had brought us closer together. I'm not sure anyone expected that to happen this time. From the outset, Gary and Martin made it clear they weren't up for a long tour. Two, three weeks at the most. The rest of us wanted to do more gigs. By then, I was feeling a lot stronger in myself. I made my feelings clear. If Gary and Martin had other plans, we'd bring in a couple of deps to cover for them. Simple. We'd already had to do that for a couple of TV shows, so there was a precedent. They backed down.

I was looking forward to playing live again although, deep down, I suspected I had made my last Spandau Ballet album; it didn't take a genius to see that the ties holding the band together were at breaking point.

After the sky-high costs of the Barricades tour, there was a half-hearted attempt to economize. One day, at the end of rehearsals, our tour manager, John Martin, showed up. He wanted to run through the rider on the last tour. It read like a stock-take for a medium-sized off-licence: twelve bottles of champagne (Bollinger), tequila, vodka, Jack Daniel's, wine, beer. He glanced round the room. We were all nodding. That sounded about right. There were no obvious savings, as far as we could see. He moved on. Two litres of fresh orange juice. Who drank orange juice? No one. What a waste. Scrub it. We shelved a couple of other sundry items, peanuts or something. Was there any point in keeping the cheese board? No one bothered with it. It usually ended up with a couple of fag ends in it. Did we need it? No. Take it off. A few minutes later, Martin spoke up. He enjoyed a bit of cheese after the show. It went back on. Forty-five minutes later, we had saved a couple of quid a night on orange juice. John Martin left, defeated.

At least we didn't add anything.

Cutting back on the rider was never going to make that much difference. We should have been looking at bigger issues, like how many people we had on the road, and whether we could afford them. We should have been asking questions about the gigs themselves. We had become a mainstream band, but we failed to capitalize on that. We never played festivals, for instance. For some bands, touring was lucrative. We struggled. There was never an explanation for that, although I think if we'd brought in a first-rate promoter like Harvey Goldsmith or a top-flight agent like Neil Warnock it might have been a different story.

The final tour took in more than forty dates across the UK and Europe. We were in Berlin in November '89, just weeks before the wall came down. We had been to Berlin a lot. It was one of my favourite cities. On previous visits, I had nipped over to East Berlin plenty of times through Checkpoint Charlie. My tendency to leave a note saying 'Back later' used to drive tour manager John Martin insane.

In January '90, we returned to Berlin for a gig. By then, locals on both sides of the wall were tearing it down. It was incredible. People were taking sledgehammers to it under the noses of the East German soldiers. We joined in. I still have my piece of the Berlin Wall.

At the same time, within the band, barriers were going up. We stopped spending time with each other after the gigs. On the road, Gary kept himself apart, buried in a book at the front of the bus. At the back of the bus, Steve did the same.

When we played our last show in Edinburgh on 6 March 1990, there was no great fanfare, no end-of-tour party. It all just fizzled out. We were just glad it was over. All I remember about that night is a row over drinks the backing singers' boyfriends had stuck on our bill.

In some respects, the tour was a success. We pulled in audiences and we sounded good, but no amount of effort could hide the fact that the heart had gone out of the band. I got the feeling that the only people performing on stage were John and I. The pair of us were still having a laugh, enjoying it. It was a chance to get out there and do what we loved, what makes us tick. On stage, the problems eating away at the band went away. For the two hours we were in front of an audience, nothing else mattered. Among the others, there seemed to be a fair bit of going through the motions, a general air of wanting to get it over with.

I'm not convinced Gary and Martin were ever all that passionate about touring, after all they haven't toured much since the band broke up. It's probably fair to say that Gary always saw himself more as a songwriter than a performer. Martin liked being on stage, but playing bass was never the be all and end all for him. He'd probably be the first to admit that. The band brought him fame and recognition. It proved a stepping stone to other things, a means to an end. I don't think he was ever as caught up in it all. For me, the thrill was singing. For John, it was being behind the drum kit.

Quite how Steve felt, I have no idea. I know he was a bit low after he and Gail broke up, but by the time we toured he had a new girlfriend. She came to some of the shows. One night we were chatting and she said, 'I don't like Spandau Ballet. I hate the music.' That probably made him feel better.

By the end of the tour, I think we all knew the game was up. I didn't want to make another album. I'm not sure if anyone else did. We needed some time apart. With *The Krays* under their belts, it seemed likely Gary and Martin would want to pursue other acting roles. The consensus seemed to be to take time out. No one talked about the band breaking up, although the thought must have occurred to all of us.

Despite the pitiful savings we made on the rider, we made little from the tour. The chances are the paid musicians (again) earned more than the band. We were partly to blame. That little heart-to-heart about tightening our belts should have rung a few warning bells. It didn't. Despite our years in the business, we were still relatively naïve. I was, anyway. I never asked the obvious questions. It was my job to sing. Other people dealt with the messy stuff, like money. It felt safe to assume the people acting on our behalf would secure the best deal possible. I trusted the band, and I trusted Steve Dagger to manage us.

At home, I was in the throes of selling the Pink House. For months I had been spinning plates, negotiating with the bank, looking for a way to keep it. The bottom line was, I didn't have enough money coming in. Earnings from the band were sporadic, and interest rates were high.

I was reluctant to put the house on the market. It was Léonie's dream home; we were happy there. She understood there was no option but to sell, but the thought of leaving broke her heart. The day we finally moved out, she was in tears.

There had been some tough moments in the years since Toni was born. We had always wanted four or five children, but when we tried for a third things started to go wrong. Léonie had the first of three miscarriages. We were both relatively accepting. We had two beautiful children. We were sure we could have more. She became pregnant again. Within a few weeks, she miscarried.

There seemed no obvious explanation for the pregnancies to terminate. Léonie was healthy, everything seemed fine. There was no reason not to keep trying. We greeted news of her next pregnancy with a mixture of caution and optimism. I was convinced everything would be fine. In the first stages of the pregnancy, we went for a scan. It was the earliest scan the nurse had ever done. Everything was as it should be. A few weeks later, we went back. Nothing. The baby was dead. We were devastated. We had coped with two miscarriages, but the third took its toll. A post-mortem revealed that Léonie had been carrying a healthy girl. That was the biggest blow. No one could explain what had gone wrong. It was an absolute mystery. We wanted answers, but there were none. Advances in ante-natal medicine still can't explain everything. We left the consulting room hand in hand, in tears.

It was a difficult time. We each questioned why this was happening. Were we to blame? Were we doing something wrong, without even knowing?

In the light of three miscarriages, we had to make a decision about whether to try for another baby.

By the time we decided to put the Pink House on the market, the pressure was getting to me. At the time, I thought I was behaving rationally. Looking back, I'm not so sure. We started looking round for another house. I wanted something with character, something that needed some attention. I walked into an estate agent in Highgate and said I was in the market for a property that would pose a challenge. I was on Planet Chaos by then. What they came up with was an eighteenth-century property in need of major refurbishment. It was right up my street. There was just one snag. There was a sitting tenant. My stress levels were already going off the scale. It was hardly sensible to take on something that was practically derelict. The estate agent, to his credit, tried to put me off. He said that the tenant had no desire to go. I didn't want to know. All I could see was the potential of the place. I wasn't thinking about its drawbacks. I asked the tenant how much he wanted to move out. He shrugged. It wasn't a question of money. He didn't want to move. I took my mate Micky Bell, a builder, to see the place. All I could see was a fabulous family home. What he saw was a building that was falling apart. He walked round the place with me looking grim.

Eventually, he said, 'Do you know what you're taking on?'

I said, 'Yeah, but it'll be brilliant.'

He said, 'You're mad.'

I was determined to buy it, so much so, I paid over the odds to compensate the tenant, and far too much for the house. Léonie probably had misgivings, but she knew that trying to talk me out of something I'd set my heart on was pointless.

When we moved in the place was in a dreadful state. It was a complete wreck, cold and uncomfortable, and we were living there with two young children. I had this romantic idea of Léonie and I working together, slowly turning the place into a fantastic home. For Christmas 1989, I presented her with a paint scraper, a light-hearted reference to the do-it-yourself challenge that lay ahead. Bearing in mind the scale of the task in front of us, a paint scraper turned out to be of little use.

Soon afterwards, Léonie discovered she was pregnant. After three miscarriages, we waited to see how this pregnancy would develop. A tense few weeks followed, during which we tried to behave as if everything was normal. We were both certain that things would work out this time, so much so that we talked about the practicalities of trying to rebuild the house with a baby on the way. When we called the builders in, it was an act of faith.

Bringing the place up to scratch cost a fortune. There was dry rot, the roof was falling in, the wiring was old, there was no heating. It all had to be done. We replaced windows, put in a new kitchen and bathroom, laid new carpets and decorated. It was like pouring money into a bottomless pit. There's a film called *The Money Pit*, which pretty much sums it up.

Meanwhile, Léonie was getting bigger. We were well past the point at which she had previously miscarried.

She finally went into labour a month before the baby was due. I called her gynaecologist, John Osbourne, who began preparing the theatre for an emergency Caesarean. Neither of us said much, but we were both nervous. This time, surely, nothing could go wrong. We called a cab and set off for the hospital. You'd have thought the driver was on a go-slow. He crawled along at a sedate twenty-five miles per hour. Léonie was hanging onto my arm. Every now and then she would grip hard. She was in agony. I told the driver to step on it. He took no notice. I caught his eye in the rear-view mirror. 'Look, mate, just get a move on, will you?' He gestured at the traffic. Everyone else seemed to be going a lot faster than us. I was getting increasingly frustrated. At every junction, he braked to let even more cars slip in front of us. A real knight of the road. I was ready to land him one. In the end, I spelled it out. I said, 'Look, mate, if you don't get a move on, I'm going to nick your car and drive there myself. Now put your foot down.' That seemed to do it.

At the Portland Hospital, we were taken straight to theatre. The sight of the medical staff, gowned up and waiting, sent a chill down my spine. I was desperate that nothing should go wrong. I stayed with Léonie, holding her hand. A green canopy obscured the surgeon from her view, but I was able to watch as he made an incision and delivered our son, Mackenzie. It was extraordinary. As the surgeon worked, I squeezed her hand. 'Wow,' I kept saying. 'Wow.'

Léonie rolled her eyes. 'Hadley,' she said, 'what are you like?'

Our family was complete. We had been told that it was not wise to try for any more children.

Chapter Fourteen

It was 8 a.m. when the phone rang. My mum, in a terrible state, told me my dad had collapsed. It was a heart attack.

In my panic, I didn't even ask which hospital he had gone to. Assuming it was St Bartholomew's – Bart's – where he went for his regular check-ups, I arranged to meet my sister Lee there. They had no record of him. He was actually at University College Hospital, a short distance away. We jumped in the car and raced over there. By now, my sister was terrified we were going to be too late. She sat in the passenger seat in tears, saying, 'He's gone, I know it.' I did my best to calm her, insisting everything would be fine. I refused to believe anything else.

At UCH, we asked for Patrick Hadley. A nurse checked the list of admissions and asked us to wait. A feeling of dread settled in my stomach. My optimism disappeared. I knew we were about to hear bad news. I had no more words of encouragement for my sister. Together, we waited in silence. A few minutes later, we were led to a room, where my mum waited. The sight of her, alone, her face crumpled with grief, tore at my insides.

It was 2 February 1991, and the worst moment of my life. My dad was sixty-three. That was too young to die.

When my brother Steve arrived at the hospital, we were ready to leave. The news had reached him later than us. The whole family was in pieces.

I last saw my dad the day before he died. Léonie and I had called in on my parents with Mack, who was just a few weeks old. My dad, perched on a footstool in the kitchen with the baby in his arms, appeared worn out. I said, 'Are you all right, Dad?'

He nodded, rocking Mack gently. 'Just a bit tired, boy,' he said.

It was hardly surprising. The night before, he and my mum had been at my sister's birthday party. Léonie and I hadn't made it, but my parents were full of it that morning. They'd had a great time. It sounded like a typical family knees-up. I suspected my dad just needed an early night.

The following morning, he woke up feeling poorly. I've gone over and over this in my head. Why didn't he get my mum to call an ambulance straight away? Maybe it would have made a difference. For whatever reason, he didn't. Instead, he got up and went to the bathroom. Perhaps he thought the feeling would pass. Moments later, there was a terrible crash. My mum found him, unconscious in the bathroom. He had collapsed against the shower screen. Instinctively, she tried to move him, but my dad was a big man, six feet tall. My mum struggled, but simply didn't have the strength.

I can't imagine what she went through in those moments, and how afraid she was waiting for the ambulance to arrive. Even now, I can't think too hard about it. It still upsets me.

I know that coping with the death of your parents is part of life. In a sense, my dad's earlier heart attack had sounded a warning for what was to come. If I thought I was in any way prepared, though, I soon discovered I was not. I had never known such loss. Without him there, the world was a different place, drab and cold. Nothing seemed the same any more. My mum was utterly bereft. Seeing her in pieces was a terrible

...... give in to grief and fall apart was
...... was not an option.

...... had to. I became harder.
...... It was the only way I was

...... e done. I went to register
...... e. He was heartbroken to
...... close to for so long. He felt
...... the natural order of things.
...... My dad had died without a
...... al and legal matters to sort

...... gathered at the crematorium
...... was a crisp winter morning.
...... covering under a clear sky.
...... clothes stood in silhouette
...... seemed appropriate; a proper
...... life, which was always black

There were plenty of ...... at day, but I kept mine inside.
Whenever I feared a crack was appearing in the wall I'd built
around myself I slapped some more mortar between the bricks
and sealed it up. I was not ready to let my feelings out. Perhaps
I'm more like my dad than I know.

I spent weeks living at my mum's, going through paper-
work, making calls to the bank and insurance companies.
Sifting through another person's legal and financial documents
was something I had never had to do. It required a clear head.
I forced myself to remain detached. Otherwise, I don't think I
could have carried on. In the background, my mum and my
sister were broken. Steve, my brother, brought the emotional

shutters down. I filled my days with phone calls to financial institutions and kept my feelings to myself.

For a while I was angry. It seemed so unfair. Just as my dad was enjoying his life, taking it easy, spending more time with my mum than ever, it was over. He had joined the print trade as an apprentice electrical engineer at fourteen. His working life spanned almost fifty years. The reward for that was early retirement, a chance to spend more time with the family, see a bit of the world. He and my mum were busy planning a trip to the Far East. He had seemed to be doing so well, keeping fit with daily two-mile walks.

I wasn't ready for him to die.

It turned out that he had suffered another minor heart attack, which I knew nothing about, before the one that killed him. I spent time wishing, uselessly, that he had sought help sooner. My dad, though, was proud. I can picture him now, thinking he would deal with things in his own way. The truth is, we all die sometime, and I'm grateful the end for him was swift. Even if it meant there was no chance to say goodbye.

During the weeks that followed his death, my concerns were with my mum and my brother and sister. I hated the idea of my mum being on her own. My dad worshipped her. I didn't want to think about her alone, getting on with things, rattling round in an empty house. My dad was always incredibly protective. When I was growing up, I felt there was nothing he wouldn't do for his family. I wanted to step into that role and take care of my mum. It was the same for my brother and sister.

In the background, Léonie was at home, coping with three young children on her own. Although Mackenzie appeared to be a robust little thing, he hadn't thrived as he should have. We had been in and out of hospital with him. Léonie had a lot on her plate and, in my efforts to remain strong and detached, I had shut her out. I wasn't even aware of how hurt she was until later. Looking back, it was incredibly difficult for her. For a while, she lost me. I wouldn't allow her in. I had seen how easily life could end, which made me take stock. I wanted to live my life, not reach the end and wonder, What if . . .? If anything positive came out of my grief, it was a sense that what counts is the present. You can learn from the past, but you can't go back and change it. As for the future, there is no certainty.

When Léonie finally got me back, I was a different person.

I was almost on automatic pilot, getting on with life, coping. On the surface, things were back to normal, but I was disengaged from day-to-day life. Months went by and I hung on to my grief, imagining I could bury it away. It was like tacking a piece of plywood over the rim of a volcano. At some point, it would blow.

About three months later, we went to Grantham to visit Léonie's parents, Helen and Nevil. There were a few of us there for dinner. I was behaving as if everything was fine, which it certainly wasn't. I was still in mourning. Across the table, Léonie's mum had a dig at her dad. He snapped back. She had another go. It was mild stuff. For as long as I've known them they've sparred with each other like that. Normally, it wouldn't bother me. I don't suppose anyone else thought anything of it, but that night it incensed me. I watched them thinking, You still have each other. I couldn't stand it. 'For God's sake, will you just *shut up*,' I yelled. 'You don't know how long you've got together.' Everyone fell silent. I left the table and went to my room. All the tears I'd kept inside came out in one big rush.

I sobbed and sobbed.

It wasn't about Helen and Nevil bickering over dinner. It was about me missing my dad and needing to express it. You can't keep that inside for ever, however strong you are. Eventually, I went back downstairs, my eyes red, and apologized for my outburst.

I miss my dad so much. He was such a huge part of my life. I had never felt I needed him less as I got older. We remained as close as ever. Even now, if I'm going through a hard time, I wish I could share it with him. In a way, I do. I may not be able to talk to him, but I have a good idea what he would say if he could.

It's thirteen years since he died but if I think too hard about it, the pain of losing him still affects me.

Everything seemed to go wrong in the year following my dad's death. My grandad, Bill Tee, died. He had been ill with emphysema. I had been close to my grandad all my life and I absolutely idolized him. He was such a character, well liked and respected in the community, and he loved a good time. When I was working at IPC magazines, I'd do the odd Saturday shift on one of the Sunday papers for a bit of spare cash. I'd often end up in the pub afterwards drinking with my grandad, who spent his working life in the print trade. We'd just about carry each other home at closing time. He was one of the funniest men I've ever met, with a dark, irreverent sense of humour at times.

A few years before he died, he was in St Bart's hospital for a minor operation. His best friend, Joe Sewell, was in another ward, seriously ill. They'd grown up together and were incredibly close. Their dads had also been lifelong friends.

As my grandad recuperated, word came through that Joe had died. My mum was in a terrible state, wondering how to break the news gently. She was dreading it. On her next visit to my grandad, she sat at the side of his bed and said, 'Dad, I'm really sorry. I've got something to tell you. Joe's died.'

My grandad stared at her for a couple of seconds then started laughing. When he pulled himself together, he said, 'Thank God the old bastard's gone before me.'

My mum was appalled, but that was my grandad's way of dealing with it. If it had been the other way round, that's probably exactly how Joe would have reacted too.

At one point, we didn't think Mackenzie would make it to his first birthday. One day he stopped breathing. Léonie was screaming for me. Our child had turned blue. I grabbed him and checked to make sure there was nothing obstructing his throat. He fell unconscious in my arms. We rushed him to hospital. It was the most frightening thing. We thought we had lost him.

The hospital diagnosed a behavioural problem; Mack had simply decided to stop breathing. There was every chance it could happen again. We were to keep a close eye on him at all times. For six months, he was on a heart monitor. We lived in absolute dread of losing him. Once you have kids, they become your world. Mack was the baby we feared we might never have.

It was another reminder of how precious life is, and how fragile too.

Léonie and I went through a period of being afraid to check on him in the morning. Perhaps that's morbid, but that's how we felt. Now, it's hard to imagine those fears, but they were real enough at the time. It later emerged that his adenoids and tonsils were enlarged to such an extent he was at risk of cot death.

The way things were, I was glad to spend time at home, but there was very little money coming in from Spandau Ballet. We had never received a regular income; that was the nature of the business, but there were still bills to be paid. It was the same for all of us. I actually had no idea how things stood with the band. We still had a record deal. Despite what had gone on during the making of the last album, and subsequent tour, no one had spoken about splitting up. Not to each other, anyway.

We decided to release another single, which triggered another payment from CBS. There was no original material, so we discussed doing a cover. Predictably, there was a difference of opinion about what we should actually do. Gary Kemp wanted to cover the Simon and Garfunkel track 'The Boxer'. I thought the Righteous Brothers song, 'You've Lost That Lovin' Feelin'' was a better bet. It was an enduring pop song. I knew we could do a good, contemporary version. John Keeble liked both tracks, but agreed we had more chance of a hit with 'You've Lost That Lovin' Feelin''. After the poor performances of the recent singles, we needed a Top 5 hit. Martin backed Gary. We all looked at Steve. He wasn't sure. In the end, he came down on the side of 'The Boxer'.

We worked on the track with a new producer, Michael Kamen. He was a good producer, but I couldn't come to terms with the track. It seemed an unlikely song for Spandau Ballet to cover. In the end, I hated our version. It felt as if we were trying to be something we weren't. Although I was never a big fan of the song, I could see it suited Simon and Garfunkel. It didn't suit us. Not that it mattered, since it never saw the light of day. We didn't release it. I'm not sure why. I don't think it was a CBS decision to bury it; I think it was ours, as a band. I know John wanted to release it. He couldn't see what harm it would do. It just might have been a hit. He had a point although, on balance, I think we were right not to. I felt it reflected badly on us all.

When we had started making *Heart Like A Sky*, no one knew that it would be the last album, although, once the process was under way, the writing was on the wall. We may have signed a six-album deal with CBS but the prospect of us making the outstanding four albums was remote.

Despite the problems during the making of *Heart Like A Sky*, we were still speaking to each other by the end of the process – just about. We had agreed to disagree, but our relationships weren't beyond repair. I didn't feel at that stage that there was no going back. For years afterwards, there was confusion. Had we split or were we just having time off? No one really knew. Our lives had been run by an office for years. All of a sudden, it all went quiet. The band didn't blow apart; it deflated. There was never any real closure.

In the light of what happened subsequently, people seem to think that I was involved in an ongoing feud with Gary Kemp. I wasn't. Most of the time we got on. We were friends. There was only one occasion when we almost came to blows and that was on tour a couple of years after Live Aid. In Germany, we met up with Bob Geldof, and were talking over the whole Feed The World experience. Geldof commented on how committed to Ethiopia all the artists who took part in Live Aid on both sides of the Atlantic had been. I said the prospect of massive worldwide publicity probably played a part. That sparked a bit of a slanging match between the three of us. I think Bob enjoys stirring up a bit of lively debate – too lively, sometimes. Gary was livid. He turned on me. 'You did it for the publicity?'

I said, 'No, I did it for Ethiopia, but we all knew how many people would be watching. The reason I was so nervous was because we were playing to eighty thousand at Wembley and another billion round the world.'

Gary was incensed. I walked away. He came after me. I told him to fuck off and leave it. He raised his hand to my face, but I don't think he had any real intention of slapping me. He just gave me a limp, half-hearted shove. In the background, Martin had appeared. I said, 'You ever touch me again and I will kick the shit out of you.'

Martin stepped up. He said, 'Gary, you're out of order.'

By now, Steve Dagger was also hovering. Martin said, 'This is ridiculous. Come on, shake hands.'

He was right. It was ridiculous. I held out my hand. Gary slapped it away. I shook my head. I said, 'You wanker.'

I went to the bar. Dagger followed. It was the most serious fall-out he'd seen. There had been plenty of raised voices over the years, but never anything physical. I think Steve Dagger was worried that this row would cause me to leave the tour.

I said, 'I'll do the tour, that's my job, but he's a wanker. Just keep him out of my way.'

It seemed pointless to carry a grudge and, as the tour wore on, we patched things up. When I started work on my solo album in LA, Gary was there at the same time, working on the Kevin Costner film, *The Bodyguard*. I got in touch and we met up. We were still on reasonable terms. I wanted the five of us to get together, just to meet for a few drinks and a chat. John was up for it, so were Martin and Steve. I thought Gary was too until Steve called him. There was an almighty row. I never found out what it was about, but it put paid to any reunion. Of course, at that point I didn't know Gary had already put a stop to the payments to Marbelow.

Once that came to light I didn't feel so much like making an effort to be friendly any more.

Chapter Fifteen

I **never wanted to be** a solo artist. I didn't know the first thing about going it alone. All I had known was being in a band and we'd had some good times together. No, rephrase that. We had some brilliant times together; at its best it was absolutely fantastic. When things fell apart with Spandau, I met up with John Keeble and Steve Norman in a pub in St John's Wood, in North London, and suggested we form a new band together. I wanted the familiarity of working with people I knew and trusted. John was interested, but Steve wanted to do his own thing. Reluctantly, I decided to give it a go on my own. The idea terrified me.

When I decided on a solo career, I decided to stick with Steve Dagger as my manager. Better the devil you know, and all that, although all I had known was life in a band, and it was the same for Steve.

I knew being a solo artist would be a completely different experience. When you're in a band, you share the load. If you're having an off day someone else can do the interview. But when you're on your own there's no one else to turn to. If there's a meeting, you have to go. If there's an interview, you have to do it.

I remember Steve told me to be prepared to take on a lot more than I had in Spandau. I was already writing songs, but had little in the way of a repertoire. Steve and I went to Los

Angeles to meet publishers and look for new material. We were complete novices, wasting our time in meetings that didn't lead anywhere. I've since discovered it makes sense to go straight to the writers. The chances that their best songs are sitting around on their publisher's books, waiting for someone to come along and find them, are slim.

At the time, I was feeling positive, though. There were a few record companies in the running, interested in a deal. It felt as if things would work out. I signed with EMI in the end, since they were offering the best deal and seemed the most committed. They made a great song and dance about it. I was introduced at their conference amid huge fanfare. Soon afterwards, I went to LA to work on the album, *State Of Play*. John Keeble came with me.

It was important to have John around at that point. Not having the comfort zone of the band was unnerving. I was about to try something new and I had no idea how it would turn out. The other musicians who worked with me were Toby Chapman, who had worked with Spandau Ballet, on keyboards, Jerry Stevenson on guitar, and Martin Kemp's TV stand-in, Kevin Miller, on bass. I knew expectations were high. The album had to succeed; there was no period of grace to find my feet. It felt like a lot of pressure. I needed a sense of continuity and, by then, I was probably closer to John than any of the others.

I brought Ron Nevison on board to produce the album. Ron had worked with bands like the Who, Heart and Kiss. He had a reputation as an excellent producer and he was the epitome of LA life. Having been in the music industry for twenty years, Ron knew everyone. He was a regular at all the best clubs, always with a glamorous woman in tow. Like so many people in LA, he had a year-round tan. Even after three weeks of rain,

Ron stayed golden brown. I couldn't understand it. That was the first time I realized that, among the LA smart set, the use of sun lamps was standard.

Ron was a hard taskmaster, but I respected him. He was an experienced, assured producer. He pushed me, stretched my voice; at times the pressure to perform was intense. John felt it too. Ron gave me the confidence to try new things. I trusted him to do a good job, and he did. At one point, John was struggling with a drum track. Ron, in his brusque LA style, was losing patience. At the drop of a hat, he would have brought in a new drummer. I was not about to see that happen. John and I had been through too much together; I wanted him on the album – not for sentimental reasons, but because he is a great drummer. Seeing him struggle stirred up painful memories of *Diamond* and *Heart Like A Sky*. Studio work can chip away at your confidence. I knew exactly what he was going through.

In the end, as he had with me, Ron managed to bring out the best in John.

We settled into LA life. For three and a half months we lived in the Le Parc Hotel, in West Hollywood, and got to know our way round. Léonie came out to visit with the kids and we went on trips to Universal Studios and Disneyland. We had a good time.

At one point, I had wanted to uproot the family and move out to LA. It seemed like a good opportunity to start again, but the time I spent there making *State Of Play* convinced me we were better off in England. There were aspects of LA life I couldn't get to grips with. There were too many guns, a drug culture that worried me. Although LA is an incredible city, it felt superficial: fake tans, plastic surgery, a sense that no one was quite what they seemed. At Le Parc, the barman behaved as if it was beneath him to serve drinks because, really, he was a screenwriter. Bar work was something he did until he got his big break. I hope he made it, because he was a crap barman. There was a lot of that in LA.

It was enough to persuade me that London is a great city, after all.

I was in LA, sitting in the bar at the hotel with John, when we caught sight of a news bulletin saying that Freddie Mercury had died. It was November '91. We had known for a while that Freddie was ill. The last time I saw him was in Barcelona at a ceremony in 1988 in which Seoul handed over the flag for the next Olympic Games. We were there to perform 'Gold'. He was singing 'Barcelona' with the opera singer, Montserrat Caballé. Freddie wasn't looking good. He was painfully thin and wearing a lot of make-up.

The show was a huge spectacle. We were part of a line-up that included Jerry Lee Lewis, Dionne Warwick and José Carreras, who sang 'My Way'. Although Carreras has a brilliant voice, an opera singer doing a pop song just didn't work for me. King Juan Carlos of Spain was the guest of honour. We met him after the show, but he didn't seem too interested in blokes in torn jeans and baseball boots. He perked up when he got to the backing singers though. The fireworks that night were fantastic. They sounded like small bombs exploding. It was an important gig but we were confident, having played 'Gold' on numerous occasions over the past seven years. There was no reason for anything to go wrong. Then we tossed a spanner in the works. For reasons I couldn't understand, we decided to 'enhance' the song with a sequence run off a computer program. It was the first time we'd done that and I was dead against it. I'm renowned for missing my cue and coming in at the wrong time. If that happens, the eight-bar intro can suddenly become a 16-bar intro, or a 32-bar intro, or even a 64-bar – well, you get the picture. It doesn't really matter. You can't really do that with a computer. It runs the way it's been programmed. I don't suppose anyone in the audience was bothered about new technology. I'm not sure they were listening out for a new horn section or an extra snare drum sound or whatever. All they wanted to do was sing along with 'Gold'. I was overruled, of course, but as it turned out, I was right to be worried. The computer cocked up halfway through and we had to switch off the sequence and carry on without it.

If it wasn't a good night for us, it was even worse for Freddie.

We were at least playing live. He and Montserrat Caballé were miming. When the intro began, you could hear the hiss on the recording. Worse, the tape was running fast. Afterwards, Freddie was furious. I could see his point.

Although we had all known for a while that he was ill, his death still came as a shock. He was, without doubt, one of the greatest performers of recent years.

I'm not sure I was ever convinced that *State Of Play* was the album I had set out to make. The truth is, post-Spandau, I wasn't sure what to do next. I needed guidance, but it wasn't there. I hoped I was moving in the right direction, but I had no way of knowing. The album seemed to have the right ingredients: a good producer, some good tracks – whether they were the kind of songs I should have been recording at that point, I'm not sure. About halfway through recording, I began to suspect I was making the wrong album. I had a sinking feeling that wouldn't go away. My debut album was turning into REO Speedwagon meets Foreigner. The songs felt too west coast for a UK audience. No one else thought so – or if they did, they weren't saying. Still, I was proud of the album. I had trusted Ron Nevison to do a good job and, in terms of production, he did. A few nagging doubts remained, though, about whether it would work.

We shot the album cover in the desert in California. The shots had a bleached, stark quality. We decided to stick with the theme for the video for the first single, 'Lost In Your Love'. Just before the shoot, the heavens opened and, for the first time in years, the desert was drenched. The cracked, alien landscape we all liked so much had been washed away.

I should have known that was a bad sign.

Instead, at enormous expense, we moved into a studio where set designers recreated the desert in painstaking detail. Artists painted a lifelike, arid backdrop. Bare trees, scrub and boulders were imported. The floor became parched and dusty. A chameleon perched on a branch. It was as real as it could be. Not surprisingly, the budget shot through the roof. All we needed now was a hit single.

I remember a meeting at which EMI's marketing team discussed what to do with 'Lost In Your Love'. I knew we needed a hit. Otherwise, everyone – myself included – would lose faith. The last thing I wanted was for anyone to assume the Spandau Ballet connection was enough in itself to produce a hit record. I wanted EMI to treat me like a new, untried artist and take nothing for granted. In the course of the marketing meeting, I suggested a poster campaign. I wanted them to pull out the stops. They didn't rate posters. People already knew who I was; a poster campaign was unnecessary. I didn't think so. The whole point was that people didn't know me as a *solo* artist. Also, the new single was a complete departure. I was extremely nervous. Apparently, there was no need to worry. When it came to marketing, this particular team knew their stuff. They would make sure 'Lost In Your Love' was a Top 40 hit. No problem. I looked around the room. No one seemed to be taking it seriously. There was no marketing strategy that I could see. The 'campaign' was built on arrogance and false assumptions, as far as I could tell. I think we should have demanded more than a show of confidence.

I remember hearing Mike Rutherford of Mike And The Mechanics review the single on the Radio 1 show, *Round Table*. He was complimentary about my voice, but surprised to hear me doing LA rock. He wasn't the only one.

When the single came out in early '92, it limped to Number 42 in the charts. I might as well have walked away there and then. The solo career had disaster written all over it. My A&R man, Nick Gatfield, had left. With perfect timing, he went while I was promoting 'Lost In Your Love'. Clive Black took over. I liked Clive, but things were already in a mess by then.

By the time we started promoting the second single, I knew there was little chance of turning things round, even though 'For Your Blue Eyes Only' was a beautiful song. Suddenly, the marketing team was talking about a poster campaign. They were too late. The single reached 67 in the chart.

I went on a promotional tour to Europe, South East Asia and South Africa to raise the profile of the album. In the end it sold reasonably well in Germany, Italy and the Far East, but not well enough.

Clive Black moved on and a new A&R man came in – Julian Close, formerly of the band Red Box. A new managing director was appointed too, a Frenchman, Jean-Francois Cecillion. I suspect we were all going through the motions at this point. I was still working on new material and I started to write and record with my very good friend, Paul Travers. Although Jean-Francois was making the right noises, nothing was actually happening. At one point, he had some disturbing advice.

He spoke with a heavy French accent, and tended to put the emphasis on the last syllable of each word. It had an air of TV's Antoine de Caunes of *Rapido* about it. 'May-bee, Ton-ee, you could go off to an island and find yourself. Then, oo knows, may-bee you could think about a new album and – may-bee – fund it your*self*.' He gave a small shrug. It was all very may-bee and may-bee not. 'Then, let's see.'

I realized my time was running out at EMI.

Julian Close turned up at the recording studio one day, where I was working on some new material. I started to play him a rough mix and he started twiddling with the controls on the desk. It's an unwritten rule in the recording studio that the desk is sacrosanct. I wasn't the only one tempted to land him one. Once it became clear he was loath to spend a few hundred pounds on making demos, there was no point in carrying on. It was time to cut and run.

It was Rupert Perry, chairman of EMI, who came to my rescue. The day I tried to reach him he was in New York. When I called, his wife answered; Rupert was in the shower. I was afraid he'd be less than pleased that one of his artists was calling him while he was out of the country but, moments later, he called back. I told him how unhappy I was. I wanted out. He probably picked up, even over a long-distance line, the desperation in my voice. He promised to arrange a meeting once he got back to London. A week later, I sat down with him. Rupert Perry knew I was in trouble. By then, I was in a huge amount of debt, with no prospect of clearing it. To my relief, he agreed to release me from the EMI deal. To this day, I'm grateful to him. He's an extremely decent man in a heartbreaking business.

I wasn't sure what to do next, although I knew that I had to keep earning money somehow. There was no time to sit around feeling bad about my solo career. I had learned some important lessons but, in the process, my career had gone down the drain. It was hugely disappointing. The only thing to do was move on.

For years, I had relied on other people. I had counted on Steve Dagger for a long time, but I wasn't happy with the handling of my solo career. I remember trying to sack him at one point. Steve was persuasive and he talked me round but, by then, we were on borrowed time. It's a bit like trying to hold a marriage together when you know it's over, hanging on out of a sense of duty. It never works. The relationship had run its course.

Finally, I began to rely on myself. Now, aged forty-three, I probably know as much about publishing and marketing as most managers. I still don't always make the right decision, but I'm a lot better than I used to be.

For a while, with the EMI deal over, I was in no-man's land, then things slowly started to pick up. I had parted company with Steve Dagger by this time. I think we both knew we were at the end of the line.

Financially, I was struggling. Having poured a fortune into the house in Wood Lane, we couldn't afford to live there. In a funny way, we didn't want to. After pulling out the stops to buy the property – against everyone's advice – we never really settled. By the time my solo career collapsed, we were living beyond our means. Interest rates were high, and we had taken on loans to renovate the property. I wasn't earning a fortune from Spandau Ballet, but regular payments of around £1,000 a month kept our heads above water. In the wake of the solo deal falling through, I noticed even that had dried up. Things were looking grim.

We sold up and moved on just before the property market collapsed. I even managed to make a profit.

By 1993, I couldn't understand why there was so little money coming through from Marbelow, the company we had set up to handle our financial affairs. I rang the office. That's when I believe I found out I was no longer receiving an income from publishing royalties. The secretary, Jackie Vickers, broke the news. Although the court later decided that I had been notified officially by Steve Dagger, I can honestly say that this was not my recollection.

It was a huge shock and made no sense. There had never been a disagreement over these payments from Gary in the past. The split had suited everyone for years. I couldn't understand why the payments had stopped.

I called John Keeble and, I think, Steve Norman, both of whom were in the same position. It was news to them. John and I went to see Steve Dagger in the office at Notting Hill Gate. He squirmed in his chair as he told us the royalties were a gift from Gary; a gift he no longer wanted us to have. We could not believe what we were hearing.

We wanted to hear this from Gary. At that stage, I thought it was a horrible misunderstanding. It had to be. I asked Dagger to arrange a band meeting. He thought that would be difficult. Gary was working on his solo album; he was too busy for meetings. Weeks went by. John Keeble tried to call Gary. For years, the two of them had been close and, though we'd all drifted apart, there had been no falling out, certainly not between them. John and his wife, Flea, had splashed out hundreds of pounds on a wedding present for Gary and Sadie.

Gary and Sadie had bought John vintage Armagnac for his thirtieth birthday. Now Gary was not available to take his calls. John waited and waited to hear from him. Nothing happened. Gary was never at home – not to us, anyway.

For months, I pressed Dagger to set up a meeting. Nothing came of it. I felt I was being fobbed off with poor excuses. It was appalling. We had suddenly lost a chunk of income and we couldn't even have a conversation about it. According to Dagger, Gary was having a hard time on his album. Oh that was all right, then. I went ballistic. I pointed out that the rest of us were having a hard time making ends meet, not that it made any difference.

I had endless conversations with John. We felt absolutely powerless. It was becoming clear to me that Dagger would stonewall us until we got tired and went away.

That was not about to happen. As far as we were concerned, what was happening was wrong.

The whole scenario had come as a complete shock. Later, Dagger claimed in court that he had spoken to myself, John and Steve, and given us notice that the publishing royalties were about to stop – and why. Neither John nor Steve nor I remembers such a conversation, and we maintained that in court, although Dagger says he came to see us at Olympic Studios when we were in the throes of recording *Heart Like A Sky* to discuss royalties. I do remember him turning up one day. It was during a break, and I was playing table tennis with John. Steve Norman wasn't there. I clearly remember that Dagger broached the subject of the separate production credit for Gary Kemp on the album. Since, in the past, we had all been credited as Spandau Ballet, I hit the roof.

I said, 'No – *fuck* him.'

John had to practically hold me back. I was ready to find

Gary and smack him. It was just another sign of a fracture. It struck me that the problems in the band went deeper than any of us had suspected. I was dead against a separate credit. It marked a worrying departure from an established way of doing things, which, until then, had suited everyone. Then again, the album *was* a departure. The whole experience had been unsettling and difficult. *Heart Like A Sky* didn't fit with my idea of a Spandau Ballet album.

The row over the credit was bad enough but, just as upsetting, was the fact that Gary left it to Dagger to break the news. We had been working together since 1976. Now, all of a sudden, he made his feelings known through our manager. If he felt he deserved a separate credit, why not just sit down and talk to us?

That day, Dagger had finally persuaded me to give way, in the interests of completing an album that had already taken far too long. The band was balancing on a precipice. I was sick of the whole thing. As far as I remember I told Dagger that *Heart Like A Sky* was the last album I'd ever do with Spandau Ballet. I wonder now if he had planned to bring up the subject of royalties that day, and lost his nerve when tempers frayed.

I just know that when I finally discovered the income from publishing royalties had stopped, I could not believe it. It took a while for it to sink in. That Gary would do such a thing just did not add up. It flew in the face of the spirit of the band. Spandau Ballet had never been about any one of us; it was always a collective. All of us, including Gary, knew that. We were in it together. It seemed inconceivable that he no longer saw things that way.

Being in a band is a bit like getting married. You start out with the best intentions, believing it will last for ever. When it doesn't, it's a shock. In the early days of Spandau we were pretty scathing about bands that went through acrimonious splits. We could never see that happening to us. We actually talked about it. We had something they didn't – trust and loyalty – which is exactly why we didn't try and tie each other up in contracts. We never felt it was necessary.

The sudden discovery that we were no longer receiving an income from publishing royalties was bad enough. It was a financial bombshell but, even worse, was the feeling of betrayal. We had always kept things tight – just the five of us and Steve Dagger. We wouldn't allow an outside manager in, preferring to handle things ourselves on the basis that an outsider in a suit might rip us off in a business where bad things do happen.

I still can't get my head round it. I had this conversation with John Keeble during the tour last year. Over lunch in Carlisle we speculated on the motivation for Gary's actions. We still can't make much sense of what happened.

For a while, I hung on to the hope that we could resolve things by sitting round the table. As the months went by, I realized that was not going to happen. I spoke to Pete Hillier, my best mate, about seeking legal advice, then I broached the subject with John Keeble and Steve Norman. We were all reluctant; it seemed an extreme step. We had long, difficult conversations about this, which always went round in circles. We had a relationship – we had thought – with Gary. We had been through an enormous amount together. Surely, we could sort this out between us. Apparently not. When I spoke to Martin, he made it clear he was in the same position. Unlike us, though, he was not in a position to consider legal action against his own brother. Presumably Steve Dagger was also affected.

In the end, we felt we had no choice. With huge reservations, we decided to seek legal advice.

No one takes the thought of legal action against someone they've known for years lightly. It was uncomfortable sitting in the office of a lawyer talking about the disintegration of Spandau Ballet. I kept wondering how it had come to this. We described how our income from publishing royalties, paid over a period of years, had come to an abrupt stop. The first lawyer we met thought we had a case, but he wanted to make it clear that legal action had considerable drawbacks.

Going to court would be a long, costly process. There was no guarantee we would win. He spoke of costs running into hundreds of thousands of pounds. It was terrifying. We went away to consider the implications of it all. There was an enormous amount of soul-searching. No one was gung-ho about legal action. None of us had much money; we were verging on broke, struggling to meet mortgage payments. We couldn't really afford to go to court.

We met with a second lawyer. He was of the same opinion as the first. There was a good case, but we had to understand it could go either way. There was no written contract outlining the division of income from publishing royalties and therefore it was likely to be a complicated case. Legal action carried an enormous risk. He estimated costs in excess of £200,000, which was an alarming thought. It was hard to know what to do. We stood to lose everything. Then again, we had already lost a source of income we had been counting on.

We went for a third opinion. By now, it seemed inevitable that we would have to take legal action. Realistically, there was no other option. We had reached the point where we felt backed into a corner. No one wanted to talk to us. We could walk away from the whole thing, but no one felt like doing that. We believed that what had happened was wrong; that we were as entitled to receive an income from publishing royalties as we had been in the past. I thought it a way of acknowledging our contribution to Spandau Ballet songs. Nothing about those songs had changed, except we no longer got paid. It was up to us. Either we turned a blind eye or we challenged Gary. There was more than a principle at stake; we were counting on the income as a kind of pension. We had to fight it.

We decided to go to court.

The period leading up to the court case was incredibly stressful. However well prepared we felt we were, the reality was about a hundred times worse. It was a constant strain. In the back of my mind was always the question of where the money was coming from to pay for it all. I couldn't allow myself to dwell too much on that. I just had to trust that it would work out somehow. For a long time, our lawyers believed there would be an out-of-court settlement. I never thought that would happen. It had gone too far. I also knew that Gary Kemp had a lot more money to spend on lawyers than we did. Why would he back down?

I took some awful gigs at this point, played depressing places just to keep the band working and keep some money coming in.

I also started drinking heavily.

We had landed a week-long residency at Ronnie Scott's in Birmingham. I was incredibly nervous. I knew that if we went down well it would generate more work. The night we opened, I was in a terrible state. It was the most nervous I've ever been. It's a small club and the audience is about a foot away from the stage. I sat in the dressing room, shaking, my heart thumping. In the end, John Keeble told me to have a drink and calm down. I never used to drink before a show, but it seemed like a good idea. It probably wasn't. I was already high on adrenalin. After a couple of drinks, I felt as if I was flying. It took care of the nerves, but I wasn't really in control.

I got into the habit of having a couple of pints at lunchtime. Then I started drinking on stage. I'd take a bottle of wine on with me. Halfway through the set, it would be empty. I'd get through another bottle before we came off. By then, I was off my head. After the show, I'd carry on drinking myself into oblivion with the band.

It had become a real problem. In some respects, it was a way of blocking out all the shit that was going on in the background. My life was a mess. My career was on the slide. I was having trouble making ends meet, and a legal action was looming. There were moments when it all got too much. A few drinks helped it go away for a while. Not that hitting the bottle changed a thing. I still woke up the next day to find the same problems there.

I knew I was drinking too much. So did everyone else. Then one day I came to my senses and stopped. That was it. No more drinking before the gig. No more booze on stage. I had enough on my plate as it was and drinking wasn't helping. These days I go on with a glass of water.

And I feel a lot better for it.

We had some good times at Ronnie Scott's. For a while we did week-long residencies and got to know the guys at the club pretty well. Whenever we could, we'd take them on at football. These were friendly games, although you'd never have guessed. We all took them as seriously as a World Cup qualifier. When it comes to football – and most other things if I'm honest – I'm incredibly competitive. So is John Keeble. Thankfully, we play on the same side, although that's not always apparent.

During one of the weeks at Ronnie Scott's, we went over to

Birmingham University for a game. It was an Astroturf pitch. No one was wearing the right boots, and we were all losing our footing a bit. Unwisely, I launched into a sliding tackle for a ball that was a good twenty yards away, skidding along the pitch, picking up speed as I went. John, who'd gone for the same ball, was in my path. I careered into him. He gasped and clutched his side. His face contorted. I was panic-stricken. With four more gigs to play, I might just have rendered the drummer incapable. I said, 'Are your arms OK?'

He grimaced. 'My arms are fine.' Other bits were hurting, though.

I've known John play drums with broken, blistered, bleeding fingers. He just gets on with it. He went on in agony for the next four nights. It was only at the end of the week when he got home and paid a visit to his local casualty department that he discovered he had cracked ribs. It was weeks before they healed. Sorry, mate.

The last time we played Ronnie Scott's was a bad experience. As far as we knew, it was meant to be a normal night. Then the manager broke the news that we were playing a corporate gig. No one was very happy. We'd been selling the place out, playing to people who wanted to see us. Suddenly, the audience was half the usual size and about half as interested too.

Throughout the set, there was a guy sitting right in front of the stage, with his back to me. He was about a foot away from where I was singing, so I couldn't exactly miss him. He didn't take a blind bit of notice of us. I got more and more annoyed. It's rare that I lose my temper but when I do, I really lose it. This guy, chatting to everyone around him, waving to people at the back of the room, puffing on big, fat cigars, was getting right on my tits. It was incredibly rude. I kept looking round at John Keeble and shaking my head. He had clocked what was going on and could tell from the look in my eye that trouble was brewing.

I didn't know the guy who was winding me up was also the boss of the company that had laid on the event, although it made perfect sense. That's why he was behaving like such an arsehole, lording it over everyone. As we were coming to the end of the set, he turned round, still waving at the room like an idiot, and gave me a smarmy smile. It was the first time he'd looked at me all night. I was ready to batter him. He got to his feet to shake my hand. I leaned forward and grabbed him. I said, 'Don't ever turn your back on me again.' His face fell. As he tried to move away, I pulled him even closer. 'Do you hear me? You ever insult me again, I'll fucking have you.'

We left the stage without doing an encore. Afterwards, the manager came into the dressing room to tell us what a great night it had been. Phil Taylor, the keyboards player, said we'd actually had a rubbish time. No one felt much like playing there any more although recently a couple of members of the band expressed an interest in going back. That's probably because it's now a lap-dancing club.

I had reached the point where I was looking at life from the bottom of a deep, dark pit. Bills were piling up. I had no money. I was running out of ideas. I considered putting on a disguise and driving cabs. I thought about disappearing into the underpass at Charing Cross Station and drinking myself into a stupor for a week, just to get away from everything. It was tempting. I think Léonie was afraid I was on the verge of a breakdown; perhaps I was.

By then we were living in Muswell Hill. One night we came in late and Léonie went straight to bed. I stayed up for a while and I drifted off to sleep on the sofa. Eventually, she came looking for me. I roused myself and went upstairs. I made it as far as the bathroom where, without warning, I passed out. I'm not sure how long I was unconscious but when I came round I had no idea what had happened. I got up and – bang – went out like a light again. This time, Léonie heard the crash and came looking for me. She had to force the bathroom door because I was slumped against it. I started to come round but I couldn't tell her what had happened because I didn't really know. Sweat ran off me. I was completely disorientated. It brought back bad memories of my dad's heart attack, but I had no chest pains and my pulse was fine. I pulled myself together and went to bed. By the next day I felt fine. Léonie insisted I went to the doctor, who checked my heart and ran blood tests. Everything was as it should be. A combination of stress, wine and jumping up too quickly had caused my blood pressure to fall and led to my losing consciousness. It's not uncommon.

I was trying all ways to earn money. I even tried management.

Paul Travers, a writer I had worked with on some of my EMI songs, suggested we look at a Sheffield band called Big Wide World. Initially I thought they already had a deal, and needed someone to produce them. The first time I saw them play at the Slug and Lettuce, in Sheffield, I thought they were an outstanding five-piece pop/rock band. The quality of the songs was impressive and the singer, Rick Baines, had a great voice. It turned out they didn't have a deal, but we were keen to work with them anyway. I formed a management company with Paul Travers and Pete Hillier, and we arranged some gigs in London. Howard Berman at A&M Records liked them enough to fund a development deal but, beyond that, we struggled.

Trying to get anyone to make a commitment to a new band is nigh on impossible.

I hoped things might change when they were picked for Manchester's annual showcase of unsigned bands, In The City, but it didn't lead anywhere. I remember seeing all the record company A&R people in the hotel bar one night, all talking about which party to go to, when they should have been out watching the bands. It was soul-destroying.

That whole period was difficult. For a while I was managing myself, and trying to get things moving for Big Wide World. I was working from home, calling people here and in the States, all day. I became obsessed, but I wasn't getting anywhere. And for all my efforts, I wasn't bringing any money in. It put a strain on things with Léonie. We went through difficult periods. There were times when I wondered if things would fall apart. Somehow, we always managed to pull through.

At times, it would have been easy to go under, but I was determined not to. I tried everything. I heard about a film being made in Sheffield called *When Saturday Comes*, with Sean Bean and Emily Lloyd, and arranged to meet the producer, Jimmy Daly. The day I went up to Sheffield, they were filming a scene in a graveyard with Sean and Emily. I had a Big Wide World demo tape with me. I wanted to persuade Jimmy to feature some of the band's tracks in the film. It seemed like a great opportunity to me – local film, local band. He loved the tracks. In the end he used three, plus one of mine, 'Build Me Up'.

By this time, Pete Hillier was tour manager with Status Quo and through their manager, David Walker – a top bloke, God bless him – we got to know Jimmy Devlin, a big, bearded, well-connected Scot with his own record label, MDMC. He introduced me to Brian Berg, John Cavanagh and Becky Hamilton from Polygram TV, who remain good friends to this day.

We signed a deal with Polygram TV for a soundtrack album. Things were looking up. We released a Big Wide World single. I thought the film would be the turning point for the band. I hoped it might also help turn things round for me. Although it generated a flurry of interest, and earned us some radio play, it wasn't enough. For all the critical success, we didn't quite pull it off commercially. The film wasn't the hit we all hoped and, consequently, the soundtrack album wasn't a massive hit either.

By now, I was perilously close to rock bottom, and that's not a comfortable place to be. The weird thing about being in the public eye is that people assume you must be doing well. There's a tendency to equate fame with prosperity. A few appearances on *Top Of The Pops*, and you're a millionaire. No one expects you to drive a beat-up car. It's not always that simple.

I had reached the point where I had to make some hard decisions. My career was in free fall. I suppose the choice facing me was whether to give up on singing and try my hand at managing full-time or working in some other capacity in the music industry, like A&R. I couldn't imagine it.

I'm a singer. That's what I do. However much of a struggle it's been, I could never give it up.

In the meantime, I worked my arse off and did some awful gigs. No one can ever accuse me of not paying my dues, because at that point I did, over and over again.

John Keeble, meanwhile, was playing all over Europe with a band called the Herbs. They covered thousands of miles – in a stolen van – played around 100 gigs, sometimes to an audience that was smaller than the band itself, and earned around seven pounds a night each. It hardly seems worth the effort, but John wanted to keep playing. It was important to him. I'm glad he did. It meant he was better than ever when we started touring again.

Everyone has off days, but most people can have those in private. The nature of my work means my life is on show, during the good times and the bad. Like everyone else, I have moments when I'm not feeling good, or I'm ill and I don't want to be Mr Happy-Smiley-Person. Sometimes, I can't manage it. Last year, on the UK tour, I was due to appear at a cricket benefit day. I knew I wasn't up to it and, within minutes of arriving, I had to excuse myself and leave. There were personal issues troubling me and it was one occasion when I couldn't fake a happy face.

At times, I have wanted to hide away, but having a face people recognize doesn't allow it. I accept that's part of what I do but, now and then, when things are going downhill, it would be nice not to be so visible. However bad it's got, Léonie has stuck by me one hundred per cent.

I think what kept me going was that I didn't know what was round the corner, good or bad. There had been so much shit that, at some point, things had to change, surely. I was never brilliant at physics, but one thing I did learn was that every action has an equal and opposite reaction. Often, if you just hang on, life gets better all by itself. That's exactly what happened in 1996.

Chapter Sixteen

Out of the blue, I got a call from Paul Fitzgerald, my new agent, at Concorde. There was an orchestral tour coming up in Europe with Joe Cocker. Six weeks' work, good money. Was I interested? The Proms tour saved my neck. We played France, Germany, Holland and Spain in front of huge audiences. We sold out twelve shows at the Sports Palace in Antwerp, playing to 15,000 people a night.

I was working with a sixty-piece orchestra, a choir, and some amazing performers and musicians. I was in heaven. It's a different discipline working with an orchestra, and it was good experience. You can't afford to mess up. They're working from sheet music and there's no room for improvisation. I'd only done it once before, a few years earlier, with George Martin conducting the Birmingham Philharmonic, for a Prince's Trust charity event.

The Proms tour went down a storm. Word filtered back to the UK. Suddenly, people were asking what I'd been doing, why I'd disappeared. I started to get my confidence back. Steve, my brother, was with me throughout the trip. We had the time of our lives, bowling and working out at the gym during the day, shows and parties by night. The atmosphere on and off stage was amazing. I became friendly on that trip with John Miles (junior). The two of us still do a lot of writing together.

After the shows, a group of us would get together for a few

drinks, sit round the piano in the hotel lobby in Antwerp and sing bawdy songs. It was a good bunch of guys. One night, one of the musicians – we'll call him X – admitted that since his divorce a couple of years earlier he hadn't been with a woman. He'd just about given up by then. I was appalled. I told him he wasn't trying hard enough, but to leave it to me; I'd sort him out.

A group of us went to a club a few nights later. Sitting at the bar with X, I caught the eye of a girl on the other side of the room. She was beautiful. I said, 'You stay there, I'll be back.' I went over and asked her to join us for a glass of champagne. Within a few minutes, Lucy and X were getting on like a house on fire. I decided to leave them to it. The club owner came over. 'Tony, be careful,' he said, nodding in Lucy's direction. 'She's not all she seems.' He made a scissors motion with his hands. Snip snip. Lucy was a transsexual. I shot back over. 'Er, Lucy, love, can I just have a word?'

There's no easy way of bringing up the subject of a sex change. I did my best to be tactful. I think X thought I'd had a brainstorm, but Lucy knew what I was getting at and she was cool about it. So were we. She was good company and she was gorgeous. In all honesty, I admired her for having the guts to go through all the trauma of such massive surgery. I said to X, 'Hey, if she's gone through all that then as far as I'm concerned, she is a woman.'

We went on to another club. In the car, Lucy decided to change. She produced a tiny, stretchy dress from her bag. The next thing, she was wriggling out of her clothes. My eyes nearly fell out of my head. She had an amazing body. She looked every bit a woman to me. I don't think things worked out with X, but we had a great night anyway.

A couple of years later, I was back in Antwerp, in the red-light district, with a group of mates. One of them wanted to find a girl. That was my cue to duck out and go to the pub.

A while later, we all met up again. My mate was jumping up and down with excitement. He said, 'I found a gorgeous girl and she knows you!'

I said, 'Me? I don't know any prostitutes.'

He said, 'Her name's Lucy.'

I thought for a second. 'Lucy?' *Lucy?*

We walked a couple of streets and there she was, sitting in the window – the girl I'd met during the Proms tour. I tapped on the glass. She leaped up. 'Tony!'

Later, my mate was raving about her. I said, 'Look there's something I should tell you . . .'

The Proms tour was one of the happiest periods in my life.

Our finale was the Beatles song 'Let It Be'. I'd carved it up, given all the singers their lines. It sounded amazing with an orchestra and choir. The first night we sang it, everyone stood in an orderly line, singing in turn, until it came to me. I was off, heading for the front of the stage, too excited to stand still. Everyone looked at each other, bemused. I was on a complete high.

When I got home, there was a gig booked at the Island, a club in Ilford, Essex. We had never played there before. It was December, raining hard as we drove out of London. It was one of those dismal winter nights when all you want to do is stay in. Still, I hadn't played with my band for a couple of months, and I was looking forward to it.

We turned up at the club. It had been closed for a couple of weeks. This was the opening night. I thought that might be a good sign. 'So, how many tickets have we sold?'

The manager said, 'I think we're up to seventy now.'

I swallowed. 'OK, seventy, that's good.'

We started getting ourselves ready. In front of the stage, someone was arranging plastic chairs and tables. That's always a bad sign.

I didn't want to go on. There were fifty people out front, if that. I stood backstage wishing the ground would swallow me up. I'm not sure how we got through the set, but somehow we did. It's the only time I've been on stage and wished I was somewhere else. The contrast with the Proms got to me. It was a real low point. In Europe, I had just played to something like half a million people, over six weeks. That seemed a long way away, although in fairness to the audience in Ilford, they were enthusiastic. They made plenty of noise. If you closed your eyes you could easily imagine there were more than fifty people out there. Ninety at least.

Later, we found out why the club had been closed: one of the bouncers had been shot. No wonder people stayed away.

Still, something good happened that night. My sister Lee gave birth to a baby girl, Josie.

The Proms prompted Brian Berg, John Cavanagh and Becky Hamilton at Polygram TV to talk to me about making a new album. They suggested mainly covers, with a few of my own songs. I approached Gary Stevenson to work with me on some of the tracks. I also wanted him to produce the album. I have huge respect for Gary. His work with Go West in the Eighties helped create their distinctive sound, which I'd always loved. When you work with Gary Stevenson you also get his partner and keyboard player, Dave West, who's a smashing bloke. With me, it's my studio partner and friend, Phil Taylor. Phil plays keyboards in my band and is someone who, thank God, understands me.

We worked hard on the arrangements and did some interesting versions of songs like 'Free Falling' and 'Woman In Chains'. Simon Le Bon did the backing vocals on 'Save A Prayer', my favourite Duran Duran song. The album went out under the title *Tony Hadley*. It did reasonably well, although we struggled to get radio play. There were a couple of tracks I was really proud of, including a cover of an old Bee Gees song, 'The First Of May', and one of my own songs, 'Dance With Me', which I'd written with my good friend Simon Baisley (Gary Kemp's TV stand-in). At one stage I thought 'Save A Prayer' might be the one to take off, but it didn't.

I had been managing myself. After parting company with Steve Dagger and EMI I hooked up with a new manager, David Godfrey. I met David through the designer, Elizabeth Emmanuelle. They had worked together and she was impressed. He was a shrewd businessman. We teamed up for a while, and we got on, but it didn't lead anywhere. I realized I needed someone with a better understanding of the music industry. David and I parted company on good terms. I managed myself again for a while, but it wasn't ideal. At one point, I approached Roger Davis, who manages Tina Turner. The word came back that he was busy. In other words, he wasn't interested.

I was in the South of France at the music industry trade fair, MIDEM, when I ran into Neil Watson. He came over and introduced himself. His area was music publishing rather than management, but we got on and he came on board for a while. That worked out pretty well. Neil was with me when I did the covers album with Polygram. Between us, we came up with a deal to go to Dubai and shoot four videos. I was funding it myself and had a budget of £75,000.

I can remember contacting Handbag Films about the shoot.

I arranged to have dinner with producer Susan Ritter and director Katie Bell, to see if they were willing to take the project on. Gary Stevenson came with me.

Katie was enthusiastic. 'We're definitely interested,' she said. 'The budget's good, we can work within that.'

I nodded. 'That's great.'

Susan said, 'So we're working with a budget of £75,000?'

I said, 'That's right.'

'On each video?'

I frowned. 'No . . . That's for the lot.'

They still took it on, and did a great job.

In terms of locations, the shoot worked out well. We filmed against a backdrop of dunes and deserted beaches. The images were simple and striking and the light was fantastic, which gave us strong, saturated colours. The only drawback was the extreme heat and the humidity which, at around ninety per cent, was crippling. In the sweltering temperatures, Neil kitted himself out in robes and headgear like a sheikh. He looked pretty authentic, so much so that when he got into the lift at the hotel with a group of British businessmen they started bowing to him. He got out a few floors up with a cheery, 'See you, lads.' In the end I told him to ditch the outfit before he landed in serious trouble with the real McCoy. I didn't think the locals would see the funny side.

A camera crew from GMTV came to Dubai with us. I was at a stage in my life where I'd been through some shit and knew, with the court case looming, that there was more to come. In terms of my career, though, I was starting to feel more optimistic than I had for a while. I was proud of the album. I was less proud of how little I had learned about the music industry during the Spandau years and the early stages of my solo career. I wasn't sure how I had managed to stay so ignorant for so long. I told the interviewer, Lucy Van Den Brul, 'I know nothing.' I also told her that things were about to change. I was ready to grow up.

Last year, the album was re-released as *True Ballads*. It has now gone silver with sales of 60,000, which isn't bad. I'm still proud of it.

In the end, Neil and I parted company. He just got too busy. I needed to find a manager I could work with long term. I went to Brian Berg at Polygram for advice. He gave me a list of names. I contacted all the names on the list and arranged a series of lunches. I finally sat down with John Glover and his son, Matt. I liked the pair of them. I felt we could work together. I'd met John a few years before when he was managing Go West, who were signed to Chrysalis around the same time as Spandau. I'd always liked him. Although he's mild-mannered, he doesn't take bullshit, and he's incredibly protective of his artists.

I have a lot of time for John and Matt. We work closely together. Because of what's happened in my past, I need to know exactly what's going on. I don't want decisions made without reference to me. That never happens with John and Matt. What exists between us is trust, and that means a lot to me.

It took years for the publishing issue to get to court. In the meantime, we all had moments when it felt like too much to cope with. None of us really wanted to go to court. There was nothing belligerent in the action, no swagger at the prospect of a courtroom battle. It was solely about standing up for something we believed in, but we were under no illusions about what we were taking on. We were shitting ourselves.

The closer we came to the hearing, the more intense the pressure became. It was a test of will, seemingly geared to breaking down your resolve. Events had gained a momentum of their own. There were moments when it felt like things were careering out of control.

About eighteen months before we were due in court John Keeble reached breaking point. The daily grind of letters and faxes from the lawyers bearing more bad news was just too much. He hardly dared answer the phone; it was all doom and gloom. John has an easy-going nature. He doesn't enjoy stress and confrontation. Suddenly, he was lying awake at night, worrying. The whole business was affecting him badly. What bothered him most was when and if all the shit hitting the fan would start to affect his family. He wanted to back out. I could see why. He said, 'I feel like I can't see any way out of this.' It was driving him nuts.

We talked things through. If he had dropped out at that point, I would have understood. It wouldn't have changed things between us. By then, we were extremely close. John and I have lots in common. We're not afraid to have a go, even when the odds are stacked against us. You can see it when we play football. We might be 3–0 down and we'll still go out to win. It's also there on stage. We both take risks; they don't always come off. It was up to John whether he wanted to take his chances with the court case. In the end, he decided to go ahead.

He felt it was the right thing to do. He still does.

At home, I know Léonie felt the strain, but she never complained. Half the time, I didn't tell her what was going on.

With Léonie and
Toni, on holiday.
I love this picture.

That's Léonie
on the right,
celebrating her
birthday with
her sister, Gail
(centre) and Shirlie,
who married
Martin Kemp.

One thing about going solo
was doing the fan club
conventions on my own.

At Ronnie Scott's, Birmingham, with guitarist Frazer T. Smith and, on the right, bass player Phil Williams.

We pulled out the stops to promote the solo album, *State of Play*, in Europe. This was an interview for Italian TV.

In Belgium during the Proms tour, 1996, with Joe Cocker on the left, and musicians Deric Dyer, Chris Stainton, Lyndon Connah and Fin O'Loughlin.

Little Mack looks a bit overwhelmed by his birthday candles. Just as well Léonie, Tom and Toni are happy to help him out.

With Léonie, living it up in Monte Carlo, in the days when I had my own private helicopter (just kidding).

That's my mum on the far right with my aunties, (left to right) Sylvie, Geraldine and Ivy.

Bosnia was still a mess when we went there in 1999 to play to the troops. They had to sweep the football pitch for mines before we could have a friendly game with the lads from one of the regiments that looked after us.

I'm not a fan of bars – I'm actually more of a pub man.

With the band in Bosnia. They're happy because they've just managed to get through a game of football without falling foul of one of my famous sliding tackles.

Kosovo, 1999, with, left to right,
Matt Glover – one half of my management
team – guitarist, Frazer T. Smith, and
keyboards player, Adam Wakeman.

One of the perks of playing to
the troops – dressing up!

I gave up smoking a few years
ago but I still love a cigar.
The bigger the better.

On top of the world, Ma! Well, kind of. This is me on my trip to Machu Picchu in Peru for Action Medical Research. One of the best adventures I've ever been on.

I loved the military trips for Combined Services Entertainments (CSE). This is me with John Keeble, Phil Williams, Matt Glover, Richie Barrett and Adam Wakeman in the Falklands. Nice uniform Tone!

With HNK we had a lot of fun, even if the reason for forming the band wasn't so funny.

When I look back at my life
I count my blessings. I've had
the most amazing time.

On the road with *Reborn in the USA*. By the end of the first week Mark Shaw had left the show, Pete Cox had flown in to replace him, and Sonia had gone – and come back again. Otherwise, it was all going to plan.

New Orleans, with Pete Cox, Gina G, Leee John – and a camera-shy Elkie 'Erica' Brooks. 'You see that nice hotel, guys? That's not where we're staying.'

There was a ding-dong in the dressing room in Philadelphia between David Van Day of Dollar and Sonia, both battling to stay on the show. It all made great TV.

I can remember hiding letters and faxes from her (sometimes I hid them from myself). I wanted to protect her from the worst of it.

In the months before we finally went to court, I was touring. John Keeble was with me. Steve Norman was, by then, living in Ibiza and one step removed from the daily madness. On tour, every day I switched on my phone to find messages from the lawyers. Almost every bit of spare time, in between playing, was spent with John discussing the case. There was virtually no escape. The only time it went away was when we were on stage, playing.

That was the only bit of the day I enjoyed. It was the only time I felt safe.

Chapter Seventeen

The Royal Courts of Justice are intimidating. They're meant to be. There's a weight about the place. The moment you set foot inside the huge entrance hall and mingle with the court officials and legal teams, you know things are about as serious as they can be. It all serves to unsettle you. We arrived for the start of our hearing, all wearing new suits, on 27 January 1999.

We were there for twenty-three days. None of us really knew what to expect. My legal knowledge came from a few dramas on TV. Actually, that was probably just as well. If I'd known what it was really going to be like – a lot more stressful than I imagined – it might have been more off-putting than it already was. As the hearing drew close, John, Steve and I had numerous meetings with our lawyers. They briefed us as best they could. We all found the idea of standing up in court daunting. Our barrister, Andrew Sutcliffe, warned us to expect some tough questioning.

As far as I could see, the most important thing was just to be truthful. I trusted that the law would back us up.

On the morning the hearing was due to start, we arrived at the court building in the Strand and were led into an ante-room before being called. John was our first witness. The first question he faced was why he had come close to pulling out of the case a few months earlier. Whether the fact he had wavered was meant to discredit him in some way, I have no idea. All credit to him, he was a lucid witness. He spent a day and a half in the witness box. We all felt he got us off to a good start.

I was next up. I was questioned for three days. It was the most nerve-racking experience. My heart was racing as I took the oath. It's a strange feeling, stepping into the witness box. I had gone over my statement, and was as prepared as I was ever going to be. All I had to do was tell the truth. Simple. On the other hand, I knew that some highly trained QC would try to trip me up with clever questioning, which was scary. I also felt a responsibility to John and Steve; I didn't want to let them down. For me, it all came down to right and wrong, although I'm not entirely sure that's how the legal system operates. It all seems a lot less black and white once you're in court. The other side was taking no chances. It appeared as if they'd had witness training. *Witness training.* Until then, I didn't know such a thing existed. Our approach was less polished. Tell it like it is. Be yourself. Steve Norman was probably the most nervous of the three of us, but he also did a good job when he gave evidence. I think we all did pretty well, on balance, but the hearing was, without question, a strain. We got into a routine of adjourning to the pub round the corner at the end of the day for a couple of pints. At home, I'd give Léonie a brief summary of the day's events. Neither of us wanted to spend hours picking over the bones of what had gone on. I needed to keep things at home separate from what was going on in court, as far as possible. Throughout the twenty-three-day hearing, home was a refuge. I tried to keep the kids out of it but the press coverage meant Tom and Toni picked up bits and pieces, second hand, at school. The playground gossip wasn't always helpful. John's daughter, Jaime, came home one day and asked if her dad was going to prison.

I found the proceedings incredibly draining. At the end of each day, I was exhausted, fit for nothing. I would eat and sleep, and that was about it. I was in bed each night by 9 o'clock.

John was busy producing a band at the time. He spent most nights in a recording studio working on tracks. I have no idea how he did it.

Most of the time I felt optimistic, although some of the evidence completely threw me. It bordered on the unbelievable in my opinion. I know everyone has their own version of events, but I couldn't help being staggered by some of what was said. Even so I had to smile.

When Gary Kemp gave evidence, I couldn't believe my ears. Gone was the Essex Road accent of old. In its place was an unfamiliar clipped, cultured sound – it wasn't anything like the Gary I remembered.

The whole process was peculiar and surreal. There we were talking about pop music and the structure of songs, what had been said in this rehearsal room and that, to a bunch of people in funny wigs a million miles removed from the world we knew. Now and then, I wondered if there was any point. Some days I woke up convinced the whole thing was a bad dream. That's how far removed from real life it felt. On balance, though, throughout the case, I remained optimistic. We were the ones who'd been in those rehearsal rooms and had those conversations. We gave the judge a truthful account as we remembered it. That gave us confidence.

In the end, I thought there would be a good outcome.

We were given the judge's ruling the day before it was made public. I remember meeting John and Steve outside Lincoln's Inn Fields. We stood on the cobbles in the sunshine waiting to see our barrister, Andrew Sutcliffe. I was feeling buoyant. Suddenly, without warning, a sense of nausea washed over me. My stomach turned over. Before anyone told us anything, I knew we had lost. We went inside and were ushered into a room. The atmosphere reminded me of being in a funeral home, everyone speaking in hushed tones. Andrew Sutcliffe ran through the ruling. He was bitterly disappointed. I think he had hoped that, at worst, the judge would find a compromise that would go some way to keeping everyone happy. He didn't. We hadn't just lost; we had lost badly. The publishing royalties were 'a gift'. Steve Dagger was 'an independent witness'. How independent he could be when he was a director of Gary's publishing company, and Gary's manager, was a mystery to me. I was staggered. I don't give a shit what the judge said in his ruling; as far as I'm concerned, I think he was wrong. I still believe we all helped make those songs what they were. Gary may have won the court case but in my mind, I believe that doesn't change what actually went on.

The next day we went back to court to hear the outcome again, this time from the judge. Our barrister immediately requested leave to appeal; it was granted at once.

We emerged from court to face the press. We agreed to handle defeat with a bit of dignity and humour. John was brilliant. A reporter asked him if he felt disappointed. He said, 'Yeah, of course I am, but I'm not nearly as gutted as when Bergkamp had his penalty saved by Peter Schmeichel in the semi-final of the FA Cup. That was much worse.' He was being serious. Football takes precedence over money any day for John. The reporter looked at him as if he was mad.

Later, over a pint in the Yorkshire Grey, the pub on the corner of Gray's Inn Road, I joked, 'I wish I'd been a bloody footballer. You earn more money than you do in the pop business.'

John said, '*You* wouldn't! You'd be playing for Chesterfield!'

He was being kind. I wouldn't even have got into the Chesterfield side.

The best thing to come out of the court case was that I stopped smoking. My youngest son, Mack, who was eight, had been begging me to give up for ages. The anti-smoking campaign on TV made a big impact on him. I had tried plenty of times to stop, but never managed it. During the case, I was smoking like a trooper. I couldn't get enough tobacco. I was having dreams about a cigarette that never went out. It was ridiculous. Mack hated seeing me with a cigarette and, at that point, I was rarely without one. I promised him I would give up the day after the court case ended, win or lose. We shook on it.

I kept my word too, although it wasn't easy. Just when I most wanted a cigarette, I couldn't have one.

We faced a legal bill of more than £500,000 and the prospect of losing our homes if we couldn't pay. We managed to pay off £100,000 but we had no idea how we were going to find the balance. Bankruptcy loomed. Borrowing the cash seemed the only way. I went to see about getting a bank loan. Although I was nervous about borrowing so much money, my bank was willing to consider it.

Another option was to sell our shares in Marbelow. None of us wanted to do that. We wanted a voice in the company we had worked at for so long. If we gave up our stake in Marbelow we would lose all royalty payments from future Spandau Ballet record sales. Having already lost our claim for publishing royalties, we were loath to go down that road. We wanted to secure at least some income from record sales. In the end, though, we had no option but to sell the shares. We offered them to Dagger and Gary Kemp as payment, hoping they might be enough to clear the debt. They came back with an offer of £200,000. We took it. We had to. We still had no idea how we were going to find another £200,000. Our houses were on the line and there were charges on our properties, which meant they could be seized and sold to pay the remaining costs. I had no doubt that was a real possibility.

All our conversations were about what would happen if we couldn't pay. If the bailiffs came round, what could they take? We spoke to a lawyer skilled in resolving difficult cases involving intransigent people. My old friend and former manager, David Godfrey, recommended David Ruben. He is used to bringing together parties locked in bloody battle with each other. He handles bitter, messy divorces between couples who want to ruin each other, negotiates between people who would happily kill one another (and may have already tried). He has seen it all. He was confident he could find some middle ground. I was less convinced. I told him, 'David, be warned – they want the shirts off our backs.'

Experience had taught him that nothing is insurmountable. He told us not to worry. He said, 'There's always a way.'

He began negotiating with Gary's legal team. A week later, he was back, looking grim. He confirmed that they did, indeed, want the shirts off our backs.

I tried to shield my family from what was going on. I promised Léonie that, whatever happened, we wouldn't lose the house. Throughout it all, she was incredible. There wasn't a moment when her support wavered. We would sit there and rationalize the worst of it away. It was only money; no one had died. We counted our blessings. We had each other; we had three amazing kids. We might have been flat broke, but it wasn't the end of the world.

Throughout the build-up to the court case, I'd remained close to Martin Kemp. He and his wife, Shirlie, lived down the road from us. We were in and out of each other's houses all the time. We shared the school runs. We had been around for each other through some difficult times. When Shirlie was declared bankrupt she sat in our kitchen and wept. Léonie helped her out with loans here and there when she was hard up. Martin was godfather to my daughter, Toni. My youngest son, Mack, was friendly with his boy, Roman. We saw a lot of each other.

The issue over royalties had made no difference to our relationship. Martin swore that he had also stopped receiving payments. When the court case loomed, I promised not to subpoena him to give evidence. He was in an impossible position. The last thing he wanted was to be called as a witness against his brother. I could see that.

After the case was over, we were thrown a lifeline by a promoter who wanted to set up a Spandau Ballet tour. It was a means of raising enough money to pay off the court debt at a stroke. All it involved was a week's rehearsal and two weeks of gigs. I broached the subject with Martin. He knew the score; I was in danger of losing my house. It was the same for John. Since Steve was living in Ibiza, it was less clear how he would be affected. I was prepared to write to Gary, see if he would consider doing the tour. By then, Martin was in *East-Enders* and didn't want to take time off to play with the band. I asked him to think again; the answer was no.

I took a different tack. I asked him to use his vote as a director of Marbelow to grant John, Steve and I permission to tour as Spandau Ballet. He was willing to consider this.

I outlined the deal. 'Twenty per cent for each of the band members on tour, ten per cent to the agent and non-touring band members, including Steve Dagger.'

He agreed to think about it.

I said, 'Martin, this is desperate. We need your agreement on this – we need your vote to make this happen. It's very simple. We just need you to say we can use the name.'

I went on my own tour with my band. In the background, everything went quiet.

I could see that Martin was in an impossible position. He and I were friends, but Gary was his brother. His loyalties were clearly divided and I suspect he was feeling the pressure. There I was, asking for his help and, at the same time, preparing an appeal against Gary.

I started to think that the only way to break the stalemate might be to drop the appeal.

I was on tour when I broached the subject to John Keeble, who was with me, and Steve Norman, at home in Ibiza. Not surprisingly, they were wary. The appeal was our one chance to try to overturn the court ruling, and I was suggesting we throw it away. What if we did and it made no difference? Although I could see their point, our backs were against the wall, and we were running out of options.

Despite everything, I was optimistic. Martin was a friend, a good friend.

I managed to talk John and Steve round, although it was clear they had reservations, and – on the eve of the appeal – we pulled out.

I was getting ready to go on stage at the Brook in South-ampton when I called Martin with the news.

'We've decided to drop the appeal,' I told him.

As far as we were aware, that was the only thing standing

in the way of the tour. I was optimistic, sure everything would work out but, as the days went by and there was no word from Martin, a sick feeling settled itself in my stomach.

I waited and waited for his call, but I never heard from him again.

By now, my financial position was no laughing matter. There was a real danger the house would have to go. A huge consolation was the way people rallied round, including David Walker, Status Quo's manager. He's dead now, bless him. During the proceedings he was a tower of strength and came with us to court almost every day. We got so many calls and letters of support. Among the people who took the trouble to write was Shirlie, Martin's wife. Her letter stood out – she suggested Léonie and I stopped harping on about the court case and got ourselves a life.

It's true what people say: when times are hard you find out who your friends are.

We had scrapped the appeal 'in the interests of goodwill between the parties', although, from where I was standing, goodwill was in short supply. I was instructed to appear before a court again, this time to have every aspect of my finances picked over. It was the same for John Keeble. Clearly, we weren't paying off the remaining costs fast enough.

Bank statements, mortgage details, bills, assets; everything was laid bare. It was demeaning and I'm not sure what it was intended to prove. It didn't take a brain surgeon to know we were struggling. You only had to look at the venues we were playing. Neither of us had any cash hidden away. We had credit card bills, overdrafts and mortgages we couldn't pay.

It's hard to lose with dignity, and it's just as hard to win with good grace.

I can remember talking to John about where it would all end. We both felt that what was going on in the aftermath of the court case was just the tip of the iceberg. I had a feeling things would get worse, much worse, before they got better.

Towards the end of '99 we went to play some gigs for the troops in Bosnia and Kosovo. We flew into Belgrade in freezing conditions. The whole place was under about three feet of snow; it was a freezing minus 15 degrees centigrade. Army Land Rovers took us to the military base in Banja Luka where, the night before, a couple of Serbs had been shot trying to lob a dummy bomb into the compound. Welcome to Bosnia.

Our accommodation was in corrugated containers. I got a place to myself since, as 'the turn', I enjoyed officer status. That was news to me, but I loved it. The band had to share. On our first night, we went for a few drinks in the Officers' Mess, moved on to the Sergeants' Mess, then the Squaddies' Bar, and a few more drinking holes I can't remember. In the early hours of the morning we ended up with the SAS in their bar, which wasn't so much a bar as a shebeen. By then, I was completely lost, and pissed. One of the lads had to show me how to get back to my tin hut.

The next morning we went for mine-awareness training. That's when it sunk in that we were in a dangerous place. Bosnia was in a mess. Landmines littered the place. I had fancied skiing while we were there; I knew there were some fantastic slopes close by. Unfortunately, they were off-limits, covered with mines. Part of the briefing was about not straying from our vehicle while we were on the move. We were due to travel around a fair bit by road. If anyone got off for a pee, the advice was to stay close to the vehicle; it wasn't safe to stray onto the grass verge. There were mines everywhere. Just in case we weren't getting the message, they showed us videos of the wreckage of an anti-tank mine. It was horrific.

Our first show was in a hangar in front of a few parked tanks and a bunch of squaddies. It was a challenge to sing love songs to a load of blokes in camouflage gear, but the set went down well. I don't think half of them had a clue about Spandau Ballet, but they joined in with songs like 'Gold' and 'True', and collected autographs afterwards for their mums.

The troops were fantastic. They pulled out the stops to make us feel welcome. One day they staged a football match. We went off to play on a field in the middle of nowhere. The pitch was buried under six inches of snow. In the wake of our mine-awareness training, we were all wary, but it had been swept. In the middle of the game, someone kicked the ball wide. It landed in the next field. Before anyone could stop him, Phil Williams, the bass player and a top bloke, hopped over the fence and ran after it. It was unbelievable. Everyone was yelling at him. '*Phil – stay where you are! Don't move!*'

Phil, by now in the middle of the field, clutching the ball, froze. It dawned on him he might just have sprinted through a minefield. A line of footprints zig-zagging through the snow separated him from us. The squaddies yelled at him to re-trace his steps. *Slowly.* He picked his way back across the field. When he reached the fence, there was a wave of nervous laughter. We had all been shitting ourselves.

In Bosnia, we moved around a fair bit, bumping along poor roads in an ancient fifty-two-seater coach with the other enter-tainers: a magician, a troop of dancing girls and a comedian. A convoy of lorries carrying generators came with us. Most of the roads are narrow, two-lane affairs. They twist their way through the mountains. Landslides are a problem. The standard of driving is not particularly good and it's not advisable to travel after dark. Getting behind the wheel should carry a health warning. On our way through the Dinaric Alps, we found the road blocked by a timber truck hanging off the edge of the highway. It had slewed to a stop with most of its wheels on the tarmac, one or two suspended in mid air. No one had actually stopped to help. Traffic was trying to nudge its way round the truck, causing jams in both directions. It was utter chaos. No one seemed bothered about whether the truck tipped over and fell several thousand feet into the ravine below, which looked likely.

We stopped. The soldiers piled out. I went with them. By now I was wearing full army kit and in my element (boys will be boys). While they began heaving the truck away from the edge, I directed the traffic. I was having a great time, marching about, barking orders. I glanced up at the coach. John Keeble had cleared a space in the condensation on the window and was peering out at me, shaking his head in disbelief.

We had all seen pictures of the conflict in Bosnia and Kosovo on TV, but it's not the same as being there. The extent of the destruction was harrowing. Spandau Ballet had played in Yugoslavia in 1990, when the country was intact. To go back and see it destroyed was a shock.

The army flew us over towns left in ruins by the conflict. We rode with our legs dangling out of the back of a Chinook helicopter – so-called ramp riding – taking it all in from 1,500 feet up. You see first-hand how people are living, some of them in houses that are virtually in ruins. We drove through areas where families had been driven out by ethnic cleansing, turned on by the neighbours they'd lived next to without incident for years. Even then, people were being killed for no reason, just for being in the wrong neighbourhood; one that no longer welcomed them, for religious and cultural reasons. It made me think about how wicked the world is. You'd see the bombed and burned remains of a single house, or a minaret, surrounded by buildings that were unscathed. It was incredible. In places, the scale of the devastation made it feel like Armageddon. In Sarajevo, we came across high-rise buildings with holes through them, wires and bits of metal sticking out, where rockets had sliced through the structure. On residential estates, the houses were riddled with bullets. Some of the stories we heard were shocking. There were tales of snipers picking off children, bombs dropped on unarmed refugees.

I've always had respect for the armed forces, but seeing how they live in Bosnia and Kosovo was humbling. A lot of them were young, nineteen, twenty years old. You knew that if there was trouble they'd be out there, putting themselves on the line, to deal with it. In Pristina, we were hosted by army and air force personnel who had been living under canvas for six months. It was minus 15 degrees centigrade. You couldn't help thinking they have amazing spirit.

We played a gig in the sports hall in town, then went back to the base. By then, in full uniform and done up like a major – full insignia, the lot – I walked into the bar, not knowing there was a no-insignia rule. Sometimes, officer status can be a handicap. As soon as I appeared I was chucked in the sin-bin and force-fed a couple of pints of lager. It turned into a wild night. We took on some of the RAF lads at table football. After a few drinks it seemed like a good idea to up the ante: whoever loses has to strip off and run round the camp. Fair enough.

Adam Wakeman, our keyboards player, and Frazer T. Smith, the guitarist, were thrashed. Outside, several inches of snow lay on the ground. Adam wasn't about to take his clothes off. John Keeble was more than happy to stand in for him. He and Frazer stripped off and ran off into the night. Frazer returned covered in mud, having fallen over on the way round. He grabbed his clothes and got dressed. John, meanwhile, was full of himself. He breezed back in, went straight up to the bar and ordered a pint of lager, which he downed in one. Still naked.

I hoped being in Bosnia would be a chance to get away from the problems at home, although it didn't quite work out that way. We still needed to meet payments on the court costs. There wasn't much money coming in at the time. At one stage, John was on a satellite phone, in tears, to Flea, his wife. It was horrible. He had to find £17,000 by the next day. He ended up borrowing it although, because he was away, it was Flea who had to call in the favours. The next morning he was at the back of the bus with his head in his hands. I had never seen him so low.

In the end, John weighed up the debts facing him and decided he couldn't hang on to his home. I know he was extremely nervous while the sale was going through, worried that the courts would seize everything. It was an anxious time.

A friend of mine bailed us out in the end with a loan of more than £100,000 to pay off the outstanding court costs. I'm not sure I would have managed to hang on to our house, had it not been for his generosity. I will always be indebted to him.

We were offered more gigs for the armed services, this time in the Falklands. It was a long way from home, but it was a way of keeping the band working when there wasn't much else around. Plus, the trips to Bosnia and Kosovo had made me want to do more work with British forces overseas.

I had my own reasons for wanting to visit the Falklands; friends of mine had fought there. On my twenty-first birthday at Dirty Dick's in Islington, Michael 'Burt' Reynolds, a Royal Marine, told me he was off to the Falklands. I'd never heard of the place. I thought it was some remote little island off the coast of Scotland. You have to remember I was only twenty-one. The next time I saw him was on the news, with his hands on his head, among a detachment of Marines captured by the Argentines.

When reports came through that HMS *Sheffield* had been hit, in May '82, Spandau were playing on *The Old Grey Whistle Test*. It was a horrible moment. Léonie's brother, Neil, a marine, was in the South Atlantic, on board a destroyer with the task force. When the first reports came through, we feared his ship had been hit. Léonie spent hours on the phone trying to find out if he was safe. Word eventually came through that he was not on the *Sheffield*. My mate, Ronnie Dunnitt, also fought in the Falklands War. He doesn't talk about it much but what he has told me is harrowing. War is a different thing when you're in the thick of it, seeing your comrades killed and wounded. A couple of good friends were injured in the conflict.

I was glad to have the chance to visit the islands, although just getting there was a lot more difficult than I'd imagined. We flew from Brize Norton with the RAF on an old Tristar plane. Before we even left Oxfordshire, word came through that there was bad weather on Ascension Island, where we were due to land for refuelling. Take-off was postponed until the next day.

After twelve hours in the air, we landed on Ascension Island. It's a tiny place, rocky and barren. Almost nothing grows there. We stepped off the plane into bright sunshine. A tropical breeze wafted over us. Looking round, it was hard to believe that just twenty-four hours earlier conditions had been treacherous. It was due to be a short stopover for refuelling. Just as we were due to board again, we got news that the weather in the Falklands was bad. Apparently, the runway at Port Stanley is exposed and vulnerable to cross winds. Our two-hour stopover became another overnight stay. We had a barbecue that night with the RAF and drank well into the night. We crashed out for a few hours in a dormitory.

The next day, we got back on the Tristar and, around ten hours later, landed at Port Stanley. The first thing that struck me was how bleak and isolated it is. There is very little there. A windswept, treeless landscape. A couple of thousand locals. We really were in the middle of nowhere. When you step off the plane, it's like entering a time warp. Port Stanley, with its timbered houses, feels like an English village from fifty years ago. It appears quaint and unspoiled, but that's just the half of it. The low-flying fighter planes that scream overhead and shatter the peace are a constant reminder that in 1982 nearly 1,000 people died here in a bloody conflict.

From the airport, we went by road to the military base, a concrete complex about thirty miles from Port Stanley. For me, it was the experience of a lifetime. We stayed on the base, did four shows in six days, and were shown terrific hospitality.

In between shows, we flew over the islands in a Sea King helicopter. From the air, you can see just how hard it would be for troops to move around undetected. There's no cover. It's incredibly barren and exposed. Even in full camouflage gear, it wouldn't take much to spot fifty guys moving cross country. We flew over Mount Tumbledown and Mount Longden, where there was hand-to-hand fighting and heavy casualties on both sides.

I was fascinated, but after a week I was ready to come home. The troops spend six months there and, in all honesty, I'm not sure how they do it. It must take some getting used to. You just feel so cut off, so far from home. The flights aren't all that frequent and, when it comes to getting on and off the island, you're at the mercy of the elements. As we found, the weather is extreme and unpredictable. You can have sunshine, savage winds, hail and horizontal rain, all in the space of a day.

For John Keeble, being in the Falklands was a depressing experience. He hated being so far from home. Our flight out depended on whether the Tristar that brought us in was able to make it back to Brize Norton, via Ascension Island, as scheduled, and then do the return trip. We knew from experience that flights were subject to last-minute, lengthy delays. The night before we were due to fly home, we got word that the plane was stuck on Ascension. It would be another day, at least, before we could leave. It was the last thing John wanted to hear. He took out his frustration on the drum kit, kicking it round the stage, and retired to his bunk with a bottle of rum. I didn't see the point of losing it; there was nothing we, or anyone else, could do about the weather. If the plane couldn't land, it was tough. The next day, we went to nearby Sea Lion Island, a marine refuge inhabited by thousands of sea mammals. John didn't want to come. He missed out. That was one of the highlights of the trip for me.

We flew in by helicopter. It's an amazing place, a tiny island, uninhabited apart from the team of scientists who run the research station. From the air, you can see the huge colonies of penguins, seals and sea lions that make up the population. The day we were there, the wind was howling. Apparently, there's a hole in the ozone layer directly overhead and, even on a cloudy day, you can feel how much stronger the sun is. In less than an hour, my skin was tight and dehydrated.

It was amazing to wander round the island and be so close to the wildlife. I'd never experienced anything like it. The penguins were comical, bumping into each other and falling down. They're incredibly friendly, and they weren't in the least bit bothered by us. It was the elephant seals we had to watch. They're enormous – great slug-like creatures with big tusks. We could see them in the distance, rearing up, grunting and snarling and sparring with each other. They're aggressive, and to be treated with respect. The guys in the research station had given us a couple of pointers: keep well away, and don't go anywhere near their young. They also advised against getting between them and the sea; they're liable to kill you.

I wandered round in a bit of a dream, watching the penguins waddle about, seals bobbing about in the sea, enjoying myself, thinking how fantastic it was to be so close to nature. I was about three feet away from a boulder when it moved. I froze. It opened its jaw. I stared at a set of impressive teeth. Several yards away, everyone else watched, thinking how brave – or mad – I was to approach a sleeping elephant seal. I have never moved so fast in my life.

The next day, the weather cleared, and we caught the flight back to Ascension Island.

The whole trip was amazing. I doubt I would have ever got to visit the Falklands, otherwise. Maybe they're not everyone's cup of tea, but I look in my passport and see the stamps for Ascension Island and the Falklands and I feel privileged to have been there. It's good to play to the armed forces too. More artists should do it, and not just when it's a high-profile gig. It's only when you visit places like the Falklands or Bosnia, or wherever, that you start to appreciate what it's like for military personnel on foreign postings. Months at a time away from home, sometimes living in tents in freezing temperatures, often in danger zones. It must be grim. And some of them are incredibly young. I've always had respect for the services, but it's even greater now.

Chapter Eighteen

It was no secret that financially things were a little bit tricky. I had lost a well-publicized, expensive legal action. I was driving a battered old Audi. When I played the Jazz Café I carried the gear in and out with the rest of the band. We couldn't afford a road crew. There was a lot of pressure and I won't deny there were times when I felt close to cracking up. I was determined I would not go under, though. The press had a field day. I remember doing a charity gig with Spike's All Stars – the SAS band. The SAS was formed by Spike Edney, Queen's former keyboards player. He brought together people like Chris Thompson from Manfred Mann, Paul Young, Roger Taylor from Queen, Cozy Powell, Neil Murray from Whitesnake; it was an interesting mix. At a time when my confidence was a bit low, joining a fun band like the SAS really gave me a boost. Working with the likes of Laurie Wisefield, of Wishbone Ash, guitarist Jamie Moses, backing singers Susie Webb and Zoe Nicholas – the Fabba Girls – and the rest of the gang (sorry, guys, if I've missed anyone out) was – and continues to be – a great pleasure. They became good mates. Some reporter got wind of the gig and wrote a piece about how I was reduced to playing in a fifty-quid-a-night covers band. No mention that it was a charity fundraiser.

I just kept my nose to the grindstone. I never stopped believing that one day things would get better. In the meantime, I was still doing what I loved, using my voice. However bad things got, it never occurred to me to stop. If anything, it just made me more determined.

You swallow your pride and get on with it. It doesn't matter whether twenty-five people turn up to see you or 25,000, they've paid their money, and they deserve a good show.

We were in Italy a few years ago, booked to play a venue an hour's drive from Rome. By the time we got there, the promoter had shifted the date several times. We were playing a club in the middle of nowhere, on an industrial estate, on a Sunday. Every building for miles around had the shutters down. There wasn't a soul in sight. At most, thirty people turned up. Backstage, we were wondering how we were going to handle things. I knew it could turn into an awkward gig with us and the audience feeling embarrassed at the poor turnout. In the end, I went out on stage alone and spoke to them. I said, 'Listen, why don't you all sit down. We're going to play some songs and have a good time.'

The band came out, we did a great set. It was intimate and the audience loved it. It turned out to be a great gig.

Fine, it's not Wembley Stadium. You still do your best. Forget your ego and make the best of it. There have been times when I've thought, What am I doing? But at least there are still people prepared to pay to see you perform. That day we behaved as if it *was* Wembley. Backstage we got showered and changed, put on our glad rags, and went on.

There's a world of difference between a gig and a personal appearance. I had never wanted to go down the PA road. Singing to a backing track in a dodgy club never appealed, but in the wake of the court case I did as many as I could to clear the debt. I appeared in some shitty places, but I always got a brilliant reception, and it was a way of keeping things going – and keeping the lawyers happy.

Every now and then, often when I least expected it, I also landed something amazing. In November 2000, I spent two weeks in South America, on an arena tour with the British Rock Symphony. My manager, John Glover, came with me. We went to Argentina, Brazil and Chile. Like the Proms tour in 1996, it was an opportunity to perform with an orchestra, which was fantastic. Without doubt, the highlight of the experience, though, was appearing on the same bill as Alice Cooper – one of my all-time rock heroes.

I was twelve years old when 'School's Out' went to Number 1 in the UK charts in 1972. I bought the single on vinyl. Alice – with his ghoulish make-up, leather gear and girl's name – was the epitome of Seventies Shock Rock. The kind of act your parents loved to hate. I idolized him.

All of a sudden, I was on tour with him. It didn't seem real.

Alice was not what I expected. Despite his snarling stage image, he turned out to be one of the nicest blokes you could hope to meet. Softly spoken. Unassuming. Courteous. By day, he'd appear in casual gear, shorts and an open-neck shirt, his curls tucked under a cap. A scratch golfer, he headed for the nearest course whenever he got a chance. I'm a bit of a golfer too, but I didn't much fancy taking him on. Alice is just a bit too good.

Before going on stage, he'd watch kung fu movies to psyche himself up. It was all part of the transformation from Mr Mild into Mr Mean. By the time he emerged from his dressing room he was a different person, his pleasant daytime features masked by menacing make-up. Skin-tight leather had replaced the golfing gear. An evil-looking bullwhip completed the effect. Nearly twenty years after 'School's Out', he had lost none of his impact. It was extraordinary.

I'm sure there are people who think being a singer is an easy ride. Try it. I can promise you, it's not. I've run into plenty of record company people who are, frankly, crap at their jobs. More often than not they just move around from one record company to the next, keeping their heads down, hoping no one's going to notice them. As a singer, that's not an option. You are who you are. There's no hiding place. I can't disappear and pop up a few months down the line in a new guise. I can only be myself.

I decided to throw a party for my fortieth birthday at Porchester Hall in London. By this time, things were looking up. I was sick of seeing stories in the press about how down on my luck I was. I wasn't about to go under, no matter what. It was a great night. All the family was there. Friends I'd grown up with in Islington turned up. My old primary school teacher, Mr Hyams, was there. There was as much food and drink as anyone wanted. The best moment in the evening for me was when I got up and sang with the band.

I've been aware of my health for a few years, but even more so since I hit forty. Even when I'm touring, I go to the gym when I can. At home, I try to go for a run three times a week, often with Abbey, our Staffie-cross for company. When the BBC approached me to do a boxing bout, three rounds against the TV reporter John Pienaar, I jumped at it. It only fell through when the British Board of Boxing Control objected. I still work out with a punch bag when I can. I try to stay fit. You can't put a price on health.

However bad things seem to be, I'm constantly reminded that I have plenty in my life to be thankful for. A couple of years ago we played to the troops in Northern Ireland. It was a strange experience, much more frightening than Bosnia and Kosovo. We were warned in advance not to bring any camouflage gear, or anything that even vaguely resembled military gear – and to make sure there were no stickers or labels on our luggage that could connect us to the British army.

We moved around Northern Ireland in unmarked, civilian vehicles, escorted by soldiers wearing plain clothes and carrying handguns. It was unnerving. The base, in South Armagh, proved to be a heavily guarded fortress. As we approached, we were aware of soldiers scanning the surrounding countryside from watchtowers, monitoring activity. Helicopters flew in and out, constantly. Inside, a roll of honour listed the many regiments that had served there since 1969.

It was a real eye-opener. I'd been to Belfast before. Spandau had played there on both the Parade and Through The Barricades tours. The reception we got at the King's Hall in 1987 was just about the best we ever experienced. A lot of bands didn't want to play Belfast because of the Troubles. My mum was anxious about us going there, but we had no problems. We'd been down the Falls Road and the Shanklin Road, but it wasn't until we visited Armagh that I got a sense of the scale of the army presence and the extreme security. There was a tension in the air around the base. Years of coming under attack from mortars meant no one was taking any chances. While we played a gig for 200 troops, another 200 were out on patrol. We stayed in the Europa Hotel in Belfast, which was a base for journalists during the height of the Troubles. It was always being bombed. We had to be careful about giving away where we were playing. I got talking to a guy in the bar one night who wanted to know what I was doing in town. I told him we were due to play a gig in a hotel near by. He was no doubt just being friendly, but it's difficult not to feel a degree of paranoia. There's a nervousness that's infectious. You can't really be yourself. It's that sense of being on your guard all the time. Paranoia creeps in.

We played in a hangar on the base – the only building that wasn't mortar-proofed. Just a few days before we arrived, it had been hit by a shell. Very reassuring. It was a scary place, filled with menace, but we were only there a few days. The troops are there a lot longer.

Chapter Nineteen

We had to find a way of paying off the loan my mate had given me to clear the court costs. John Keeble, Steve Norman and I put our heads together. I think it was John who came up with the idea of forming Hadley, Norman and Keeble, and playing old Spandau songs. It made perfect sense. We became HNK and went on tour.

In no time at all, we were up to our necks in legal shit again with the arrival of a writ on Christmas Eve 2001.

Apparently, there was a problem with the posters for the tour. Under the words, Hadley, Norman and Keeble was a line which read 'ex-Spandau Ballet'. The lettering was larger than it was meant to be, apparently. We spoke to the promoter. He admitted there had been a mistake. He changed the posters, but that was far from the end of it.

The writ, issued by Gary and Martin Kemp, and Steve Dagger, withdrew permission for us to call ourselves ex-Spandau Ballet. Hang on a second – we *are* ex-Spandau Ballet. We spent *ten years* as part of Spandau Ballet. In my opinion, we don't *need* permission to say so. The animosity had reached a new level. I tried to get my head round how we could cause any confusion by using our own names – Hadley, Norman and Keeble – and telling people which band we used to be in. I'm sorry, I still can't work it out.

While the HNK tour went ahead, the lawyers got busy. The

Kemp brothers and Dagger wanted damages. They'd lost me. *Damages?* If anything, we were promoting Spandau Ballet's hits. For all we knew, we were sparking record sales from which we earned nothing. Quite how that could be construed as damaging was beyond me. Meanwhile, new legal bills began to pile up, as we tried to pay off the loan to clear the existing ones.

As I have found, litigation is a costly exercise. Exeperience has taught me the civil law system in this country is seriously flawed. It's possible to find yourself at the receiving end of a legal action that goes nowhere but could bankrupt you in the process.

HNK was the only means we could think of to pay back the money we owed my mate. The court case had been a joint effort and HNK seemed the fairest means of tackling the debt. It was a device. My band had become the HNK band – with Steve Norman bolted on. Steve hadn't played for a while and we didn't have much rehearsal time, but everyone worked hard. Phil Taylor, our musical director and keyboards player, put a huge amount of effort into pulling it all together. Our first show was in Dublin. The audience was fantastic. The next night we were due to play the Forum in London. I was nervous. I think a few other people were too. We wanted to do the best show we could. Phil Williams, the bass player, had been away in the States. We didn't want to play London without him. He agreed to fly back. The guitarist at the time, Frazer T. Smith, was playing his last gig with us before leaving to join Craig David. Richie Barrett was lined up to replace him.

Before we came on, John Keeble wandered into the audience. He bumped into a gang of blokes from Essex singing 'Gold'. We all thought that was a good sign. It turned out to be a brilliant gig. After the encore, Steve Norman picked up his guitar and smashed it to bits on stage. I had no idea what was going on. For most of the night, he'd been playing a white Stratocaster belonging to Phil Taylor. Phil's an easy-going guy, but he went white at the sight of Steve laying into what he thought was his precious Strat. It turned out that the guitar was on a list of equipment which Marbelow – Gary and Martin Kemp and Steve Dagger – claimed to own, and wanted us to return. The saga was never-ending. We had paid the money we owed and *still* they wouldn't go away. Actually, the guitar wasn't theirs. Like much of our gear, it came our way as part of an endorsement deal. No one ever paid for it, and no one ever will. Steve was just making a point.

It was tempting to put the pieces in a box and mail them to the Kemps but, in the end, Steve gave away the neck to a fan. We left the body with the Forum as a memento. Someone nailed it to the wall.

We joined the Here and Now tour, an Eighties retrospective, with artists like ABC, Belinda Carlisle and Howard Jones, and put together a set of Spandau Ballet songs. I wasn't sure I wanted to play Spandau songs night after night. Although I'll always be proud to include some, a whole night of nostalgia seemed a bit much. I'd been working on a solo career, which was suddenly on hold. It felt like a backward step. I kept reminding myself why we were doing it: to pay back the loan. We had to make it work, otherwise we were fucked.

In the end, Here and Now was a fun tour. We played some good venues, including Wembley and the NEC in Birmingham. It was good to be on the road with other bands. The playing side of things turned out a lot better than I'd imagined. Once it was over, we kept going and played more dates in our own right as HNK.

Touring as HNK was never about making us any money. It

was about clearing a debt. Everything we earned went into a pot to pay off my mate. At least, that was the idea.

With the writ hanging over us, we began settlement discussions. There was a trademark issue, which was dealt with straight away. The 'ex-Spandau Ballet' issue remained. This stemmed from a clause in the Marbelow contract relating to the use of the band name, a contract we had signed without any independent legal advice several years earlier. It was madness, a joke. Not a very funny one, granted. We *were* ex-Spandau Ballet and always would be. Surely no one in their right mind would seriously challenge our right to use the term. They did. Various sessions to hammer out an agreement were scheduled; I turned up with John Keeble and our lawyer, Tony Willoughby. Steve Norman was in Ibiza.

There was no sign of Gary and Martin Kemp, which really pissed us off. Steve Dagger did show, however. With the best will in the world, this kind of negotiation is a slow, tortuous process. It's not cheap either. Our costs ran into several thousands of pounds. An intermediary went from one party to another, trying to get agreement. It dragged on for hours. By around 10 p.m., when we thought we were getting close to some sort of agreement, the intermediary appeared. Everyone was worn down by now. We looked at him hopefully. He had news, but the look on his face told us it wasn't the kind we wanted to hear.

I was ready to kick the shit out of Steve Dagger. I got up. John Keeble put a hand on my arm. I said, 'That's it. Session over.'

No amount of talking was going to make a difference. If they really wanted to go to court, that was up to them. Meanwhile, the abortive discussion simply served to drive our costs up even higher.

John and I went to the pub, ordered a couple of pints and I lit up a la-di (la-di-da – cigar). I was shaking with rage. Suddenly, I burst out laughing. It just wasn't worth getting wound up about. Why waste the energy?

There was no way I was going to back down. The whole basis of the action, in my opinion, was wrong. There was no way anyone was going to tell me I was no longer entitled to call myself ex-Spandau Ballet. You just need to look at an album cover or watch a video to see that there were five of us in that band.

As the action rumbled on, the costs topped £100,000. Yet again, I was working to pay off legal bills. It was crazy, but I was not about to give in. I couldn't afford to. John and Steve, meanwhile, dropped out. They were less affected by the issue than me. Hadley, Norman and Keeble had split by then. Of the three of us, I was the only one pursuing a solo career. I didn't need a lawyer to tell me that the Spandau connection would sometimes be of help when it came to breaking other countries. Give up my right to use it, and I would live to regret it. The whole issue of whether or not I could tell people the name of my old band dragged on for months and months. It was insane. The lawyers must have been rubbing their hands.

It was during the *Reborn In The USA* series that the case was finally dropped. At that stage, it had been active for more than a year. During the early part of the tour, faxes on some legal point or other arrived almost daily. Meanwhile, I was in the middle of a reality TV show. It was hard to block out the shit and get on with my life with all that going on.

Months later, I'm still trying to sort out astronomical legal costs incurred over a writ that, in my view, should never have been served in the first place.

Some people may say I brought it all on myself by taking

Gary Kemp to court over the issue of publishing royalties, but I did what I felt was right. It's true, I didn't have to take legal action, but I couldn't have lived with myself otherwise. Faced with the same situation today, I would do it all again.

For me, life is about sticking to your principles and standing up for what you believe in, even if it's difficult. Some people choose to lead safe lives; I don't. If I think something is wrong, I take it on. If needs be, I'll pay the price.

I'm very much like my dad in that respect.

At the end of the day, it's only money and I can deal with that. Much worse things happen in life. I may not be rich by some people's standards, but I do have plenty to be grateful for. Recently, I became patron to the Shooting Star Trust, a hospice charity for sick children. One little girl with horrific burns was about the most feisty kid I've ever met. She wasn't about to let anything get her down.

When you meet kids with terrible injuries and life-threatening illnesses it doesn't half make you appreciate your own life. You hear what they've been through and you wonder how they keep going. It's incredibly moving and humbling too.

It makes you realize there are more important things in life than money.

Chapter Twenty

I've never wanted to settle for a comfortable life. In fact, I'm as ambitious now as I ever was. At forty-three, I'm still hungry. I'll always want to sing. I can't ever imagine not being on the road. I still want hit records. I'm not content to look for another way of making a living, something more reliable, less stressful. I'm more driven than ever before.

That probably makes things hard for the people around me – especially my family – but I can't help it; that's how I am.

I already had a major UK tour scheduled for 2003 when ITV1 got in touch about a new reality series they were planning to film in the States. I liked the basic premise of *Reborn In The USA*: touring America with a bunch of singers for a prime-time Saturday show. At best, I'd be on the road for seven weeks, on a trip that would take me from New Orleans to New York. At worst, I'd be voted off first and on my way home at the end of a fortnight. I did have some reservations about appearing on a reality TV show. More than anything, I was wary of hidden cameras. After much deliberation, and having received assurances that there would be no secret filming, I decided it was a good opportunity, although the timing of the series wasn't ideal. We were on the verge of war with Iraq and there was a groundswell of anti-American feeling in the country. Just before the series was launched, the opening title sequence was amended in case the sight of the Stars and Stripes made people set fire to their TV sets. Still, when we set off for New Orleans in late February everyone was in good spirits. The series was generating huge publicity and the spin-off was extra dates added to the UK tour.

I loved the idea of being able to perform in a different city each week, on a show millions of people would see. I could cope with the reality element of the show. It seemed harmless enough. It would be a laugh. The one thing that bothered me was that the music – the most important thing, as far as I was concerned – would come second to everything else. Television has a tendency to treat music like a poor relation and *Reborn* was no exception. Sure enough, just before we left for the States, we found there wasn't money in the budget for a band, which pissed me off. We would be singing to backing tracks instead.

I flew to New Orleans, our first destination, with Leee John and Elkie Brooks. David Van Day of Dollar, Haydon Eshun, Sonia, Michelle Gayle and Mark Shaw arrived on a later flight. Thereza Bazar, the rest of Dollar, and Gina G flew in separately from Australia.

I'm not sure what I expected from the show. I went into it wanting to win, but thinking it wouldn't be the end of the world if I didn't. It was just television, nothing to get in a state about. Not everyone else was as relaxed.

I've known Mark Shaw, lead singer with Then Jericho, for a long time. He's always been a bit of a wild man. We've done gigs together here and there, some with the SAS band. On stage during one of my shows, he joined me as a guest for the encore, and smacked me in the face with a microphone. By accident, I think.

A couple of years ago, he got carried away and fell off a PA stack during a gig at the Café Royal in London, crushing both his heels. Doctors told him he wouldn't walk again. After months in a wheelchair, he was back on his feet and as excitable as ever.

As soon as he stepped off the plane in New Orleans, there was trouble. A lap dancer had attached herself to him on the flight from Chicago. He wanted to bring her on the tour bus, but Michelle Gayle objected. It was a sign of things to come. Twenty-four hours later, he was off the show.

It wasn't what anyone had predicted and I think Mark probably regretted what happened. I'm still not sure how things got so out of hand. We had spent the day shopping for costumes to wear at the Mardi Gras parade. We all got together for dinner in the evening in Tujaques, one of the oldest and smartest restaurants in New Orleans, and it was all going well until Mark and Michelle started having words. Mark left the table. When Thereza Bazar tried to persuade him to finish his meal, he told her he would rather eat his own vomit. I didn't think the food was that bad.

Things went from bad to worse back at the motel when he lobbed a camera off the balcony and threw a drink over Gina G.

I missed all that because I stayed behind at the restaurant. By the time I got back to the motel, Mark had packed his bags and was leaving. Even as a friend, I couldn't persuade him to stay. That was the last I saw of him until I got back to England. I still don't know what got into him. The whole thing was bizarre. To come so far and leave before anyone had heard him sing a note didn't make sense. I think what happened was he started to play to the cameras – acting up, doing all this panto-mime theatrical wild man of rock 'n' roll routine – and he just took it too far. In the end, the edges between play-acting and reality were so confused he couldn't find his way back. That's my theory. Or maybe he'd just had too much Jack Daniel's.

Whatever, it was the start of an eventful week.

On our first morning we were taken to the city's most famous diner, the Camellia Grill, for breakfast. There was a queue of people waiting outside but we were ushered straight in so I assumed we had a reservation. We didn't. It turned out you can't make reservations there. Everyone waiting patiently for a table was muttering about how rude we were for pushing in. I agreed. We'd just arrived in New Orleans. The last thing we wanted to do was start pissing off the locals. I left and went over the road while the others had breakfast, with a side order of abuse from customers who'd seen them queue jump.

After a couple of days, there were the first mutterings of mutiny. The Super 8 wasn't the best hotel in the world. I didn't mind it. I've stayed in much worse places, although it wasn't ideal, since there was no bar and no restaurant. Nowhere for us all to get together, in other words, which didn't make sense. Also, it wasn't in a great neighbourhood. It turned out to be a magnet for drug pushers and prostitutes. There were some worrying goings-on. Thereza Bazar was kept awake one night by a woman in the room next door threatening to stab some-one. I was told not to go for early-morning runs because of shootings near by. Instead, I worked out in the gym at the production team's hotel. They had more sense than to stay at the Super 8.

Mark Shaw's departure was unsettling enough, but what no one knew was that Sonia was also ready to pack her bags and go. In the first couple of days, she spent hundreds of dollars crying down the telephone to her husband, Mark, in England.

By the end of the week, he was on his way to get her. The flight was probably cheaper than the phone bill.

Meanwhile, Pete Cox from Go West, another mate of mine, was on his way from London to take Mark Shaw's place. Pete, who likes to mull over major decisions, barely had time to pack and get to the airport. When he arrived in New Orleans, he was straight in at the deep end, inheriting the song Mark was meant to sing – 'House Of The Rising Sun' – in the wrong key. He had packed in such a rush he didn't even have a shirt to wear for the show. In between rehearsals, he went shopping.

Already, there were stories circulating in the press that everyone was ready to walk off the show. It was rubbish. I was having a great time. The weather was lousy but the Mardi Gras celebrations were in full swing. Leee John and I took full advantage, believe me. People go crazy during the festival, and not just in the parades. There's a lot of dressing up. Anyone who can't think of a good costume just strips off. There's an awful lot of bare flesh about. For ten days, the whole place turns into Sodom and Gomorrah.

We ran into a guy playing guitar in his underpants and a Stetson – the Naked Cowboy – who turned up again a few weeks later in New York's Times Square.

At the end of the week, we did a final run-through for the first show. It wasn't exactly hitch-free. The technical crew had flown in from New York and no one knew who anyone was. For two days, the assistant floor manager called Elkie Brooks 'Erica'. We were recording in Generations Hall, a small club venue on the edge of town and, at one point, it was touch and go whether we'd get an audience. Optimistically, someone had put crash barriers along the side of the venue. There was no need. Most people were in Bourbon Street getting drunk and taking their clothes off.

In the end, someone persuaded a stag party to fill the empty seats, in exchange for a few free beers.

Meanwhile, Sonia's husband had slipped into town, unnoticed. That night, along with Dollar, she ended up with the least votes from the American audience. She decided she didn't want to hang around to find out if the British TV audience would vote to keep her on the show. While the rest of us went out for dinner, she went back to the Super 8 and packed. In the early hours, I arrived back at the motel and bumped into her leaving with her husband. I could feel a pattern developing. First, Mark Shaw, then Sonia. Later that day, it was confirmed that Sonia had left the show and was on her way back to London with Mark.

I began to wonder if we'd get to the end of the show, with people leaving before anyone had a chance to vote for them. Meanwhile, the rest of us prepared to get on the *Reborn* bus for the three-day trip to Philadelphia.

I had a lot of time for Henry Lynch, our driver, a rough, gruff, no-nonsense Texan. He'd been on the road with all kinds of bands, from Elton John to the Pretenders. You wouldn't want to get on the wrong side of Henry, as you could tell from his T-shirts. One said, 'Don't mess with me – I'm running out of places to hide the bodies.' According to legend, when he was on the road with the band Gay Dad a 6,000-pound trailer fell on his foot. While Cliff, Gay Dad's singer, was on the phone, frantically warning Henry's kids their dad might lose his foot, Henry was having an Incredible Hulk moment and easing himself out from under the trailer. Before Cliff had a chance to finish the call, Henry was back behind the wheel, behaving as if being crushed by a 6,000-pound trailer was nothing unusual, which, in his case, is probably true.

I'm not sure, though, that Henry was prepared for the *Reborn* trip. For one thing, there was a camera crew on board, with every intention of filming him as well as us. That drew a few expletives. For another, he was part of a convoy that included a press bus and a fleet of production vehicles. Every time we stopped – which was roughly every couple of hours – it took another two hours to round everyone up and get going again. On day one, his patience started wearing thin.

He also had a few choice words about the itinerary, which wasn't exactly direct.

From New Orleans it took us north of Memphis and Nash-ville to Philadelphia, then west to Detroit – passing Cleveland on the way. From Detroit we went south to Memphis, then doubled back to Nashville. Finally, we went north again to Cleveland, then east to New York. Seven thousand miles in all, much of it doubling back on ourselves. What he had to say about that is unprintable.

I didn't mind the journey. I settled myself with Pete and Leee in the back lounge and watched *This Is Spinal Tap* for the umpteenth time. My main concern was getting some decent food inside me at the truck stops. I knew the temptation would be to eat too much in the States. They just don't understand about small portions. The first time I was in New York in 1982 I ordered a simple beef sandwich. It had seventeen slices of meat in it. At the truck stops I tried to stick to the salad bar. The trouble was, there wasn't always one. It was mainly fast food. As you stepped off the bus, the smell of grease hit you. In most places, the healthiest option was a foot-long sandwich. Otherwise, it was junk. Fries, fries and more fries. You had more chance of finding a doughnut than a piece of fruit. I ate a lot more rubbish than I'd have liked.

That first day, we were on the road for more than twelve hours. With just an hour left before we were due to arrive in Peach Tree City, Atlanta, one of the other vehicles had a blowout. We all ended up in a truck stop while the tyre was changed.

When we finally arrived at our motel, there was a camera crew already in place. To our amazement, Sonia was waiting. She had got as far as the airport in Atlanta and changed her mind about going home. She was back on the tour. David Van Day and Thereza weren't happy; they felt they'd been stitched up by the production team.

It turned out the producers had known for several hours that Sonia was back in the running. Just as the bus was leaving New Orleans, she called to say she'd had a change of heart. She was told to go on to the motel in Peach Tree City and wait for everyone. I felt a bit sorry for David and Thereza, but I wasn't all that surprised. We were making a TV show, after all, and TV is about ratings. Catching everyone off guard at the end of a long day is probably someone's idea of good television.

By the next morning there were conspiracy theories flying left, right and centre. No one was sure any more whether the blowout that had held us up was real – or whether it was just a means of making us hang back while a camera crew went on ahead to the motel. There was a bit of an atmosphere on the bus. Sonia sat at the front. David and Thereza kept their distance. David produced a video camera and started filming the *Reborn* crew filming him. This went on until the bus pulled off the road and David had a full and frank exchange on the hard shoulder with one of the producers. I couldn't help wondering whether the people I was on the road with had done any serious touring before. And whether it was the first time they'd had a camera shoved in their faces. I mean, that's what we were there for. What was the problem?

Meanwhile, I settled down in the back lounge with Pete and Leee to watch a rerun of *This Is Spinal Tap*.

Philadelphia sticks in my mind for a few reasons. After three days on the road, we arrived at the Society Hill Hotel. It didn't look open. There were notices pasted on the windows: *Closed For Painting And Cleaning*. Not a good start. I think someone had persuaded the owner to reopen before the place was ready. None of the phones worked, there were workmen banging about in the basement, and the building stank of paint fumes. There were bugs in some of the bathrooms. For two days, Sonia refused to have a wash because she reckoned the bathroom was unhygienic. I actually didn't mind the place, and I liked the area. Plus, I'd got lucky. I had a suite, which was very nice.

Everyone else was up in arms.

Still, I think people were coping pretty well until someone saw a mouse on the stairs. That was probably the final straw. Either that or the workmen turning off the water supply the day after we arrived.

I'd been at the gym and by the time I got back the place was in chaos. Everyone was packing, except David Van Day, who was ill in bed. A camera crew plus a director and researcher had squeezed into his cramped bedroom to capture the moment. In the thick of it, trying to calm everyone down, was Terrie Doherty, the artist liaison manager. Thereza Bazar was in tears. She was upset because she thought the production team was trying to wind everyone up (they were staying at the swish Westin Hotel, which was definitely open, a few blocks away); she was probably right. At the end of the day, their job was to make entertaining TV. I don't suppose they wanted us all to be happy. You could tell that people were getting to the end of their tethers. It didn't really bother me. I was still having a good time.

One of the best things about being in Philadelphia was that I got to meet Kenny Gamble and Leon Huff, who are absolute giants in the music industry. There's a tendency to overuse the word 'legendary' but in the case of these two, it's spot on. Between them, they created the sound of Philadelphia, working with artists like the O'Jays, Harold Melvin & the Blue Notes, the Three Degrees and McFadden and Whitehead. When we went to their offices, there were gold and platinum discs all over the walls of the lobby, glass cabinets crammed with awards. Over the years, they've collected 175 discs in recognition of millions of record sales. That's pretty impressive stuff. Apparently, a Gamble and Huff record is played somewhere in the world every thirteen minutes, which is a staggering thought. And they're really lovely blokes.

It's funny, but we were all a bit nervous about meeting them. They're among the most successful writer-producers in the world, after all. Thankfully, they were down-to-earth guys. I know that whole encounter was a big moment for Leee John – he is a huge fan.

They took us into the old Philadelphia International Records Studio, which is like a 1940s museum piece. Before Gamble and Huff moved in, it was the Cameo Parkway Records studio, where Chubby Checker recorded 'Let's Twist Again'.

I was knocked out by the whole experience of being there and meeting them. What was amazing was that, in an unplanned, magical moment, Leon Huff sat at the piano and played the O'Jays hit, 'Love Train', while we sang along.

The hairs on the back of my neck were on end. The whole

thing was filmed, but it never made it into the TV show, which was a huge shame. Before I left, I got Kenny and Leon to sign something for me. That visit was one of the highlights of the whole tour for me.

Philadelphia was a strange week though. There were loads of tensions. The night we moved out of the Society Hill Hotel Sonia went missing again, Leee discovered he had lost his wallet, and news came through from London that Dollar were under attack in a *Reborn* diary on Sonia's web site. A game invited fans to blow Dollar to oblivion. On screen, a gun sight roamed across David and Thereza's disembodied heads. It was all getting a bit ugly. Back home, the tabloids were having a field day. I wrote an update for my web site, which I read out to Pete and Elkie during rehearsals. It was along the lines of what a great time I was having and that, contrary to reports in the UK press, we weren't all on the verge of leaving. I said, 'I won't read out the bit that says what a set of bastards you all are, of course.'

During rehearsals for the show, David and Thereza went to Sonia's dressing room for a quiet word. A camera crew trailed them. Predictably, nothing was resolved. It turned into a huge bust-up with Sonia in tears. All on camera, of course. It probably wasn't ideal preparation for a show.

I think having cameras around all the time got to some people. It really didn't bother me. It was part of the deal, what I'd signed up for. I just thought, Be yourself, and you can't really go wrong. Not everyone's going to like you, that's OK. But some of the others hated it. The whole Sonia's-gone-now-she's-back episode had made Pete Cox wary. He didn't believe anything anyone said any more. And he thought there was some behind-the-scenes plotting going on to throw him and

Gina together, which wound him up. Thereza was unhappy too. By the time we did the show in Philadelphia the strain was starting to show. She looked pale and tired and, between rehearsals, she stayed in her dressing room. I felt for her. It was a tough decision to leave her family in Australia to do the show. I'm not sure *Reborn* turned out anything like she expected. In the end it was probably a relief to lose the vote and go home.

I'd chosen a Harold Melvin & the Bluenotes song – 'If You Don't Know Me By Now' – for Philadelphia. The theme of that week's show was the sound of Philadelphia. Gina was also doing a Harold Melvin number, 'Don't Leave Me This Way'. In rehearsals, I felt pretty good, although Harold Melvin's not my style at all. I'm much more into rock music. You're more likely to find me listening to Weezer, the Red Hot Chili Peppers or Blink 182 than the sound of Philly. When it came to the show, I had a horrible moment. On the third or fourth line, my mind went a complete blank. I couldn't remember what came next. I held on to one word as long as I could – *wroooooooooong* – until the next one popped into my head. By then I was in a cold sweat. That frightened the pigging daylights out of me.

After the show, there was a strange atmosphere backstage. Pete Cox had won the audience vote, with a brilliant version of 'Me And Mrs Jones', but, with Dollar packing to leave, it didn't seem right to celebrate. It was all very weird. Gina was upset because Davina McCall had peered down the back of her dress on stage to check if she was wearing anything underneath, which Gina said made her feel like trash. Elkie Brooks, up for eviction with Gina, was her usual easy come, easy go self. She didn't give a toss.

We moved on to Detroit. I loved it. It's a cool city. When you drive in it feels like the set of a sci-fi movie, a bit gloomy and industrial with run-down, boarded-up buildings. It built its name as the home of America's car industry but what's striking is how little traffic there is on the streets. At night, it feels quite spooky, no one around, steam rising out of manhole covers on empty four-lane highways.

We stayed in a great hotel, the Inn on Ferry Street, a restored nineteenth-century mansion. From the outside, it was gothic and eerie-looking. It reminded me of the Munsters' house. Inside, it was so plush everyone was suspicious. We were all thinking, OK, what's the catch? Why are they being so nice to us?

Paranoia was setting in. A sense of 'us and them' had developed, which I think is inevitable on a reality show. Occasionally, the cameras would appear when you least expected them. They caught Sonia washing her knickers in the bathroom sink. They caught me ironing in my underpants. I didn't mind. I like ironing and I'm good at it. I'd rather be filmed ironing than line dancing any day.

In Detroit, everyone was starting to feel the strain of long days and late nights. A couple of people were battling colds and throat problems. I felt like I'd been pushing the social side of things a bit hard. I decided to lay off the booze until after the show. I'm not sure anyone thought I'd manage it, but I did. The funny thing was, back home, it made the papers, and Paul Ross, who I've known for years, brought it up on *This Morning*.

A couple of days later, on 19 March, there was more bad news: the US had launched the first strikes against Iraq. The war had started. The front page headline in the *Detroit Free Press* simply read '*WAR*' in big, bold letters.

The strange thing was how far removed we all felt from what was going on in the outside world. We were living in our own little TV bubble. The main talking point in Detroit was whether there was anything going on between Pete and Gina (there wasn't).

One of the things to remember is that, after just a few weeks, missing your home and family really begins to take hold. It's hard to be away, but it's especially hard for your family back home. Other than phone calls, they really only get to know what you're doing by seeing an edited version on TV every week, which must be strange.

It was a good move to stop drinking. I felt really good in the run-up to the show. The venue was an amazing little theatre called the Gem, one of the most historic buildings in Detroit. The Gem's a survivor. Built in 1927, it was due to be flattened seventy years later to make way for a sports stadium, but the owner couldn't bear to see it destroyed. He came up with a plan to move it to a new site five blocks away. The entire structure was raised, intact, placed on wheels, and inched down the street to its new home. In the lobby, there are photographs of the theatre trundling along Madison to its new location. It ended up in the *Guinness Book of Records*.

One of my best moments in Detroit was meeting one of the Four Tops. Abdul Fakir – 'Duke' – came to the hotel one afternoon. He turned out to be a snake-hipped, energetic sixty-seven-year-old. He arrived wearing a pair of blue mirrored shades, which he kept on the whole time he was with us.

I'm always fascinated by people who've been in the business for years and are still passionate about music. I can't get over the fact the Four Tops were together for more than forty years. It's hard to imagine in today's pop industry.

Duke had a great story for us. Apparently, in 1965, when the group was at Number 1 with 'Sugar Pie Honey Bunch', the pressure was on to find a follow-up hit, but the writers Holland-Dozier-Holland had nothing up their sleeves. Their first few efforts came out sounding like a variation on 'Sugar Pie Honey Bunch'. Someone happened to say that all they were doing was coming up with the same old song. Within a few hours, they had their new track. The Four Tops recorded it the following day and acetate copies were pressed over the weekend. Just three days later, 'The Same Old Song' was getting radio play and on its way to being another hit. It's amazing that songs were turned around at that kind of speed. Good songs too.

I was a bit nervous about performing in Detroit. We'd all chosen Motown tracks, which isn't really my style of music. Also, forgetting my words in Philadelphia had given me a fright. I've been forgetting lyrics since I got up to sing 'Lady Madonna' on stage at Pontin's when I was thirteen, but I didn't fancy the idea of drying up in front of millions of TV viewers. We'd all been told we had just one chance. Forget the words, mess up the phrasing, sing out of tune, and you'd had it. It was playing havoc with my nerves. On stage, there's usually a chance to ease into things. You've got a band around you, who can go with you if you cock up. TV is different. You're on your own with a backing track. You have to be spot on straight away. We had two minutes to get it right.

I was doing 'For Once In My Life'. I wasn't sure how I was going to sing it, but I knew it wouldn't bear much resemblance to Stevie Wonder's version. Duke had some advice. He said, 'Just do it your own way. The audience is not going to compare you to the originals. If you're good and comfortable they'll clap, believe me.'

They did too. I crooned the song in the end, but singing Stevie Wonder in the style of Frank Sinatra was probably a mistake in Detroit. Despite the applause, I was on probation by the end of the show.

The first thing I did when we came off air was crack open a beer. We were all sharing one cramped dressing room at the back of the theatre. You could hardly breathe for all the competing scents in the air. Gina, who'd been voted off, was in tears. Elkie, on probation for the second week running, was as cool as ever. She got straight on the phone to her husband, Trevor, who was pissed off because he'd been looking forward to having her home. At the stage door, Haydon, who'd won the vote, signed autographs.

The following week in Memphis was crunch time for me. Another few days and I could be on my way home. At that point, I was just glad to have come so far. I'd still get to visit Graceland, spend some time in the bars on Beale Street. I couldn't complain.

I thought Memphis was amazing. It's Elvis's town and Graceland, the house he bought for just over $100,000 in 1957, is a shrine to him. When you go there, it's a reminder that there was no one like him. He was the genuine rock 'n' roll article – and way ahead of his time. Wandering round Graceland, you get a sense of the scale of his success too. There's one particular corridor that's like a trophy room. As you walk along it, the walls on either side are covered with gold and platinum discs. In all, more than 100 in the collection were awarded for record sales that topped one billion. Elvis was a phenomenon. When his Hawaiian concert was televised in

1973 it drew a worldwide audience of 1.5 billion – more people than watched the *Apollo* moon landing.

I loved Graceland, although everyone else thought it was tacky. It is in a sense, but that's only because it's exactly as it was in 1977 when Elvis died. Everything has been preserved. The house is a museum piece. The Seventies *were* tacky. Elvis wasn't the only one who went for shag-pile carpets. We all did.

It doesn't seem to matter to anyone that Elvis has been dead for more years than he spent at Graceland. In Memphis, he's still the King. Every year visitors from all over the world arrive to pay their respects. The Elvis connection is everywhere: Elvis Presley diners, Elvis memorabilia, Elvis's old tailor. We played the Gibson Lounge that week. Part of the building houses the factory that made Elvis's guitars.

On our first night, we ate in a restaurant on Beale Street called Elvis Presley's Memphis (once the site of Elvis's favourite clothing store), which prides itself on the full-fat, deep-fried peanut butter and banana sandwiches the singer loved. I tried to order a low-fat salad dressing. The waitress looked at me as if I was mad. No wonder Elvis had a weight problem.

Memphis more or less marked the halfway point of the tour. That week was pretty stressful for everyone. No one liked the idea of singing Elvis songs in the town he made his own; it was asking for trouble. I'd managed to avoid doing an Elvis song by choosing the Marc Cohn track, 'Walking In Memphis', a song I know well.

At least I thought I knew it well until we got to Memphis and I heard the new arrangement for the first time. I couldn't get my head round it. It wasn't what I was expecting at all. I listened to it again. And again. It's quite a difficult song, anyway, in terms of timing, but I was suddenly hearing a version that felt odd and unfamiliar. I couldn't even work out where the vocals came in. I just didn't get it.

I was relieved that Pete Murray, *Reborn*'s music associate, was due in from London the following day. We got a chance to work on the track together but I still wasn't confident. I felt I was jumping in with the vocals in the wrong place, which throws you for the rest of the song. I'd had my own version of 'Walking In Memphis' flown in from London, and I'd much rather have worked with that, but it was too long. All the arrangements on *Reborn* had to be just two minutes long. There was no room to stray from that.

I was quite nervous in the days leading up to the show. I don't like rehearsing anyway. Singing without an audience feels sterile. Each time I performed the song, it made me anxious about the timing. The Gibson Lounge is a fairly small venue, with seating almost up to the edge of the stage. During rehearsals, I got Pete Murray and Rachel Williams, Granada's Head of Music, to sit in the front row and cue me. I wasn't sure I'd manage to come in at the right point without them when it came to the actual performance.

On the day of the show, I got up early and went to do a radio interview with Leee John at a local station, FM100. Inside, the lobby was littered with audience flyers for *Reborn*. A line about pop stars 'whose fame has slipped a bit' killed the show stone dead as far as I was concerned. I couldn't see why anyone reading that would want to bother coming. Still, there was a good omen for me. FM100 was the first station to play the original version of 'Walking In Memphis'. According to Ron Olsen, one of the breakfast show presenters, that was a good sign. I hoped he was right. I still couldn't get to grips with the track.

I also had something else on my mind by then. A couple of

nights earlier, I'd lost an antique bracelet, a Christmas present from Léonie. I'd been out in Beale Street and when I got back to my hotel room, it was gone. I think maybe the clasp just went and I didn't notice. I went straight back to see if I could find it, but there was no sign. I asked FM100 to let their listeners know there was a reward for its safe return. As a last resort, I decided to try the local pawnbrokers. There are plenty in Memphis and I reckoned they'd remember something in eighteen-carat gold, with each link individually hallmarked.

When we broke for lunch I trawled the pawn shops on Poplar Avenue. They're weird places, full of guns – hand guns, semi-automatics, you name it. I don't even think you need a licence to buy one in Memphis. There were bits and pieces of jewellery, but no sign of my bracelet. As I trailed from one to the next, John Glover, my manager, called to wish me luck. He wanted to know where I was. I told him. He seemed surprised. I said, 'No, John – a P-A-W-N shop.'

All day, my phone bleeped at me with good-luck text messages from the UK. There was one from my good friend Shane Richie, who encouraged me with calls and messages throughout the US tour. His read, 'Kick arse, my son!'

Meanwhile, I was wading through yet more legal crap. This was all happening off-camera. Before I'd left for the States, Granada TV, the makers of the series, had received a letter from Gary Kemp's legal team which prevented me from talking on camera about the dispute which rumbled on in the background. Although the issue of whether or not I could let people know I was ex-Spandau Ballet was resolved a few days before the *Reborn* tour began, there was still a question mark over damages. A fax, several pages long, had arrived outlining best- and worst-case scenarios, and the likely cost of one course of action versus another. While the others had breakfast in Elvis Presley's favourite diner, I paced up and down outside trying to make sense of this latest document and wondering what to do next. I had enough on my plate as it was.

It was strange knowing I might be voted off the show, that in a few days I could be back in London, although at least I'd get to see the family. By then I'd been gone almost a month and I was missing them. While I was gone Mack had ended up in casualty after injuring himself playing football. Apart from a bump the size of a golf ball on his head, he was fine and there was no need to panic, but I was feeling a long way from home.

I never expected to survive the vote *and* win the show that week. The audience in Memphis was fantastic, but you just don't know how people are going to vote, and there were some good performances that week. Pete did a great version of 'Always On My Mind'. When the result was announced my jaw just about fell open. It was a boost for me, especially after a difficult week, but I felt for Elkie Brooks when she was voted off. She'd had two weeks on probation, which seemed harsh. I did feel a bit of a bastard but, predictably, she was fine, happy to be going home to her husband. Afterwards, the first thing I did was light up a cigar and call Léonie and my mum to tell them I was staying. Then I went out with the others and got very, very drunk.

At the end of the week we headed north a couple of hundred miles to Nashville, Tennessee. America's Music City, Nashville has an amazing pedigree. There's a district called Music Row where all the record companies have studios. Elvis recorded in Nashville, and the old RCA studio where he worked is still there. So did Johnny Cash and Patsy Cline. The city lives and breathes music. In every bar along Broadway, in the heart of Downtown, there's live music. Good music, too.

If Nashville has a distinctive sound, it also has its own particular style of dress. This is the home of cowboy boots and big belt buckles. If you're not wearing rhinestones and a Stetson – as we found out within seconds of getting off the tour bus – you're underdressed. We arrived looking like a bunch of city slickers. On our first morning, we toured the city in a bright pink bus with a couple of larger-than-life locals, the Jugg sisters, who took one look at me and shook their heads.

Sherri-Lynn Jugg told me, 'You need to get yourself a cowboy hat – and wear it on stage.'

I already had a black Stetson, which I was more than happy to wear around town, but nothing was going to make me go on stage at the end of the week looking like a cowboy. I'd never live it down.

Still, being in Nashville does have a strange effect. Within the space of a few hours practically everyone had bought cowboy hats – and had them on. It was the people who didn't who looked out of place. After a couple of days, you start to think that maybe rhinestones aren't so bad after all. A fringed shirt seems like a good idea. It's bizarre. We went shopping at Manuel's, the city's most exclusive – and expensive – clothing store. The owner, Manuel Cuevas, designs for celebrity clients like Mick Jagger, Bob Dylan and Elton John and his shop is a temple to the rhinestone. Everything sparkled. There were no prices on anything, which is always a worry. We spent hours there. Sonia eventually found an outfit she liked, a Stars and Stripes jacket and a silver cowboy hat. It was very Wonder Woman and had a price tag of around $4,000. She ended up hiring it. No one could accuse her of being underdressed.

I already had a stage outfit. In Memphis, I'd bought a cheap white suit and a pair of black and white brogues, but I was having second thoughts. It made me think of old gangster films.

I tried on the suit with a black shirt for the benefit of Jessica, our American wardrobe supervisor. She searched for something polite to say.

'I think you can look sleeker than that,' is what she finally came up with.

Joanne, the make-up artist, was more direct: 'I think you look like a pimp.'

I looked at my reflection in a full-length mirror. Al Capone came to mind. Those shoes. What was I thinking? I put the suit back on a hanger. At least it hadn't cost much. I decided to stick with a navy pinstripe – another $100 purchase in Memphis – instead.

I was a bit under the weather in Nashville. I felt quite homesick. I suppose I'd got used to the idea of going back if the vote had gone against me in Memphis. Suddenly, I was around for at least another couple of weeks, which was great – I wanted to win – but I was also starting to feel I'd been away a bit too long. I was doing my best to keep in touch but at times I did feel remote from home and family. My phone bills were astronomical. Much to everyone's amusement, I had bought another mobile phone, an American one, to try and keep the cost of calls down. Everywhere I went, I had a phone in each hand. It wasn't unusual to have two calls on the go at the same time. It became a standing joke. Two Phone Tone.

My throat was also bothering me. Pete Cox had a theory about that – too many late-night cigars and brandies. I'm not sure I agreed. Brandy's medicinal, after all. One of the locals thought it might be an allergy to elm pollen, which is a problem in Nashville in springtime. That made sense to me. When I told Pete he just rolled his eyes.

You can't come to Nashville and not go line dancing. Actually, I could, quite easily, but we didn't have a choice. Someone thought it would make good television. I'd rather have visited the Jack Daniel's distillery, a few miles out of town, at Lynchburg. That's my idea of an outing, but, instead, we went to the Wildhorse Saloon.

I'm really not a dancer, but someone told me that line dancing is not difficult. They were lying. The fact that someone takes you through the steps first – making it sound a lot easier than it actually is – means you just feel worse when you can't do it. Once the music started up, it was a nightmare. All around, rows of people moved in one direction at the same time. In the middle of them I went forward when I should have gone back, slid to the left when the rest of the room was going right, bumped into people, stepped on toes, and generally caused mayhem. Captain Chaos strikes again. I gave up before someone got hurt. What really pissed me off was that Pete Cox didn't put a foot wrong. At home, all my friends cried with laughter when they saw me on TV stumbling round in my cowboy hat. It probably made about two minutes of television, if that, but I don't think I'll ever live it down. I still get asked about it. On stage in Skegness, halfway through my UK tour in 2003, the band decided it would be funny to line dance around me. There wasn't anyone to take them through the steps, and they still had more coordination than I managed in Nashville.

We were doing the show from the Ryman Auditorium, once home of the *Grand Ole Opry* – the world's longest-running live radio show. The Ryman is one of the most famous venues for country music in the States. All the big names – Dolly Parton, Willie Nelson, the Dixie Chicks, Emmylou Harris and plenty of others – have played there. Fans come to worship country music's greatest stars, which is appropriate since the theatre used to be a church and still has its rows of wooden pews.

We all felt under pressure to perform well in such a hallowed place. In the end, it was Sonia who went home that week. Leee, who had spent the week on probation with her, stayed, but was up for eviction again, this time with Michelle.

We were nearing the end of the tour. Just two more American cities – Cleveland and New York. Cleveland was great. It's not an obvious tourist destination, but it's a cool city and it's home to the Rock and Roll Hall of Fame, which is incredible. I could have spent days wandering round there. It has the most amazing collection, which ranges from David Bowie's stage gear to one of John Lennon's school reports. There's a wedding invitation with the lyrics to 'Save The Last Dance For Me' scribbled on it. I didn't expect to find myself in there, but I am, along with the other Band Aid artists featured on the cover of the single, 'Do They Know It's Christmas?'.

We went there a couple of times, once to have a look round the exhibits, and once to take part in a live broadcast for a local breakfast TV show. That morning, we were up before it was even light, ready for the first broadcast, just after 7 a.m. The show was pretty chaotic. One of the things the station had set up was a blind tasting session with a local brewery. I got that bit right. The brewery people had brought twelve bottles of beer along. By 9 a.m., when we came off air, it was all gone. That was the only day on the whole US trip that I had a mid-morning nap. I wonder why.

For most of the tour, Pete had been having sleepless nights. While I was out having fun every night, Pete was being sensible. I felt great, but he was feeling awful. For weeks he'd been taking sleeping pills, but was still awake night after night. In Cleveland, after a particularly bad night, he decided he needed help. He had woken in the early hours with his heart thumping. In the emergency room at the local hospital, they hooked him up to a heart monitor and ran blood tests. Four hours later, he was given a clean bill of health. Everything was normal. The doctors diagnosed stress and anxiety and told him to stop taking sleeping pills. He returned to the hotel looking – and feeling – sheepish. That night he had his best night's sleep in weeks.

For the Cleveland show, we all chose songs from members of the Hall of Fame. I sang David Bowie's 'Changes' and Bonnie Raitt's 'I Can't Make You Love Me'. It's one of my favourite songs of all time and I think I know how to sing it now. When I sing about love or heartache or missing someone I know what I'm talking about. I can feel it, and I think that comes across. I can get really emotional when I'm singing. I get so wrapped up in certain songs. Maybe that's why you go through loss and disappointment. I really believe that the knocks life throws at you make you a better singer.

That week in Cleveland was a strange one for all of us. There were only five singers left and, by the end of the week, Leee was on his way home. I knew I'd miss him. We had got along really well. A lot of the time, he was my drinking buddy. It was just Pete and me, Michelle and Haydon, going on to the last US show in New York. If I'm honest, I wanted it to be Pete and me in the final in London. He's a good mate and a talented singer. Before we left Nashville, we were asked on camera for our favourite to win the contest. I went for Pete because he'd sung so well all the way through. Pete was thinking along the same lines. He picked himself too.

In New York I hung out mostly with Pete. On the first night the four of us went for dinner at a revolving restaurant. Michelle got travel sick. Pete and I were sick too – of stage-managed dinners. Someone pointed out that it was our 127th meal together. No wonder the company was starting to wear a bit thin.

It was great to get to the final week. I wanted to be home. Being away for seven weeks was a bigger strain than I'd imagined. It was certainly a lot for Léonie to keep things going single-handedly. When I left for the States, we'd hoped she and the kids would be able to join me if I ended up being there more than a couple of weeks. I had visions of being able to get away with the family for a long weekend, maybe go to a ski resort, or nip to Florida. In the end, it didn't work out. The filming commitments, which were pretty relentless, would have meant we'd have had virtually no time together. By the time I finally got back Léonie was just about at the end of her tether.

That trip was one of the longest we had ever been apart.

The New York show at the Roseland Ballroom, just off Broadway, was scary. New Yorkers are a tough lot, although the atmosphere in the city seemed a lot less abrasive than it was a few years ago. Maybe that's an after-effect of 9/11. With just four of us left, we were each singing two songs. The Roseland is a massive venue, but we filled it. On the day of the show, I was nervous. I was performing a couple of old songs – 'That's Life' and 'Mack The Knife'. It suddenly struck me that a young audience wouldn't know them. I wasn't sure how well *I* knew them, especially the lyrics to 'Mack The Knife'. All through rehearsals I'd struggled with them. On every run-through I got the words wrong. The closer we got to going on air, the more desperate I felt. Minutes before the show was due to start I was in the doorway of the make-up room, scribbling the words onto the palm of my hand. Pete Cox caught me. He shook his head. 'Tone, that's not a good idea,' he said. I stopped in my tracks. There was still time to run through the lyrics another couple of times. I scrubbed my hand. 'You're right,' I said. 'Thanks, Pete.'

Less than half an hour later, on stage, a few lines into the Norah Jones song 'Don't Know Why', it was Pete who forgot the words. Being Pete, he didn't even try to cover it up. He just grinned at the audience. 'Does anybody remember the words?' he said.

Backstage, I had my head in my hands. So did most of the crew. I still hoped the audience would vote him through on the strength of his voice; he'd already done a great version of Cyndi Lauper's 'I Drove All Night'. They didn't. Pete was out. I was shocked. Haydon was also voted off. I would take on Michelle Gayle in the final in London a week later. After the show, we all went to a nearby bar for drinks, minus the road crew who stayed behind in the venue, taking the set apart. After seven weeks on the road, it was our last night together. Pete put on a brave face, but he was a lot more upset than he let on.

A couple of days later, on Easter Holiday Monday, we were all back in London and facing reporters at a press conference at the LWT studios on the South Bank. I was so glad to be home, but in no time I was off again. Once the press conference was over, I went straight to join the band, already rehearsing for the first date of the tour later in the week. The next few days were hectic. Suddenly life felt a lot more pressured than it had in the States, and there was nothing I could do about it. It had its own momentum. After weeks away, I was home, but I wasn't there much. The night before the *Reborn* final, I had a gig arranged in Darlington. That meant a late finish and an early flight back to London on the day of the show. It was madness, but I was happy enough. I was running on adrenalin. Meanwhile, I still had a camera crew trailing round with me.

The Darlington gig kicked off the UK tour. I think that's

when I got a sense of how much the tide had turned in the space of a few weeks. I walked on stage and the audience went wild. I looked round at the band. Everyone was grinning. John Keeble, behind his drum kit, was laughing. It was our best reception for years. I nodded at John. Between us, we had gone through shit, always believing things would eventually get better. That night in Darlington set the tone for the rest of the tour. The next morning, at 6 a.m., I was at Newcastle airport, checking in for the flight to London. A few hours later, I won *Reborn In The USA*. It was a live show and seemed to flash past. The best thing for me was that I finally got to sing with a band, and my whole family was in the audience watching. Since then my life has been in overdrive, although I have to say it was already hectic enough even before *Reborn*.

I don't know what this 'rebirth' means, but I do know I feel as if I've entered a new phase in my career. I feel more positive now than I have for years. I'm on a bit of a high. Things are looking up.

The atmosphere on the tour last year was amazing. We sold out every venue. The reviews were good. I felt like we were reaching a new audience. The people who came to see us weren't just ex-Spandau fans. Some were too young to remember Spandau Ballet. It seemed I had picked up a whole new set of fans following *Reborn*.

I was happy to be back on the road. I love the routine, the late-night sessions, band and crew squashed into the back lounge of the tour bus air drumming to *Hocus Pocus* and downing brown-blue-green (an evil concoction of Jack Daniel's with a blue cordial mixer, dreamed up by John Keeble). It's usually the early hours before people start falling into their bunks. It's mental, but that's what makes being on the road manageable. You couldn't do it otherwise. I'm fortunate because I have a brilliant bunch of people around me. John Keeble on drums, of course. We go back for ever. There's Phil Taylor on keyboards, who has been with me since we worked together in Germany when I was promoting my solo album more than ten years ago. We now share a studio and do a lot of writing together. He's a really good friend. My bass player, Phil Williams – P Dub – has been with me almost as long. He's a real asset when it comes to working on the arrangements for songs. Richie Barrett, who took over from Frazer T. Smith on guitar and is a top musician, joined the band on the recommendation of P Dub. Richie sometimes tries to sneak an early night in on the tour bus, but John Keeble rarely lets him. On backing vocals are Andrea 'Angie' Grant and Shelley Preston, who's now Steve Norman's girlfriend. The road crew are a great bunch too. Richard Baker handles sound and production, Richard John looks after monitors, Dave 'Gibbo' Gibbon takes care of lights. Bones and Scary Paul complete the team. On tour in 2003 our stage manager was Graham Bowden, although he has now moved on. Doing his best to keep everyone in line is Dave Williams, my tour manager, who has possibly the scariest mug shot I've ever seen on his Access All Areas laminate. Matt Glover joins us on the road from time to time and keeps the whole thing ticking over, which can't be easy.

I don't set myself apart on tour. We're all in it together, which is why it works, and I regard the band and crew as mates. Over the years they've proved extremely loyal and supportive, and I have enormous respect for all of them. They're a major part of my life. They know how to party, but they're a disciplined bunch too.

Touring, for all it's fun, is a slog. Not everyone manages to sleep on the bus. The bunks are narrow and confined. We call them coffins, for obvious reasons. With fourteen people on board, it's stuffy and claustrophobic, and there's no privacy. Also, it can be a bumpy ride. On the tour last year, one of the drivers hit every overhanging branch between Carlisle and Wolverhampton. The sound of wood clattering against metal at speed is enough to wake the dead, although I managed to sleep through it. The next day we got up to find the bus filled with bits of foliage that had come through the open skylights overnight.

After a night on the bus all you want is a shower, but sometimes you get to a venue and find the facilities aren't great. There's one shower between everyone, and no clean towels. After a few days, you lose track of what's going on in the world beyond the bus. A fog of tiredness sets in. Knowing you can let rip at the end of the day keeps you sane, just about. Occasionally, it has the opposite effect and sends us all a bit mad.

I know the tour, hard on the heels of the *Reborn* trip, was tough for Léonie. Ideally, she would have liked me to be at home and for life to be less frenetic, although I'm not sure that would work.

As I get older, I find I want to do more with my life, not less. In the middle of the tour last year, I took off to Peru for ten days to walk the Inca Trail for Action Medical Research. It turned out to be the trip of a lifetime, and it paid dividends for the charity. The publicity resulted in all the places on their next few trips selling out – a potential fundraiser of around 1.2 million pounds. Five of us walked the trail together – John and Matt Glover, the ex-Arsenal player Brian Hornsby, and Matt's friend, James Watson. There were around sixty people – all ages and backgrounds – in the group in total.

The trek to Machu Picchu blew me away. We flew into Lima and then onto Cuzco for the start of the trek. You can feel the effects of the altitude straight away. It makes you a bit dizzy and out of breath. We were told to take it easy and give our bodies a chance to get used to the conditions, but I was too excited for that. I didn't want an early night. I was in a new, exciting country. I wanted a night on the town. I ended up in a pub getting wrecked on *agua libre* cocktails – a lethal mix of just about every white spirit. True to form, I bumped into someone I used to play football with years ago. It doesn't matter where I go, I bump into someone from my past. It used to be a standing joke with the Spandau boys. I finally turned in at 4 a.m. I was up and ready to start the trail three hours later. The scenery along the way is spectacular. It was probably adrenalin that kept me going that first day. Although you don't cover vast distances, the air is thin and it's a steep climb. I had decided to wear my army boots, which was a mistake. They weren't properly broken in and by the end of the day I was in agony. When I took them off at our first camp, the skin on my heels peeled away with them. It was two days before I could put them back on. My feet were raw. Luckily, in the meantime, one of the team leaders loaned me some trekking sandals.

Our first night on the trail was amazing. I arrived at camp gasping for a cold beer. The consensus was, 'You'll be lucky.' As it happened, I was. Waiting for us was a Peruvian woman with a bucket of beers submerged in the icy mountain stream. I bought the lot. It turned into another late night, drinking in one of the tents with James, a couple of the team leaders, and the team doctors, until the early hours.

The Inca Trail is short, around thirty miles, but it's tough. You're a long way up and, at times, the views make you dizzy. Brian Hornsby got altitude sickness. One of the women in the group was too ill to complete the trail and made the descent on a stretcher. On day two, when we reached Dead Woman's Pass, we got a sense of how far we'd come. It was breathtaking. It does give you an amazing sense of achievement.

I found the whole experience exhilarating. It made me realize how much of the world I haven't seen. Life is short. At the Sun Gate, looking down on Machu Picchu, I made a promise to myself to make the most of it. The older I get, the more I appreciate life. Experience has taught me not to take things for granted. I actually like getting older. I prefer myself now. I'm wiser, I hope. I'm still a dreamer – more so than ever, probably – but my head's screwed on. I'll probably always be Captain Chaos, but I can live with that.

I'm in love with life. I notice things around me. I think I must have spent half my life with my eyes shut, missing so much. Now I find myself looking at buildings, looking at the sky. When Mars was close enough to the earth for us to see it last year, I was out almost every night looking. I hope I have another forty years in front of me, and I'd like to think I'm not going to waste them.

In between shows last year, I spent a lot of time with John Keeble, working on this book. Most of our reminiscing was done over lunch and a couple of bottles of breakfast wine in places like Newark and Telford. We talked about things that had been buried for years and, mostly, the memories made us smile. An awful lot of shit has hit the fan in the past few years, but that doesn't change the fact that the Spandau era was, by and large, pretty good. It's all part of what has brought me to this point in my life. I don't have any regrets.

I see the hardships – the times I struggled to get gigs – as good preparation for what's happening now. So much of this business is about having faith that if you keep going it will come right eventually. I'm getting there.

I've had my fill of legal disputes. I hope I've seen the end of all that, although I'm under no illusions about the extent of the bitterness some of my old band mates feel towards me. Last summer, the day before I was due to perform Spandau Ballet songs at the Party In The Park for the Prince's Trust, word came through that Gary Kemp had refused Channel 5 the rights to broadcast them. Even after everything that's happened so far, I was amazed. The Prince's Trust concert is a charitable event. It struck me as well and truly below the belt. That's how deep the rift now goes.

Chapter Twenty-One

I'm not sure ambition leads to happiness. I am rarely content, always striving to do more, do better. In the States last year, on the *Reborn* tour, I had endless conversations with Pete Cox about what we wanted from life. We would find a gym in whichever town we happened to be in and sit in the steam room, mulling things over. We both want pretty much the same thing: the freedom to make the music we love, to tour and perform. It's not all that complicated. It's only on odd occasions I've felt at peace; a few fleeting moments here and there. They don't last. I suspect if you settle for less you may end up with a greater degree of contentment. Life seemed a lot simpler for my mum and dad. Their happiness came from bringing up their kids, living a decent life, a holiday once a year. They didn't seem to need anything else. I'm not saying those things don't matter to me; they do. I do count my blessings. I've had an amazing life. I've made a living singing and performing for twenty-three years which, in this industry, is extraordinary in itself.

The older I get, the more aware I am that we only have one shot at life. None of us knows what's around the corner, good or bad. That's why I want to make the most of every moment. I don't want to end up wishing I'd done things differently. Some of that's to do with losing my dad. His death made me think hard about my own life. Ironically, it didn't make me want to take things any easier. There isn't time.

I actually work harder now than ever before. For much of the past year, I've lived out of a suitcase. I've been away a lot. I know how hard that is for Léonie. Given the success of Spandau, I don't suppose she thought I'd still be touring twenty years on. She probably thought our lives would have settled into an easier rhythm by now. Instead, I'm away more than ever, and the chances are it's always going to be like this. Léonie has put up with a lot over the years. It *is* hard being the wife or girlfriend, always the one left behind.

Maybe I had a better idea of how things might go than she did. I never expected my life to be conventional. When I think back to the weeks leading up to the wedding, we talked things through and went into it with our eyes open. We both knew what we were taking on – at least, we thought so – but sometimes life throws you a curve ball. It rarely turns out the way you think it will. That's certainly been true for me. When I married Léonie, I believed it was for ever. We both did.

Sadly, a few months ago, we separated.

It was my decision to leave, and it's one of the hardest things I've ever done. I don't think anyone walks away from a marriage without an awful lot of soul-searching. Over the past twenty-three years, Léonie and I have been through an awful lot together. We've managed to have three beautiful, kind children. We've certainly had our share of ups and downs. Throughout, Léonie has been an absolute tower of strength, but I've no doubt that in recent years the career insecurities, financial worries – and, not least, the court battles – have taken their toll. On both of us.

I'm pretty sure I've changed as a result of everything that's happened. I've had to. I've become a lot harder, less tolerant, as the disputes over Spandau Ballet have rumbled on – and, incidentally, still do. We're still paying for all that, and I don't just mean in terms of the lawyers' bills. Perhaps, in some respects, our relationship was a casualty.

Increasingly, in recent months, we seem to have been looking for different things from life. For both of us, the long separations while I'm on the road have been far from easy, but I'm as passionate about touring as ever. That's one thing that hasn't changed – and won't. The trouble is, I know I haven't spent as much time at home as perhaps I should have over the years. I'm never going to reach the point where I'll willingly give up what I do in exchange for a more conventional life and Léonie's never asked me to. I'm not being pig-headed – just honest. I'm doing what makes me happy – singing – and I don't want to stop. It's not about money, it's about being fulfilled. I look around and see artists like Tony Bennett, still performing at seventy-seven, appearing on MTV, appealing to a new, young audience. There's no generation gap where he's concerned. The fact that he's a great singer and passionate about performing cuts across all ages. He's sold more than 50 million records. He could stop any time if he wanted, but he chooses not to. B.B. King is seventy-eight and still touring, playing around 250 gigs a year. I don't suppose he tours because he needs the money. He does it because he wants to. I think that's what audiences identify with. They respect passion. You can be the most gifted singer in the world but if you're going through the motions, the audience will catch you out. Frank Sinatra, another hero of mine, survived being dropped by his record company and ended up performing into his eighties. There's nothing to say you have to stop when you reach a certain age.

I don't see an alternative to what I do. Perhaps that's selfish, but all I can say in my defence is that I've never pretended to want any life other than this. Retirement is not an option. It never was. If I can grow old gracefully, still singing and performing, I'll be thankful.

I know the hurt and pain I've caused Léonie these past few months but, if I'm honest, I don't think either of us has been truly happy for some time. I still think the world of her and the children, and I always will. I just hope they know how much I love them.

It's sad how things turned out with Spandau Ballet. For a long time, we did have something special. We grew up together, shared some good times. We enjoyed being a gang. What blew us out of the water was a row over royalties. Without that, I'm sure we would still be on speaking terms. I have no doubt we would have collaborated on some new material by now. The chances are we'd have toured. Other bands manage it, stay on speaking terms long enough to collect lifetime achievement awards – and good luck to them. Ironically, our supposed arch rivals from the Eighties, Duran Duran, have reformed in their original line-up and are being recognised by the industry for past and present achievements. It's rather sad that, given different circumstances, Spandau could have one day enjoyed the same accolades. As the saying goes, That's life. As it is, there's no chance that we will ever play together again. You reach a point of no return, which is where I am now.

These last few years have taught me plenty. I've discovered that life goes by at a rate of knots, and rarely turns out the way you think it will. If you can get through whatever it throws at you, without regrets, that's half the battle. I'll probably always be searching for that elusive thing, happiness. I suspect it's less to do with what's already happened in my life than what might be about to happen. One thing I have worked out, though, is that while you can't do much about the past, you can make the most of the present. I don't know what else life has in store and I've learned from experience that looking too far ahead is asking for trouble. Just take the rough with the smooth, and move on. Even so – and perhaps I'm tempting fate here – I am optimistic about the future.

I'm ready for the next chapter, whatever it may be.

Postscript

If there's one thing you can say with any certainty about life, it's that it's full of surprises. Mine is, anyway. I suppose the trick is to expect the unexpected, although that's easier said than done. I'm not sure you can ever be prepared for everything that comes your way.

In August 2004, I was asked to do a Spandau Ballet reunion tour.

The offer came from Gary and Martin Kemp and our old manager Steve Dagger. Was I surprised? You could say so. Staggered more like, although there had been speculation in the press about us getting back together and, a while back, Steve Norman had hinted something was in the offing.

Still, when an eight-page proposal arrived, outlining costs, promoters and territories, I thought, bloody hell, they're serious. It was unbelievable really.

Not so very long ago, the same people proposing a tour were taking legal action to stop me from saying I was ex Spandau Ballet. Now here they were, acting as if we were all pals again.

As far as I was concerned, Spandau Ballet belonged to a part of my life that was over. It was the past, not the present. Hadn't I told myself countless times that after all the legal shit over the past few years we would never play together again? *Never.* I'd meant it, too.

As it was, I couldn't have done the tour even if I'd wanted to, since the dates, in May 2005, clashed with gigs I was already committed to with Martin Fry of ABC.

I turned it down, although I couldn't help thinking that wouldn't be the end of it, and I was right. A few weeks later, during a lengthy conversation with Steve Norman, the whole thing surfaced again. Clearly, it wasn't about to go away, and I knew I'd have to give it some serious thought.

I turned the idea over in my mind, trying to imagine the five of us back on the road together, playing and performing, but I couldn't quite see it. I know Duran Duran pulled it off, but they never fell out the way we did. I kept thinking there'd have to be one hell of a making-up to get Spandau back together, although quite how we'd manage that wasn't something covered in the tour proposal.

I wasn't really sure where Gary and Martin were coming from; remembering the good times, perhaps, and thinking that's how it would be again. I can't pretend to feel any great nostalgia for what went before; I don't think of the eighties as the be-all and end-all. Maybe it was for some of the others, but not for me. And I'm not sure it's ever a great idea to dig around too much in the past. It's a bit like going back to a place you love and finding it's not the same any more. You can end up very disappointed.

With the best will in the world, I couldn't see how we would even begin to recreate what we once had. Our differences ran too deep. By the time the band broke up we were barely on speaking terms and, since then, there's been the bust-up over publishing royalties and all kinds of horrible – and expensive – legal wrangling. Even now, I'm still paying off costs from the most recent Spandau-related disputes.

It's all been an enormous strain these last few years – not just for me, but for the people closest to me. Not everyone might have agreed with my decision to go to court over publishing royalties, but I did what I believed was right and, thank God, my family and friends were with me every step of the way. They'd have every reason to wonder what all the heartache had been about if I suddenly announced I was going back on the road with the very people I've been in dispute with for so long.

I know there are plenty of examples of bands that don't necessarily get on, yet still manage to go out and play together and I'm sure I could too, if I had to. I don't suppose it would be much fun, though. When I tour with my band, we have an absolute ball. I love being on the road, having a few drinks in the back of the tour bus after the gig, falling into my bunk in the early hours, and no egos getting in the way of having a good time.

It wasn't anything like that the last time Spandau went on the road.

I also have to consider my solo career. I'm busier than ever with a touring and recording schedule that means I pretty much know what I'm going to be doing for at least the next twelve months. As well as a major UK tour, there is a lot of orchestral work in the diary, a tour of stately homes, one-off gigs here and around the world, and a jazz-swing album scheduled for release in 2005.

Under the terms of the Spandau tour proposal, the whole lot would have had to be shelved, and an awful lot of people let down.

It's been bloody hard work establishing myself as a solo artist and it's not something I'd put on hold lightly. The tours are getting bigger, and so are the venues. A few years ago, I was playing Ronnie Scott's in Birmingham, now I'm selling out the city's Symphony Hall.

Twenty years ago I enjoyed the security of being part of a band, but now I'm happy as a solo performer. I like the freedom it brings, the fact I'm in control – which makes me wonder if I'd really want to be part of a set-up like Spandau again.

It's something I'm still trying to figure out.

In 2004, a gig came up in New Zealand, a private show for the airline, Emirates. The last time I was in New Zealand – the only time, in fact – was in 1985 when I got drunk with Freddie Mercury and appeared on stage with Queen. I'd not managed to see much of the country on that occasion, since most of the time I was in Freddie's hotel room getting caned. Anyway, I jumped at the chance of going back, thinking I might even manage a bit of sightseeing second-time round, although I knew the schedule would be tight.

I didn't appreciate just how tight, however.

The night before leaving for New Zealand, I was on stage with Pete Cox at the Opera House in Blackpool. Early the next morning I set off for Heathrow with my band and checked in for the flight to Auckland via Los Angeles. Two days and 13,000 miles later we landed on New Zealand's North Island. From there, it was a short hop down to Christchurch on South Island, where we were just in time for lunch. That afternoon we did a sound check and waited for the jet lag to kick in. Strangely, nothing happened. A few hours later we did the gig, which went down a storm, had a few drinks, and turned in. You'd think by then our body clocks would have been all over the place, but everyone managed a decent night's sleep. Next morning we met in the hotel lobby and headed to the airport for the trip home. We'd been in the country less than twenty-four hours. The sightseeing would have to wait (again). Just to spice things up a bit, we came home by a different route, stopping briefly in Melbourne, Australia, where a customs official did a double take when he checked my passport.

He frowned. 'You arrived . . . yesterday?'

I said, 'That's right.'

He looked doubtful. 'You were in New Zealand for *one day*?'

I nodded.

He shook his head. 'Mate, are you mad?'

He had a point.

From Melbourne, we flew via Dubai to London, arriving the following morning. Then it was straight off to Broadlands, near Southampton, where we played a festival. Round the world in four days. Funnily enough, none of us suffered jet lag at all, probably because we had crossed time zones in both directions so fast that our bodies – God help them – didn't have time to work out what was going on.

I know, it's a crazy way to live but, believe me, the job has some phenomenal perks.

In May, 2004, I got to play at Highbury in the testimonial game for the ex-Arsenal defender and England player, Martin Keown. We took on an England XI side in front of 38,000 fans, and beat them 6–0. When you're a lifelong Arsenal fan, things don't get much better than that.

For as long as I can remember my life has been hectic. Actually, that's an understatement. I suppose I'm always trying to do more, even if it means operating at full tilt most of the time, which can be trying for the people around me. I carry a diary stuffed with important notes and reminders, names and numbers, meetings, interviews, rehearsals, gigs. I'd be lost without it. When I look back at where I've been and how much I've crammed into the past twelve months, it hardly seems possible. However busy things are, though, I try to see as much as I can of my kids, Tom, Toni and Mack. It's scary how fast they're growing up. Tom's already been off travelling the world, Toni's set her heart on a career in acting, and Mack's a great little footballer. They're all doing well and I'm incredibly proud of them.

I do feel I've reached a point in my life where the pieces are starting to fall into place. As a solo artist, I'm more confident than I've ever been and the work is increasingly diverse. Contemporary music is just a part of what I do these days. At an orchestral concert at Rochester Castle in the summer of 2004, working with conductor Mike Reed and the Royal Philharmonic Concert Orchestra, I sang a duet with the opera singer Alison Buchanan. The week before, I'd been on stage in a dinner suit and dickie bow with an orchestra led by conductor Martin Yates, singing James Bond classics at an event staged by Robert Mackintosh. It's as though the older I get, the greater the opportunities become.

The funny thing is, although everything's looking good, I still have the same recurring dream that's plagued me since I was seventeen, of walking on stage to find half the audience missing. I'm not sure what that's about, but maybe it's a reminder that I'll always have moments of doubt. I don't think I'm the only singer who feels like that and I don't think it's necessarily a bad thing. Maybe it helps keep me on my toes, reminds me not to take things for granted, and makes me want to keep finding new challenges.

In 2005 I celebrate twenty-five years in the music business. It's rare to survive that long in an industry where artists are disposable, and I'm grateful I'm still singing and recording, still making a living from doing what I love. One of my proudest moments in 2004 was receiving a Gold Badge Award for outstanding achievement from the British Academy of Composers and Songwriters. I feel as though I've come a long way since the days I struggled to fill venues.

As I write this, in October 2004, I'm still wrangling with the question of a Spandau Ballet reunion.

Obviously, Gary and Martin want the tour to happen. Steve Norman's up for it too, as far as I know. For John Keeble, like me, it's far from clear-cut. I'm well aware that if I say no it might scupper something the others badly want, which is obviously a concern. I'm still close to Steve Norman, and John Keeble remains one of my best friends. If both of them were in favour, would I still say no? It's a huge dilemma. I'd never want to hold anyone back, but I could never agree to something that doesn't feel right.

I can't help thinking it's more than a touch ironic that when *I* wanted us to tour again in 1999, some of the people now showing the most enthusiasm weren't in the least bit interested. I couldn't even get my calls returned.

A few weeks after I turned down the initial proposal a second letter arrived, asking me to reconsider. It sounds so simple: we go back on the road, have a great time and, a few months or years down the line, return to our day jobs. That's the theory, anyway.

As I've said, we didn't fall out over something petty. Our disagreements were about as big as these things get.

I'm just not sure what it would be like to put the five of us in the same room, let alone go on the road together. We might think we could handle it, but the reality could be very different. Perhaps we'd hate it, which would be incredibly stressful for everyone. I'm no good at pretending. If I'm not happy, it's written all over my face.

Whether we like it or not, a reunion would inevitably open old wounds. I can just picture us facing the press and the kinds of questions that would come up. It could be extremely uncomfortable for all of us.

However, I must admit that I've wondered how I'd feel about all this if there was a life-changing sum of money on offer. Would it make a difference if doing the tour meant being able to set my family up for life? Although I really don't think money is everything, something like that might sway me, but I would still have serious doubts about compromising my principles for the sake of a fat cheque. I'm not rich by any stretch of the imagination, but I'm doing OK and, after years of seeing my earnings eaten up by court costs, I can now see light at the end of the tunnel. I suppose what I'm trying to say is that I'm in a good and happy place with my career and the question is whether it's worth jeopardizing all that for the sake of being part of Spandau Ballet again.

And that's where I am now and it feels like I'm back at the beginning, considering being part of a band that dominated my life for so long. I'm doing a lot of soul-searching trying to come to a decision I can live with – one that the people who matter most to me will, I hope, understand.

Index

J. RANDY TARABORRELLI

Michael Jackson: The Magic and the Madness

PAN BOOKS

**By the bestselling author of *Madonna: An Intimate
Biography* – the acclaimed biographer on his
greatest subject**

So much has now been said and written about the life and
career of Michael Jackson that it has become almost impossible to disentangle the man from the myth. The truth may be
stranger than any fiction; such is the uniqueness of the world
in which he lives, and his vision of the world. Recent revela-
tions are of course only the latest instalments of a saga that
began decades ago, and simply add more twists to an already-
tangled family epic.

This book reveals the behind-the-scenes story to many of
the landmarks in Jackson's life: his legal and commercial
battles, his marriages, his passions and addictions, his children. Objective and revealing, it carries the hallmarks of all of
Taraborrelli's bestsellers: impeccable research, brilliant story-
telling and definitive documentation.

'I feel I can learn more about Madonna and
Michael Jackson by talking to Taraborrelli than by talking
to the artists themselves . . . Already I feel closer to
the unreachable, thanks to his work'
Tom Payne, *Telegraph*

J. RANDY TARABORRELLI

Madonna

An Intimate Biography

PAN BOOKS

The massive bestselling biography of this international diva – updated with three new chapters

Whereas other books about Madonna have been based on previously published material, this biography is the result of ten years of exclusive interviews with people who are speaking publicly for the first time, including close friends, business associates and even family members. Bestselling author J. Randy Taraborrelli has also interviewed the star herself on numerous occasions and he draws on these first-hand experiences to bring Madonna to life as not merely a tabloid delight, but as a flesh-and-blood woman with human foibles and weaknesses, as well as great strengths and ambitions. This paperback edition includes three new chapters that discuss the 'Drowned World' tour, marriage and motherhood.

This is as close as you can get without being
Guy, Rocco or Lourdes!

'A thoroughly professional job . . . makes her more,
not less, fascinating'
Lynn Barber, Daily Telegraph

'A book you will find yourself "just dipping into"
for hours at a stretch'
Evening Standard

MARC ALMOND

Tainted Life

The Autobiography

PAN BOOKS

'There was always something attractively decadent about Marc Almond . . . you sensed that here was the real thing: an artist set on self-destruction. Many pop stars play at nihilism; Almond meant it . . .

'Today the delight with which Almond flouts conventional expectations still rankles with some. He writes well . . . about the drug abuse, the promiscuity, the false friends, the broken lives and the recklessness that drove him to the edge of madness . . . One cannot but respond to the spirit of the man, to his self-lacerating honesty, the sympathy with which he writes about his unhappy boyhood in a broken home in Southport, and the undeniable excitement of the pop adventures he describes . . .

'This excellent book also sends you to the music, to the traumas of late adolescence, and to the first time you saw that effete man-boy smothered in make-up on *Top of the Pops*'
Jason Cowley, *The Times*

'Jaw-dropping'
Q

GEORGE JACOBS AND WILLIAM STADIEM

Mr S: The Last Word on Frank Sinatra

PAN BOOKS

**An insider's account of life with Sinatra during the
heady years of the Rat Pack that's as cool, original and
dazzling as the man himself**

Generally considered 'the last of the Rat Pack', George Jacobs
was Sinatra's valet and confidant from 1953, when Ava Gard-
ner had just left him, until the end of his short-lived marriage
to Mia Farrow in 1968. In *Mr S*, George describes one of the
longest and most outrageous midlife crises ever.

'I doubt you'll find anything as memorable . . .
so wittily and stylishly written that it goes straight
to the top of my showbiz memoir league'
Lynn Barber, *Daily Telegraph*

'A unique, gossipy perspective on Sinatra's relationships
with some of the glossiest women and dodgiest
men mid-century Hollywood has to offer'
Observer

'Juicy tidbits concerning the Mob, Marilyn, the Kennedys
and other cool stuff Robbie Williams can but dream of'

Q

CYNTHIA TRUE

American Scream

The Bill Hicks Story

PAN BOOKS

The first ever biography of the cult anti-hero comedian

You know who's bugging me these days? The pro-lifers . . . if you're so pro-life, do me a favour – don't lock arms and block medical clinics. Lock arms and block cemeteries.

A lot of Christians . . . wear crosses around their necks. Nice sentiment, but do you think when Jesus comes back he's really going to want to look at a cross? . . . Ow! Maybe that's why he hasn't shown up yet.

It is this kind of humour that made Bill Hicks 'an exhilarating comic thinker in a renegade class all his own' (*New Yorker*). But it also led to the notorious censorship of his entire twelfth performance on the *Late Show with David Letterman*. Hicks's response was typical: 'Why are people so afraid of jokes?'

Bill Hicks died of pancreatic cancer in 1994, just four months after the Letterman incident. He had been selling out theatres all over Britain and at thirty-two was on the brink of becoming a major voice in America. His popularity has mushroomed since his death, with the video and CD legacy of his anarchic talent consistently occupying the comedy best-seller lists.

'The future, past and present of stand-up comedy'
Sean Hughes, from the Foreword

RUSTY YOUNG

Marching Powder

PAN BOOKS

A darkly comic, sometimes shocking account of life in the world's most bizarre prison

When Thomas McFadden was arrested trying to smuggle five kilos of cocaine out of Bolivia, he was thrown inside the notorious San Pedro prison. He found himself in a bizarre world, where corrupt politicians and major-league drug smugglers lived in luxury apartments in one wing while the poorer sections of the prison were too dangerous to enter after dark. To survive in San Pedro you needed an income – and so prisoners turned to the trade they knew best: manufacturing cocaine. Even the prison cat was addicted to crack. After spells as a drug dealer, shop keeper and Mormon pastor, Thomas hit upon the idea of giving guided tours of the prison, and as a result became legendary on the South American backpacking circuit. But behind the show he put on was a much darker reality, where brutality and death were common currency, and sometimes even the strongest did not survive.

'Awesome. Astonishing real-life story of a Brit drug smuggler banged up in Bolivia's most notorious jail. Another world seen through the terrified eyes of a likeable Englishman'
***FHM* (5 Stars)**

OTHER PAN BOOKS
AVAILABLE FROM PAN MACMILLAN

J. RANDY TARABORRELLI
MICHAEL JACKSON   0 330 42005 4   £8.99
MADONNA   0 330 48164 9   £7.99

MARC ALMOND
TAINTED LIFE   0 330 37201 7   £10.99

GEORGE JACOBS AND WILLIAM STADIEM
MR S   0 330 41229 9   £7.99

CYNTHIA TRUE
AMERICAN SCREAM   0 330 43806 9   £7.99

All Pan Macmillan titles can be ordered from our website,
www.panmacmillan.com, or from your local bookshop
and are also available by post from:

Bookpost, PO Box 29, Douglas, Isle of Man IM99 1BQ
Credit cards accepted. For details:
Telephone: 01624 677237
Fax: 01624 670923
E-mail: bookshop@enterprise.net
www.bookpost.co.uk

Free postage and packing in the United Kingdom

Prices shown above were correct at the time of going to press.
Pan Macmillan reserve the right to show new retail prices on covers
which may differ from those previously advertised in the text
or elsewhere.